EXPERIENCING QUALITY

A SHOPPER'S GUIDE TO

WHOLE FOODS

BY MARGARET M. WITTENBERG

Illustrated by David Paul Butler

Published by Whole Foods Market, Inc., Austin, Texas.

Publication support and book design by Silent Partners, Inc., Austin, Texas.

Cover design by Jane Wu.
Food Stylist, Fran Gerling.
Photography by Rick Patrick.

Printed in the United States of America
First Edition: December 1987
Second Edition: June 1988

Library of Congress Catalog Card Number 87-051460

ISBN 0-9619616-0-0

Cautionary Note: The recipes, instructions, and nutritional information contained in this book are in no way intended as a substitute for medical counseling. Please do not attempt self-treatment of a medical problem without consulting a qualified health practitioner.

DEDICATED TO EVERYONE
STRIVING FOR QUALITY OF LIFE,
HARMONY, AND HAPPINESS

TABLE OF CONTENTS

PREFACE

I first walked into a natural foods store thirteen years ago with my husband, Terry, soon after I had first met him. I'll never forget the mixed emotions I had as he boldly ran armed with paper sacks towards the dozens of drawers of bulk beans and grains and gingerly began to fill them with items I had never seen in my life. Feelings of "This is really exciting!" intermingled with thoughts of "What am I getting myself into?" and "Where are the cans of Van Camp's Pork and Beans?"

Nevertheless, I bought some of the bulk foods for myself along with a cookbook (to do some major research). Once home, I transferred the sacked items into glass jars. At least they looked nice sitting on my counter. A couple of days later I decided to impress Terry by inviting him over for a dinner featuring soybeans. My only problem was that I had forgotten what soybeans even looked like, much less how to cook them. My roommates had no idea either, so with pride cast to the wind, I called Terry again and asked as brightly as possible, "Uh...by the way, can you describe the appearance of a soybean?"

Despite the fact that I forgot about the water level while cooking them, and consequently, burned the soybeans, I became fascinated with the concepts, cooking techniques, and especially the flavors of the "new" foods. Having only been familiar with Rice Crispies, Frosted Flakes, and white bread as my grains, the sweet, chewy fullness of whole grains intrigued me. Naturally raised meat and poultry were more tender and delicious. Beans were a welcome protein alternative that were inexpensive and very versatile. Cheeses that did not have the same color, flavor, and texture as my staple, Velveeta, brought new meaning to the word "cheese". I realized there were more vegetables in life than carrots, green beans, and iceberg lettuce. And...they even tasted better when fresh instead of canned!

I also discovered that unlike processed foods, it was not necessary for foods to be sweetened to taste good. As if all of these revelations and experiences were not enough, chronic health problems diminished as alertness and vibrancy increased.

I'm still fascinated with foods and still love to experiment. Whole, minimally processed foods are delicious prepared simply or with a gourmet touch. However, quality convenience foods are also part of my whole food's picture when I lack the time or even the desire to cook.

EXPERIENCING QUALITY is a sharing of the experience and knowledge I have amassed during the past thirteen years, half of which have been involved with Whole Foods Market, Inc. Based in Austin, Texas, with locations throughout Texas and projected sites in other areas of the country, the standards of quality and service in addition to its extensive selection have made Whole Foods Market a hub for those interested in good food and good health. Functioning as a tour of the stores in print, this book features descriptions, uses, quality standards, and noteworthy details of all the products sold in the stores, from basic, gourmet, or ethnic foods to supplements and bodycare. Specific interests such as sports, allergy cooking, and pet care are also covered to discuss the healthy alternatives available. Easy and delicious recipes follow the major food sections to give the opportunity to try some of the more unfamiliar foods as well as traditional favorites.

EXPERIENCING QUALITY was designed to make the transition to using whole foods and natural alternatives easy and exciting for the novice. At the same time, the experienced may discover products they never knew existed. Anything but trendy, the use of whole foods and chemical-free products have been used for centuries. Rediscover them as I did.

Experience, enjoy, read on!

Margaret Moothart Wittenberg
September, 1987

ACKNOWLEDGMENTS

Many people have made this book possible. Thank you to all the people at Whole Foods Market, Inc.— particularly John Mackey and Craig Weller for their support and encouragement and for the opportunity to write.

Many, many thank you's to Patti Lang for her excellent job of supervising the production of the book.

Thanks also to David Butler for his beautiful illustrations, Jewelle Yamada, David Matthis, and Don Moffitt for initial technical and production support, Steve Adams for his help typing the first draft of the manuscript, and to Terry Shaw, M.A., L.D., for reviewing and offering suggestions concerning nutritional information.

Love and thanks to my parents, Dolores and Merle Moothart, who have been a constant source of inspiration in generosity, diligence, and patience throughout all my explorations.

And especially to my husband and friend, Terry, who has played a significant part in my journey— challenging me, providing feedback, tolerating my excitement and absorption with learning, and reminding me to relax.

And last, but not least, to my "kids", Bud, Kitten, Betty, Mochi, and Scooter, whose animal antics remind me that life really is magical!

1

ADDITIVES & ALTERNATIVES

100%
NATURAL

Food, Glorious, Food: The nutritive material taken into the body to keep it alive and to enable it to grow. Fruits, vegetables, meats, fish, poultry, beans, grains, dairy products, nuts, and seeds. Protein, carbohydrates, fats, vitamins, minerals, and water. Sustenance, nourishment, provisions, grub, chow, victuals. Luscious, savory, delicious, choice. Holidays, families, weddings, celebrations, picnics. Kitchens, restaurants, cafeterias, barbeque pits. Omnivorous, carnivorous, herbivorous, granivorous. Ideal weight, overweight, underweight, obese, malnourished. Mention food and each person has a different connotation.

We eat according to personal preference, habit or tradition, social pressure, immediate availability, convenience, economy, and nutritional value. Recently, however, more people are becoming interested in the actual nutritional value of the food they are consuming. How is it grown? How is it prepared? How old is it? How is it processed? Does it contain any questionable additives? While food technology flourishes, answers to these questions become even more important to know.

Artificial, synthetic chemicals are added to food to extend shelf life, to replace nutrients lost in processing, to enhance flavors, to improve color, to improve baking quality, to impart body or texture in foods, to cut costs for the manufacturer, and to mask deterioration of the food.

Unfortunately these additions are not without their drawbacks. Large scale processing and manipulation of foods is new technology that initially was more of a novelty for people than the norm. However, in the 34 years after World War II, the percentage of calories that the average person derived from chemically fabricated and modified food jumped from 10% to 70% of their total diet.

Tampering with the basic structure of a food radically disrupts the balance of nutrients that are needed for proper building and maintenance of health. Some companies try to compensate by adding some minerals and synthetic vitamins, but fail in providing all the nutrients known to be lost and those which have not been synthesized yet.

Chemically processed and preserved foods can also be a direct harm to one's health as illustrated by the use of artificial colors, flavors and preservatives.

COLORS

Seven synthetic dyes are allowed to be used in foods at this time: Blues #1 & #2, Green #3, Reds #3 and #40, and Yellows #5 & #6. Early manufacture of synthetic color additives was based on combining coal tar, a black viscous liquid by-product produced from coal heated in the absence of oxygen, with other chemicals. Most artificial colors can now be synthesized from chemicals more pure than coal tar.

Prior to 1960, a food color additive could be added to food until the government proved that it was harmful. Since then, many artificial colors have been banned after having been proven carcinogenic or otherwise harmful to the body.

The artificial colors currently used are under further study or have been provisionally listed. Furthermore, interpretations of test results on those approved have been controversial and politically twisted. The Food, Drug, and Cosmetic Act's Delaney clause forbids any additive that causes cancer in any animal when given in any amount. Despite the fact that in 1984, the FDA proposed to the Department of Health and Human Services that approval for Red #3 (used often on cherries in canned fruit cocktail and to dye pistachios red) be withdrawn from the approved color listing since it induced thyroid tumors in rats, the request was denied. The decision was based on the belief that sophisticated scientific research techniques makes the Delaney clause more and more constricting because even minute amounts not detected previously can now be shown as *capable* in leading to a carcinogenic response. Currently, the FDA policy is that Red #3 should be allowed if it poses no problems at levels usually consumed. Meanwhile, Red #3 is still allowed to be used as testing continues. Nonetheless, the question still remains: how can risk really be calculated?

Yellow #5 is the most widely used artificial color in processed foods. Although it is not suspected of causing cancer or birth defects, it does cause allergic reactions in some people such as asthma symptoms, hives, and "runny" or "stuffy" nose. Oddly enough, those allergic to aspirin also seem to be allergic to Yellow #5. Because of numerous documented allergies to Yellow #5, since 1981, the FDA requires that ingredient labels specifically list the presence of Yellow #5 in order to alert sensitive individuals.

All other artificial colors used in a product can be listed simply as "artificial color". The term "U.S. certified food color" has nothing to do with toxicity testing. It means that a batch of coloring has been inspected only for a certain level of impurities.

Artificial colors may also be linked to behavioral problems in sensitive individuals. Although not conclusive, many people have found good results when artificial colors were removed from their diet.

In contrast, natural colors can be derived from foods, minerals, insects, seeds, and flowers. Tumeric, an herb, and annatto, a seed, serve to tint foods yellow and can be used instead of Yellow #5. Dehydrated beets impart a red coloring while carob yields a dark brown. Although not as vibrant and stable, most natural colors have been found to be safe.

FLAVORINGS

Artificial flavors mimic natural flavors that would be present if the actual food had been used, such as a cherry flavored lozenge containing a red artificial color and an artificial cherry flavor instead of using real cherries. Because the artificial flavor contains none of the nutrients present in the actual food its flavor is imitating, artificial flavors are generally found in lower quality, less nutritious foods. Since many of the components for artificial flavors are derived from natural sources and only small amounts of the resulting artificial flavor are used, its toxicity is much less than other additives. However, many have not been subject to detailed toxicological tests and remain under scrutiny. Some sensitive individuals may also manifest behavioral problems. Labels require only the phrase "artificial flavor" or "natural flavor" on ingredient listings, not the particular chemical or flavor actually used.

PRESERVATIVES

Preservatives are used to retard food spoilage caused by microorganisms. Antioxidants prevent rancidity in fats and foods containing fats. The use of both preservatives and antioxidants enables the manufacturer to produce, store, and ship extra large batches of their food product and stock up on ingredients when their cost is low.

Both sugar and salt have been used for centuries as effective preservatives since their presence in foods cause the cells of microorganisms to dehydrate. Products made with honey stay moist for a longer period of time due to its capacity to retain water. Citric acid and other acids provide an environment that is unfavorable to the growth of many microorganisms. Drying or dehydrating, canning, and freezing are other traditional methods of preservation.

Modern artificial preservatives such as BHA and BHT have been linked as possible carcinogens.   Like artificial colors and flavors, BHA and BHT may also cause behavioral changes and allergic reactions in sensitive individuals. Other questionable preservatives include sodium nitrite and sulphur dioxide. (See MEATS and DRIED FRUIT for more details.)

IRRADIATION

The most recent concern is food irradiation. Irradiation does not make food radioactive. It is yet another method of food preservation. The food is placed in metal boxes, crates, or airtight containers, led into closed chambers, and exposed to specific doses of gamma rays emitted from radioactive forms of cobalt 60 or from the more abundant source, cesium-137 (the by-product of nuclear weapons production and nuclear power generation) for 1-2 minutes. Gamma rays are measured in terms of "rads" (radiant energy absorbed) or, more recently, in terms of "grays". One gray = 100 rads. One kilogray = 100,000 rads. One kilogray is used for irradiating fruits and vegetables while 30 kilograys are used for some dried herbs, spices, and teas. More radiation is needed for more simple organisms. Five-hundred rads or five grays over a short period of time is a lethal dose of radiation for most humans. In comparison, a typical chest x-ray produces less than 0.035 rads.

Its effectiveness in preservation lies in the chemical alteration of the foods. This alteration destroys insect larvae, bacteria, and other microorgansms in order to delay ripening of perishable foods, retard sprouting of potatoes, annihilate the parasite responsible for trichinosis in pork, and to preserve foods indefinitely, if sealed airtight. In effect, irradiation makes food sterile.

Long term effects of human beings eating sterile foods are unknown. Various animal studies have resulted in tumors, cataracts, kidney damage, chromosome breakage, and fewer offspring. However, some facts *are* known, based on the research done on irradiation since the 1940's.

The irradiation process affects vitamins, proteins, amino acids, carbohydrates, nucleic acids, and enzymes adversely. In particular, vitamin C is destroyed and vitamins A, E, K, B_1, B_2, B_6, and folic acid are dramatically reduced. Beyond the depletion of nutrients in foods irradiated, many irradiated foods are then involved as ingredients in further food processing, such as canning, which contributes to additional nutrient loss.

The chemical changes in the food produce unique, unknown, untested compounds now coined as URPs (unique radiolytic products), many feared to be powerful potential carcinogens. Studies have shown that grains and nuts are more susceptible to a mold called aflatoxin, a recognized potentially carcinogenic substance. In addition, the bacteria that causes botulism, a highly toxic food borne illness that can form in canned goods and products wrapped in airtight casings, is not killed in the irradiation process. Unfortunately, the bacteria that provide the usual warning smells or other usual signs of spoilage *are* destroyed, thus creating a potentially dangerous situation.

Irradiation also causes cosmetic changes. Undesirable changes in color, flavor, and texture occur in some foods.

The environmental impact of thousands of irradiation plants, the dangers transporting radioactive materials to food processors and the safety of the workers involved complicate matter even more.

Safe alternatives to irradiation include the traditional methods of food preservation: cold storage, drying, fermentation, to the more high tech methods: oxygen deprivation through nitrogen flushing or carbon dioxide blasting, heating foods before cold storage, and infrared treatments.

Not surprisingly, representatives from states involved in nuclear power, the Atomic Energy Commission, and the Department of Defense are urging for approval from both consumers and the government to increase usage of irradiation. They cite numerous studies done in the past to support their stand; however, most of the early studies were done by their own agencies instead of independent research and 80% of those are now considered inconclusive. The remaining 20% are split 50/50 on safety and adverse effects of irradiation.

The FDA has approved irradiation of some foods already. In 1963 wheat and wheat flour were approved for irradiation treatment followed by potatoes in 1964 (although neither are generally irradiated since other commercial methods of preservation are cheaper). Recent additions include irradiation approval for some dried herbs, spices, and teas in 1983, pork in 1985, and, in 1986, approval for fruits and vegetables as well as an increased level of irradiation for herbs, spices, and teas. Although irradiated foods require proper labeling, prepared foods that contain irradiated products require no special labeling!

FOOD LABELING

There is no need to feel helpless, paranoid, or scared about choosing the most nutritious foods with the least amount of questionable additives. Certainly, the ultimate decision depends upon you, but the choices are there and the means to decide which foods to buy are there also, namely, food labels.

As set by the U.S. Food and Drug Administration (FDA), **labeling laws** require that food labels must state 1) the common name of the product, 2) the name and address of the manufacturer, packer, or distributor, and 3) the net contents in terms of weight, measure, or count, and 4) the ingredients, in descending order of predominance by weight.

If any nutritional claims are made or if **nutrition information** is included on the label, the following must be present: 1) the serving or portion size, 2) servings or portions per container, 3) food energy in kilocalories per serving, 3) grams of protein per serving, 4) grams of carbohydrate per serving, 5) grams of fat per serving, 6) and the percentage of the U.S. RDA per serving of protein, vitamins A, C, thiamin (B_1), riboflavin (B_2), niacin (B_3), and the minerals calcium and iron. Phosphorus and magnesium are sometimes added but are not required.

The **U.S. RDA** is based upon the RDA levels, the recommended daily intakes for normal, healthy people according to age, sex, and the special needs of pregnancy and lactation. The U.S. RDA amounts chosen by the FDA represent one level for each nutrient for children above the age of four through adulthood to use as a standard guide to evaluate and compare various foods. The values are about equal to the highest values for each nutrient found on the RDA table. This includes a 30-50% margin to allow for individual variations.

Food amounts on nutrition information labels are listed according to the metric system, specifically in **grams** and **milligrams** since many food components are present in very small amounts. Grams can easily be converted into ounces, if desired. 16 ounces (oz.) or 1 pound (lb.) = 454 grams (g.). 1 ounce (oz.) = 28 grams (g.) Also, 1 gram (g.) = 1,000 milligrams (mg.) and 1 milligram (mg.) = 1,000 micrograms (mcg.)

Wherever **additives** are listed on labels, their functions must be stated. For example, foods that list BHT must indicate that the substance is used as an antioxidant. Additives described as "conditioners" are used to keep food from losing texture, body, or photogenic appearance and/or to enhance flavors that may have been removed in processing. Emulsifiers help ingredients to mix and stay in suspension.

Not all ingredients need to be listed, however. If a product has a **standard of identity** classification, simply the name of the type of product is required, such as "mayonnaise" or "bread". In order to qualify for the standard of identity classification, certain ingredients must be present in a specific percentage before the food can use the standard name. Mandatory ingredients in standardized foods do not need to be listed on the label.

Products must labeled as **"imitations"** of other foods if the product is not as nutritious as the product it resembles or if it is similar and just as nutritious, but differs in

standard ingredients. A classic example of this is unsweetened ketchup or ketchup sweetened with honey instead of using white sugar as the standard sweetening agent. Up to a
few years ago, the "alternative" ketchups were labeled as "imitation ketchup" and mainly
served to confuse health conscious shoppers who equated the word "imitation" with something inferior. However, it is permissible to give a new name to similar, nutritious products
instead of calling them "imitation". Now shoppers can buy unsweetened ketchup labeled as
"Unketchup" and honey sweetened varieties as "Table Sauce" or "Natural Catsup".

   Food grading used in phrases such as "U.S. Grade A" is based on quality standards of
taste, texture, and appearance as set by the U.S. Department of Agriculture and has nothing to do with the actual nutritional content of the product. Food grading is strictly voluntary and is not required to be on the label.

   The most sought after information on a food label these days, seems to be the **sodium**
level of the product. Labeling laws also specify how terms relating to sodium levels must be
used.

   •**sodium free**– less than 5 mg. per serving
   •**very low sodium**– 35 mg. or less per serving
   •**low sodium**– 140 mg. or less per serving
   •**reduced sodium**– processed to reduce the usual level of sodium by 75%
   •**unsalted**– processed without the normally used salt but may still contain the sodium
originally present in the food

   Enrichment of a product occurs when nutrients are added to meet a standard. A
survey in the 1930s in the United States showed that people were suffering nutritional
deficiences due to the refinement of whole grains (removing the bran and wheat germ).
Early research found that four nutrients, thiamin (B_1), riboflavin (B_2), niacin (B_3), and iron,
were especially affected. As a result, the Enrichment Act of 1942 was enacted to require
that these nutrients be added back to flour to boost them back to the levels found in whole
wheat. Riboflavin is an exception; twice the amount of riboflavin originally present in the
whole grain is added. Since then, research has shown that many more nutrients as well as
fiber are also depleted in the refinement of grain. Nonetheless, a food labeled as "enriched"
must supply only thiamin, riboflavin, niacin, and iron.

   A **"fortified"** food is one that has nutrients added to it to make it richer in nutrients
than the original unprocessed food. Examples include the addition of vitamins A and D to
milk and iodine added to salt, neither of which is naturally high in those specific nutrients.

   If **"low calorie"** is listed on the label, it means that the product contains no more
than 40 calories per serving or 0.4 calories per gram. **"Reduced calorie"** indicates that the
particular product contains at least 1/3 less calories that the food it substitutes or resembles.

   The phrase **"sugar free"** is one of the most misunderstood phrases on food labels.
Although it may not contain sucrose (white table sugar) it may contain any number of other
sugars such as fructose, corn syrup, high fructose corn syrup, sorbitol, mannitol, honey,
molasses, barley malt, or artificial sweeteners. All sugars basically do the same thing: they
sweeten the product and raise blood sugar levels quite high for a period of time. Some
sugars may metabolize somewhat slower than others but all should be used in moderation.

AVAILABLE ALTERNATIVES

What types of alternatives are available? Alternatives to chemically manipulated food are provided by offering what many people refer to as "natural foods". But the terms "natural" and "organic" have been used so loosely that they have lost their true meaning. You can go into a grocery store and find "natural" peanut brittle and "organic" shampoo.

So what is a natural food? **"Natural foods"** are chemically free, minimally processed foods. Minimally processed means that the food is manipulated only to the extent that is necessary while still retaining a high degree of nutrition. Fruits, vegetables, beans, dairy products, meat, fish, poultry, whole grains, nuts, seeds, herbs, and spices are considered "natural" foods. Likewise, whole wheat bread, pasta, oatmeal, and even falafel mix are examples of "natural" foods. Some foods even require the removal of an indigestible, fibrous hull in order to be utilized in the body, such as the black outer hull on buckwheat. The key is how and to what degree the food is processed and the nutritional value that is retained.

"Natural" foods are whole foods. Partitioned foods have been peeled, separated, refined, purified, sweetened, enriched, and dried. A diet consisting of a greater percentage of "natural" whole foods is more nutritious.

These "natural" foods may or may not be "organic". Chemists define "organic" as any substance containing a carbon compound. Under that definition, even DDT is organic! In the natural foods industry, "organic" basically describes foods grown without any synthetic fertilizers or chemical pesticides.

WHAT IS ORGANIC?

Growing foods organically is much more involved than planting a few seeds and watching them grow. Organically grown foods are produced within a sophisticated system of ecological soil management that relies on building humus levels through crop rotation, recycling organic wastes, and applying balanced mineral adjustments. This approach, along with the use of resistant crop varieties, minimizes disease and pest problems. When necessary, mechanical, botanical, or biological controls which have minimum impact on health and environment may be used. Chemical pesticides and herbicides including fungicides, rodenticides, growth regulators, fruiting agents, and defoliants are strictly avoided.

Although nutritional studies vary on whether organically grown foods are superior in individual nutrient values when compared with comparable foods grown with synthesized chemical pesticides and herbicides, the main issue primarily concerns its environmental impact on not only our own health and the health of the farm worker, but of our planet, as well. Consider the following facts:

•More than 1.1 billion pounds of chemical compounds intended to kill or control weeds, fungi, rodents, insects, and other pests are used in the United States each year, more than double the quantities of the early 1960s. Meanwhile, the number of insects resistant to pesticides roughly doubled between 1970 and 1980, and more than 150 species of weeds were found to be resistant to one or more pesticides during that 10-year period.

•Reports of pesticide contamination of ground water, the source of drinking water for about half of the U.S. population, are increasing. Residues of at least 17 pesticides have been found in ground water in 23 states.

•Declining populations of wildlife have been linked to pesticides.

•Despite a congressional mandate to the Environmental Protection Agency in 1972 to reassess pesticide products for long-term health and environmental effects, so far only 2 out of 600 have been fully studied.

Even the tests have their flaws. Maximum residues allowed in a food assume that people will eat only moderate amounts of that food. (How often have you eaten more than a moderate quantity of a particular food?) Physical examinations may not tell the whole story. Toxicity to nerves can lie dormant years before overt symptoms appear.

Furthermore, the National Cancer Institute has found that farm workers are at a heightened risk for several malignancies including leukemia, Hodgkin's disease, non-Hodgkin's lymphoma, and cancers of the brain, stomach, prostate, skin, and lip. And, just recently, the National Academy of Science released a study stating that the dietary risk of cancer is particularly pronounced for 10 of the 53 pesticides used in growing food and fiber.

As of September 1987, nine states— California, Oregon, Maine, Minnesota, New Hampshire, Nebraska, North Dakota, Washington, and Montana— have standards for what can legally be called "organically grown". Actual certification that a food is truly "organically grown", however, is levied by both third party agencies and self-regulating farmer's associations. These certification agencies must conform to the standards of the Organic Foods Production Association of North America (OFPANA) which acts as the "certifier of certifiers".

Texas is working on being the tenth state to recognize a legal definition of "organically grown" foods. It is estimated that at least 70 growers in Texas use strict organic growing methods based upon the standards of the California Organic Foods Act. Initiated by Texas' Agricultural Commissioner Jim Hightower in early 1987, work is in process to initiate legal standards governing what could be considered an "organically grown" Texas commodity and also concerning what information must be included on the label. Additionally, unlike the other nine states who depend on the private sector to actually certify the food as being organic, plans are to make the State of Texas itself an impartial third party certification group. Not only would the eventual Texas state certified organic logo indicate state support and recognition of organic farming practices in Texas, but it would highlight quality Texas produce to the rest of the country.

Produce is not the only food that is organically grown. Several companies insist on selling only the quality and purity of organically grown foods such as grains, beans, nut butters, and flour. Others use primarily organically grown foods as ingredients for prepared foods. Look for foods made by Arrowhead Mills, Café Altura, Cascadian Farms, Chico San, DeBoles, Eden Foods, Erewhon, Grainaissance, Lima, Knudsen Juices, Kashi, Kyolic Garlic, Lundberg, Mountain Sun Juices, Natural and Kosher, Soyfoods Unlimited, Timbercrest, Westbrae, and White Wave.

Eden Foods has their own very *strict* certification program based on a strong working relationship with their growers including farm visits and regular communication, farm and crop questionaires, and thorough nutritional and chemical residue testing.

Arrowhead Mills, based in Hereford, Texas, is in the midst of helping organize a grower's certification group that would be independent of Arrowhead Mills, patterned after certification groups in other states. Meanwhile, all products labeled as organic conform to the California certification standards. Like Eden Foods, Arrowhead Mills maintains a close relationship with their growers, requires notarized affidavits from the growers concerning particular farming methods utilized, and conducts tests for nutritional content and chemical residue.

In addition to the ecological and health aspects, most organically grown foods have a much better flavor due to natural maturation and the lack of pesticide residue that can produce "off" flavors. Occasionally the appearance may not be perfect, but it is no indication of the flavor or nutritional quality. Organic bananas are a good example. Often they appear small and somewhat bruised on the outside. However, their flavor far surpasses the more perfect looking commercial bananas which may have been sprayed up to 20 times during growth.

Organically grown foods are also processed, packaged, transported, and stored to retain maximum nutritional value without the use of artificial preservatives, coloring, other additives, or irradiation.

WHAT DIET IS BEST?

None in particular. There are as many dietary regimes as there are people, and rightly so. The term "biochemical individuality" was coined by Dr. Roger Williams, a noted bio-chemist from the University of Texas - Austin, to explain that one person's requirements vary from another's. Heredity, environment, and stress levels determine each person's unique nutritional needs.

Quality food stores should support "biochemical individuality" along with regard for individual preferences. A varied product mix ranging from T-bone steaks to tofu and beer as well as fruit juice enables customers to make their own choices, whether they are based on actual dietary needs, philosophy, or simply desires. The choice of quality, chemical-free, minimally processed alternatives are offered alternatives, not a specific way of eating.

COMPLEMENTARY PROTEINS

Eating less meat or none at all has become more popular lately for moral, ecological, monetary, or allergy considerations. Whatever the reasons, vegetarianism can be as balanced as an animal protein-based diet if careful planning is used to ensure that the combination of vegetable proteins eaten at a meal makes a "complete protein".

Protein is made up of chains of amino acids, the building blocks of protein. It is these building blocks that the body needs from food to perform its myriad of roles in the body. Of the 22 amino acids which comprise protein, 8 must be supplied by the diet while the others can be manufactured by the body. These 8 "essential amino acids" include isoleucine, leucine, lysine, methionine, phenylalanine, threonine, tryptophan, and valine.

In order to have a "complete" protein, all 8 essential amino acids must be present in the proportion (there is not an equal one-to-one relationship) that the human body needs. Animal proteins such as meat, poultry, fish, dairy products, and eggs are "complete" proteins. Except for soy protein isolate, quinoa, and amaranth, plant proteins such as grains, legumes, nuts and seeds, and vegetables are considered "incomplete" proteins since they are low in one or another of the essential amino acids.

However, different plant proteins can be combined with each other's proteins to produce a high quality "complete" protein—the essence of the "complementary" protein system. For example, grains are low in lysine but high in methionine, whereas beans are low in methionine but high in lysine. When supplied separately, the body uses the essential amino acids at the level of the poorly supplied "limiting amino acid". If the grain and the bean are consumed together, the protein quality is increased dramatically and is biologically the same as eating a complete protein.

The book that made "complementary protein" a household phrase for vegetarians, Frances Moore Lappe's *Diet for a Small Planet,* published in 1971, gave the impression that to get enough protein on a meatless diet, considerable attention was needed in choosing foods in the right combinations. In her completely revised and updated version, she has since claimed that studies have shown that it is much easier than previously thought. If a diet is varied with little emphasis on "junk food" devoid of nutrients and protein or dependent on mono-diets such as an exclusively fruit diet, there is little danger of protein deficiency in a plant food diet.

In all other diets, if enough calories are consumed, protein is probably sufficient and there is no need to consciously calculate complementary proteins. However, if too few calories are supplied in the diet to support an individual's energy needs, some of the protein is utilized as an energy source, thus increasing the protein requirements to cover the loss. Notice all the "ifs". A good, well balanced diet geared to the individual is a prerequisite to adequate protein as well as other nutrients which allow the protein to do its job.

Another qualification is in order. Some people's protein needs are significantly higher than others and some situations warrant an increase in protein. Growing children, pregnant and lactating women, people under extreme physical or mental stress, including recovery from an accident, infections, or prolonged illness, generally need more than the "average" person. Since many people normally ingest more protein than they probably need, the excess can often cover any extra needs, but, even so, it is wise to be aware of the complementary protein system.

Controversy continues whether proteins need to be complemented at the same time or whether an "amino acid pool" exists within the digestive tract containing complete protein supplied daily from the breakdown of cells in the normal course of metabolism. Consensus seems to be that if it does exist, dietary deficiencies of protein quality could be made up by the "amino acid pool" only for short periods of time, within 3-4 hours.

Unless a person "grazes" throughout the day with frequent meals, the most convenient way to insure complete proteins is to eat complementary proteins in the same meal. Not every dish in the meal or even the main entree itself needs to be complemented. The soup, salad, vegetable dish, or dessert can serve as the combined protein course. Additionally, the incomplete protein in any one of the dishes can serve to complement the incomplete protein in another dish or course, i.e., the legumes in a bean soup would complete the amino acids found in the meal's grain.

But don't worry; no calculator is needed and over-preoccupation with menu construction is not necessary. For many, combining plant proteins is an unconscious habit. Most people prefer to eat foods such as grains and beans or cereals and milk together simply because they taste good that way!

The complementary protein system does not exclude the use of animal products. Small amounts of animal protein can supplement a plant protein to make it more complete. It is also possible to go completely without meat, fish, or poultry. Dairy and eggs can be included, if desired. However, the more limited one's diet, the more conscientious one should be about the quality and quantity of all foods that are consumed.

Complementary proteins are not only for vegetarians. Knowledge of the principles enables a person to take advantage of the lower cholesterol, generally lower fat content, and lower price of plant foods.

Below is a general summary of complementary protein relationships. Note that in a few instances, depending upon the specific limiting amino acids in the actual foods being combined, a complete protein cannot always be assumed. Make sure to include in the diet a majority of the confirmed relationships. For more specific limiting amino acid information, refer to Frances Moore Lappe's *Diet for a Small Planet, the 10th Anniversary Edition,* published by Ballentine Books.

COMPLEMENTARY PROTEINS

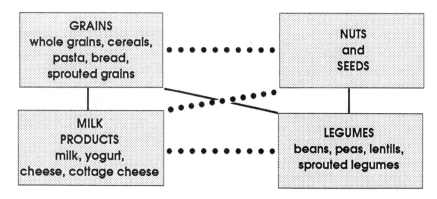

Some vegetarians prefer not to eat eggs or dairy products. Since B_{12} is mainly present in animal products, it is critical that the person avoiding all animal products obtain a B_{12} source. The earliest symptom of B_{12} deficiency is an anemia which could appear within 1-3 years of consumption of no animal products. The danger is that the anemia can disappear with adequate folic acid intake and the B_{12} deficient person can be asymptomatic for several years until the more serious damage to the central nervous system results, namely, pernicious anemia. Symptoms of pernicious anemia include unsteadiness, poor memory, confusion, moodiness, delusion, overt psychosis, and eventually death. Remember: any vegetarian who includes dairy or eggs in their diet will receive adequate amounts of B_{12}. Those who eschew any animal products will find B_{12} supplements or fortified nutritional yeast as good sources of B_{12}. Miso, spirulina, and sea vegetables may also provide some B_{12}, but other more reliable sources should also be included.

DIETARY GUIDELINES FOR AMERICANS

In September, 1985, the U.S. Department of Agriculture and the Department of Health and Human Services published seven general guidelines to improve one's diet:

•Eat a variety of foods.
There is no such thing as a "super food" that provides in significant amounts the more than 40 different nutrients we need. Eating a wide spectrum of foods will satisfy the gaps in nutrition from one food to another.

•Maintain a desirable weight.
Obesity increases the risk of chronic diseases such as high blood pressure, heart disease, strokes, and diabetes. Lose weight by eating foods high in nutritional value but with fewer calories, getting more exercise and shedding weight at a sensible, gradual rate—one or two pounds per week.

•Avoid too much fat, saturated fat, and cholesterol.
Eat leaner cuts of meat, poultry, fish, and dried beans for protein, limit foods high in fats, and broil or bake instead of frying foods.

•Eat foods with adequate starch and fiber.
Eat more whole grains, beans, fresh fruits and vegetables.

•Avoid too much sugar.
Reduce concentrated sweets including not only white and brown sugars, but also fructose, molasses, honey, maple syrup, and malt syrup. Select more fresh fruit as an alternative.

•Avoid too much sodium.
Learn to flavor foods with herbs, spices, and lemon juice. Refrain from adding salt to foods at the table.

•If you drink alcoholic beverages, do so in moderation.
Investigate other modes of relaxation. Try sparkling mineral water for an alternative.

The remainder of this book will introduce foods and methods to achieve these goals. Learning about whole grains is a good place to start.

2

GREAT GRAINS

GRAINS

Grains are low in fat, low in cost, and low in calories while high in fiber, trace minerals, B-vitamins, and protein (when combined with a complementary protein). They should be stored in a tightly covered container in a cool place during the winter but preferably stored in the refrigerator during the summer in order to protect the grain from rancidity and insects.

There are a variety of ways that grains can be cooked: simmered in liquid until tender, pressure cooked, baked, or "cooked" in a thermos. Whatever method is used, remember to use a pot large enough to account for the expansion of the grain. Millet and barley expand to four times their original size, while other grains usually expand two to three times their original size.

To cook in liquid, rinse the raw grain in water to remove surface grit. In a pot, bring the correct amount of liquid, grain, and a pinch of salt (optional) to a boil and stir once. Allow the liquid to return to a boil and then reduce the heat to low and cover until the grain is cooked and the liquid is absorbed.

When pressure cooking grain, generally 1/2 cup less water than normal per 1 cup dry grain is required, unless a softer consistency is desired. Add the washed grain, salt, and water to the pressure cooker and bring to full pressure. Place a flame deflector under the pressure cooker to distribute the heat evenly and to prevent burning. Reduce the heat to medium low and start gauging the cooking time. When done, remove the pressure cooker from the heat and let the pressure come down naturally. If pressed for time, place the pressure cooker in the sink and run cold water over the lid until the pressure comes down. If possible with either method, let the grain sit in the unopened pressure cooker for five to ten minutes before serving.

In a 400 ° oven, the grain will cook in about the same length of time as when cooked on a stovetop. First, sauté 1 cup of grain in 1 tablespoon of oil or butter. Then add the water, cover, and bake until the water is absorbed and the grain is tender.

When using a quart thermos, place 1 cup of grain and boiling water 1" short of the thermos stopper. Stir the grain to distribute the water around the grain. Close the thermos and let set 8-12 hours. Brown rice, for example, requires only 1 1/2 cups of boiling water and 8 hours length of time.

Adding a pinch of salt per cup of grain brings out the sweet delicious flavor and decreases the tendency of wanting to salt the dish at the table. Since the salt permeates the food while cooking, a larger amount of raw salt added after cooking would be needed to simulate the "cooked-in" flavor.

TYPES of GRAINS:

Amaranth is a rediscovered ancient Aztec grain now dubbed "the grain of the future." Its seeds are about the size of millet, ranging in color from purple-black to buff yellow. Amaranth contains protein that is of higher quality than any other grain, except quinoa, due to its high concentration of lysine, an amino acid lacking in most grains. It can be cooked into a cereal, but more frequently is added to other grains to improve the protein balance. Amaranth has a slightly nutty flavor. When cooked, it has a jelly-like consistency similar to soaked psyllium seeds. To cook, use 3 parts water to 1 part amaranth and cook 20-25 min. When combining amaranth with other grains, use 1 part amaranth to 3 parts grain and cook according to the predominant grain's instructions.

Barley has short, stubby kernels with a hard outer shell. Whole grain barley must be soaked overnight before cooking.

The most readily available form of barley is **pearled barley** which has the outer husk removed to reduce the cooking time. Barley can be used as a thickener for soups and stews, as a cereal, and as a main grain at a meal. It is also used as an ingredient in making beer, as a coffee substitute when roasted and ground, and as a sweetener known as malt when the grain is sprouted, dried, and ground. To cook pearled barley as a main grain, use 3-4 parts water to 1 part grain and cook for 1 hour.

Another type of barley used mainly in Japan, **hatomugi**, looks similar to barley, but actually is a pearl shaped seed of a wild grass called "Job's tears." Most often it is added to other grains, soups, or stews rather than used alone, due to its firm texture and expense. Like wild rice, even a small amount will permeate the dish in which it is cooked. Its unique, delicious flavor make it worth the splurge! Traditional oriental medicine use of hatomugi is to dissolve accumulated fat within the body. Use 1 part hatomugi with 3 parts of another grain and cook about 10 minutes longer than is usually required for the main grain.

Buckwheat, technically, is not a grain but a member of the rhubarb family. Buckwheat contains high quality protein, calcium, riboflavin, minerals, and B vitamins. Buckwheat with the black hull intact is suitable for sprouting, however, the hull must be removed before buckwheat can be cooked. Once the indigestible outer hull is removed, the familiar three-cornered, tan colored seeds of buckwheat appear.

Buckwheat without the hull is available roasted and unroasted. Roasted buckwheat is known as **kasha** and has a delicious nutty flavor. The unroasted variety, although tasty, has a less hearty flavor. Unroasted buckwheat can be roasted at home with or without oil or butter. To roast dry, toast in a dry saucepan, stirring until the groats become brown and fragrant. For a richer flavor, sauté groats in 1 tablespoon oil or butter, stirring constantly for 2-3 minutes.

Buckwheat can be used as a substitute for grain or potatoes. It makes delicious croquettes and stuffing for vegetables, meats, and pastries. Also, it is delicious as a breakfast cereal when combined with dried fruit and nuts. Buckwheat cooks very quickly. Use 2 parts water to 1 part buckwheat and cook for 15-20 minutes.

Corn is one of the few native grains of the western hemisphere. The most popular variety, **sweet corn**, is always eaten fresh as a vegetable.

Popcorn is derived from another variety of corn that has a hard outer layer that encases soft, moister layers in a pressured situation which explode as the interior layers heat up.

Ground, mature, dry, whole **flint or dent corn** is the basis for cornmeal mush, tortillas and polenta. It is especially good cooked whole. Wood-ash or limestone is cooked along with the corn to remove the tough outer skin and enhance the corn's nutritional content. After a period of time, the ash is rinsed from the corn. Then the corn is cooked somewhat longer with salt. The cooked whole corn can be eaten in its whole form or puréed as a grain dish or used as masa for the basis of tamales.

Masa Harina is fine cornmeal soaked in limewater to be used in making tortillas.

Hominy grits are a highly refined product of corn. The hull and corngerm have been removed, reducing nutritional content considerably.

Blue corn contains 21 percent more protein, twice the manganese and potassium, and up to 50 percent more iron than other varieties of corn. Although seemingly a new hybrid, on the contrary, blue corn has been used for thousands of years by Hopi and Navajo Indians of the Southwestern United States. A longer growing season, lower yields, and manual harvesting contribute to its higher price. Blue corn's deep, purplish-blue kernels turn pale grey when ground, and lavender when mixed with water. It has a coarser texture than yellow or white cornmeal, and a sweet, nut-like taste.

Corn contains the least amount of the amino acid lysine than any other grain. To enhance the amino acid profile, a **high lysine corn** was developed that contains up to 70% more lysine than ordinary corn, along with higher levels of tryptophan, isoleucine, threonine, and other amino acids. The cornmeal ground from this strain has an exceptionally nutty, sweet, delicious flavor.

Degerminated cornmeal has the bran layer and the germ removed to extend shelf life. Use undegerminated cornmeal ground from whole corn for superior flavor and nutrition. Since undegerminated cornmeal contains the oil-rich corngerm, refrigerate to prevent rancidity.

To cook cornmeal as a cereal, use 4 parts water to 1 part cornmeal and cook for 25 minutes.

Millet has tiny, round, yellow kernels that look like birdseed, and unfortunately, is most often used for that purpose! When cooked, millet has a delicious flavor that is appropriate for breakfast, lunch, or dinner. It has a better balance of essential amino acids than any other grain, except for amaranth and quinoa. To cook, use 3 parts water to 1 part millet. Bring to a boil, cover with a lid, reduce heat to medium, and cook for 12 minutes. Remove from heat and let sit uncovered for 20 minutes to prevent a mushy consistency. Many people prefer a softer textured millet, similar to mashed potatoes. For soft millet use 4 parts water to 1 part millet and simmer, covered, 45 minutes to 1 hour.

Oats have regained popularity lately, especially among those who are concerned about cholesterol since the bran layer of oats has been found to be an excellent soluble fiber which helps lower cholesterol. Although pure oat bran is a more concentrated source, all forms of oats contain some of this type of fiber.

Whole **oat groats** are long and light brown. Good at breakfast or as a pilaf at lunch or dinner, whole oats need approximately 2 1/2 hours cooking. They absorb a great deal of water, so cook 1 cup groats with 4-5 cups water.

Steel cut or **scotch oats** are whole oat groats that have been steamed and cut into small, coarse pieces with sharp steel blades. Cooking time is reduced from 2 1/2 hours to 45 minutes.

Oat flakes or table cut rolled oats are steamed and pressed flat between steel rollers to reduce cooking time even more— 15 to 20 minutes.

Quick cooking oats have been cut into pieces before they are rolled to make a thinner flake for 5 minute cooking.

Instant oatmeals are pre-cooked, extremely thin oat flakes that are often sugar laden, artificially flavored, highly salted, and sometimes treated with proteolytic enzymes or disodium phosphate. However, new processes have been devised to produce an instant oatmeal with no additives, preservatives, or chemical fortification for those who want convenience without chemicals. Again, read your labels to get the quality you deserve.

Oats are most often used as a cereal, but they can thicken soups or stews, add a chewy, moist texture to breads, and even serve as the main grain at lunch or dinner. (For more information, see CEREALS and FIBER.)

Quinoa (pronounced keen-wa), a grain that has been cultivated for centuries by Inca tribes in the Andes Mountains of South America and now in Colorado, is quickly becoming a staple in the diets of many. Its nicknames, "supergrain" and "the mother grain" refer to its amazing nutritional profile and delicious flavor.

Not only does quinoa contain more protein than any other grain, its amino acid profile shows it already to be a complete protein— similar to the protein quality of milk! Therefore, quinoa can be served as the main course or combined with other grains or beans to boost their protein values.

Quinoa's light texture and delicious flavor underlie its versatility from the main grain dish to breakfast, salads, and desserts. It can also be ground into a flour. However, similar to rice, corn, and millet, it contains no gluten so it should be combined with other flours for best results.

Quinoa is also easy and quick to prepare. Rinse the grain thoroughly before cooking to remove the naturally occurring bitter tasting resin that coats the grain. Although most of this is removed before packaging, it still is a good idea to rinse it before cooking. Combine 2 cups water, 1 cup quinoa, a pinch of salt, and cook 15-20 minutes. Quinoa expands almost 5 times compared with 3 times for rice. So, although it seems expensive, a little *does* go a long way.

Rice has long, medium, and short grains covered with a green-brown husk. Organic rice is difficult to grow and therefore costs more. **Brown rice** has this outer indigestable husk removed while white rice has this plus several more outer layers as well as the germ removed. **White rice** is often polished with glucose or talc to make it look even whiter. Brown rice has a delicious nutty flavor far surpassing the bland flavor of white rice. Several varieties of rice are available.

Long-grain rice cooks up dry and fluffy with separated grains whereas **short-grain rice** is soft and sticky. **Medium-grain rice** is more similar to long-grain but has some of the stickiness of short-grain rice. Texture, not nutritional content, is the main difference between the long, medium, or short grains. They can be used interchangeably in recipes, but most often long-grain is used for Chinese, Indian, Indonesian, and Middle-Eastern cooking, rice salads, and general warm weather cooking. The short-grain is used most often for desserts, Japanese cooking, and general cold weather cooking.

Contrary to what TV commercials tend to portray, cooking rice is really simple. Use 2 parts water to 1 part rice and cook 45 minutes for long-grain or 50 minutes for short-grain. The secret to perfect rice is to refrain from lifting the lid of the pan until the rice should be done. Experiment with your stove to maintain a simmer that is not too high and yet high enough to cook the grain.

Sweet brown rice is a short, round shaped rice that develops a sticky consistency and sweet flavor when cooked due to its high carbohydrate content. It is used to make amasake, mochi, and desserts, but need not stop there. Try sweet brown rice as a main grain or cooked with other types of rice for a festive flair.

Parboiled or converted rice is rice that is steamed before being dried and then polished to make it look white. The steaming forces 70% of the B-vitamins and minerals from the bran and germ into the rice kernel. Nutritionally, it lies between brown and white rice.

Enriched, non-converted white rice is dusted with a powder containing thiamin, niacin, and iron. Do not rinse this rice before cooking in order to retain the added enrichment nutrients.

Basmati rice is a unique, delicious, aromatic, easily digested rice that can be grown only in the mineral-rich foothills of the Himilayas. Although traditionally eaten in its lightly milled white form, the whole grain brown basmati is now available. Although no East Indian meal is complete without basmati rice, it is perfect with any type of meal, especially during the summertime. To cook basmati rice, use slightly less than 2 cups of water per cup of rice. White basmati requires only 15 minutes cooking while brown basmati needs 45 minutes, similar to cooking regular brown rice. Substitute basmati rice for white rice for better nutrition and flavor. Because of limited quantities and importation costs, basmati rice is more expensive than brown rice.

To provide a less expensive alternative, a hybrid that could be grown in the United States, primarily in Texas, was developed by crossing basmati with long-grain rice. This variety is called **Texmati rice** and has a similar flavor to basmati rice. Brown texmati is the whole grain version while the white texmati is lightly polished. Use the same cooking methods as basmati rice. Texmati is also an excellent substitution for regular white rice.

Wild rice with its long, dark-brown kernel, is neither a rice nor a grain but the seed of a grass which grows in the marshy areas of northern Minnesota, Wisconsin, and southern Canada. Although still found growing wild, much wild rice is produced by conventional growers. Limited quantities and a method of harvesting controlled by law and custom contribute to its high price. The flavor is so predominant that it can be combined with brown rice without sacrificing the heartiness of the wild rice. To cook, use 3 parts water to 1 part wild rice and cook 1 hour or more.

Wehani rice is a beautiful rose colored hybrid rice developed by the Lundberg Family Rice Farms in California. The nutty flavor, light texture and unusual color make this special whole grain rice. Combine 2 cups water, 1 cup rice, a pinch of salt and cook 30 minutes. Then let it sit, covered, 10 minutes before serving.

Sushi rice is a semi-polished white, short grain rice traditionally used in making nori wrapped sushi rolls. Sushi rice should be rinsed and drained several times until the rinse water is almost clear. At this point, the rice should be allowed to drain for 30-60 minutes.

Using equal amounts of water to rice, bring to a boil over medium heat, and cook for 1 minute. Reduce heat to low and cook for 8-10 minutes; then reduce heat to very low for 10 minutes more. Do not remove cover while cooking. Remove from heat and let rice stand, covered, for 10 minutes more before fluffing and using in the sushi.

Quick cooking brown rice is now available for those whose cooking time is limited and want a more nutritious alternative to quick cooking white rice. A special process formulated by Arrowhead Mills involves exposing individual whole grains of rice to dry heat for minute amounts of time. The moisture inside the grain turns to steam and exits the grain by creating tunnels within the rice. This effect gives the rice its quick cooking properties while retaining its rich natural nutrition. Quick cooking brown rice requires only 10-12 minutes cooking. After removing the rice from the heat and letting it set 2 minutes, the rice is ready to eat! (Almost makes one feel guilty, doesn't it?) The texture, nutritional content, and flavor are somewhat similar to the traditional brown rice.

Rye has dark-brown kernels that are longer and thinner than wheat. Rye is usually found in the flour form but can be cooked in its whole form to be used as a cereal or combined with other grains for a main dish rice substitute. Most people falsely equate the flavor of caraway seeds to rye since most rye bread is seasoned with them. Rye, however, has a delicious, hearty flavor of its own. To cook whole rye, use 4 parts water to 1 part rye and cook for 1 hour for a chewy consistency. For a softer grain, soak 6 hours and simmer 2-3 hours or pressure cook in the soaking water for 45 minutes.

Triticale has gray-brown, oval-shaped kernels which are larger than wheat grains and plumper than rye grains. Most often it is sold as flour rather than as a whole grain. Triticale is a hybrid developed in the 1930's by crossing wheat and rye that is higher in protein because of its improved amino acid balance. With similar properties to rye berries, it can be cooked by using 4 parts water to 1 part triticale and cooking for 1 hour or more. Most often it is found in the form of flour.

Wheat is utilized in many ways. Wheat bran, wheat germ, whole wheat flour, cracked wheat, and pasta are the most common forms. See CEREALS and FIBER for more information.

Wheat, in its whole grain form, is known as **wheat berries** characterized by short, rounded kernels of varying shades of brown. After cooking, the "berries" can be added to rice for texture or used in stuffings, casseroles, or breads. Use 3 parts water to 1 part wheat and cook for 2 or more hours.

Cracked wheat is made by cracking the wheat berries between rollers resulting in a considerably reduced cooking time. Use 2 parts water to 1 part wheat and cook for only 25 minutes. Use cracked wheat as a cereal, a rice substitute, in casseroles, stuffings, or in making tabouleh, a Lebanese grain-based salad.

Bulgur is cracked wheat that has been partially cooked and then toasted. Since it is partially cooked, the cooking time is even less than cracked wheat. Use 2 parts water to 1 part bulgur and cook 15 minutes. Another method is to boil the water, pour it over the bulgur, cover, and set aside for 1 hour.

Farina is a refined cereal made from wheat that is ground and sifted. The bran and most of the germ is removed in the process.

Cous-Cous is made from coarsely-ground semolina which has been pre-cooked. (Semolina is durum wheat with the bran and germ removed.) Cous-cous is the traditional dish of the North African countries of Morroco, Algeria, and Tunisia. It is a refreshingly light grain used as a main or side dish, a breakfast cereal, a salad, or as a dessert. To cook, use equal parts of water and cous-cous. Boil the water, add the cous-cous, stir, cover, remove from the heat, and let stand 5 minutes. That's all the time it takes!

Recipes

MUSHROOM BARLEY PILAF   *serves 3-4*
Sautéed mushrooms added to cooked barley give that extra zip that enhances plain barley.

1 cup pearled barley
3 cups water
1/4 tsp. salt

1/2-1 lb. mushrooms, quartered
2 TB. olive oil or butter
1 TB. naturally aged soy sauce (tamari shoyu)

1. Rinse barley and place in pot with water and salt.
2. Bring to a boil and simmer 1 1/2 hours until grains have expanded and water has evaporated.
3. Meanwhile, heat oil or butter and add mushrooms and soy sauce. Sauté until mushrooms are golden and smell wonderfully!
4. Add mushrooms to cooked barley while barley is still hot. Let flavors blend about 10 minutes, taste, and adjust seasoning.
5. Serve as an accompaniment to beans, fish, or meat. As a main dish entrée, garnish with roasted sunflower seeds and serve with your favorite vegetables.

BUCKWHEAT PILAF   *serves 4*
Cooks in 20 minutes!

1 1/2 cups white or toasted buckwheat groats
1 onion, diced
3 medium potatoes (1 inch chunks)
3 cups boiling water
1/2 tsp. thyme
1/4 tsp. salt or 1 tsp. naturally aged soy sauce (tamari shoyu)
Oil (optional)

1. Roast white buckwheat in dry skillet or with 1 tsp. of unrefined oil for a richer flavor. (Toasted buckwheat needs no further roasting.)
2. Sauté onion in oil if desired.
3. Combine all ingredients in pot. Bring to a boil, cover, reduce heat, and simmer 20 minutes.
4. Serve with fish and steamed vegetables or with a chunky soup for a hearty meal.

Recipes

SAVORY BULGUR   *serves 3-4*

Although the oil is optional when preparing bulgur, it adds a rich flavor. Preparation time is minimal for this recipe, but it tastes as though hours of your time went into it.

2 cups bulgur
3 cloves garlic minced
1 TB. unrefined oil
4 scallions, thinly sliced including the green
3 cups boiling water
1/4 tsp. salt

1. In a cooking pot, sauté garlic in oil for 2 minutes.
2. Add bulgur and sauté another couple minutes until bulgur is coated with oil.
3. Add salt, boiling water, and scallions.
4. Stir, remove from heat cover, and let sit 1 hour.
5. Garnish with chopped parsley and serve.

SIMPLE, BUT DELICIOUS CORNBREAD   *makes 13 X 9 1/2" pan*

Hearty, wheat-free flat bread is a wonderful accompaniment to soups or stews. Also try it as the basis for an open faced sandwich.

2 cups high lysine cornmeal
pinch of salt
water (boiling)

1. Preheat oven to 350°.
2. Add salt to cornmeal and toast over a low flame in a dry skillet being careful not to burn.
3. Add enough boiling water to make a thick batter.
4. Let rest 10 minutes and then spread in a 13" by 9 1/2" oiled baking dish.
5. Bake 30 minutes at 350°.
6. Serve with your favorite spread, sweet or savory.

Recipes

PECANOA PILAF   *serves 4*
This is excellent as a main dish, as a stuffing for vegetables, fish, or poultry, served as a side dish accompanied with beans or other protein dish, as a basis for a grain salad (add peas and celery), or even for breakfast!

1 TB. safflower oil
1 small onion, diced
1/2 bunch parsley, chopped
1/2 teaspoon each: ground cumin, coriander, curry powder
1 1/3 cup quinoa, thoroughly rinsed
3 cups water
1/8-1/4 teaspoon sea salt
1/2 cup pecans

1. Preheat oven to 300°. Place pecans on a cookie sheet and dry roast for 20 minutes while pilaf cooks. Stir occasionally to prevent burning.
2. Heat oil in a saucepan and add onions.
3. Sauté 3 minutes and add parsley and spices.
4. Sauté an additional 3 minutes and then add quinoa, water, and salt. Bring to a boil and cover.
5. Reduce heat and simmer 15 minutes.
6. Remove from heat and stir in coarsely chopped pecans. Let sit at least 10 minutes and serve.

PEACHY QUINOA   *serves 4*
Great for breakfast or for a quick dessert! Mention the name and everybody will want to try it!

1 cup quinoa, thoroughly rinsed
3 cups water
pinch of salt
4 dried peaches or other dried fruit, cut into small pieces
roasted almonds, walnuts, or pecans

1. Place all ingredients into a saucepan.
2. Bring to a boil, cover, and reduce heat to simmer.
3. Cook for 25 minutes or until all the water is absorbed.
4. Divide into bowls and sprinkle each serving with nuts.

CEREALS

Many of the grains are also available in flake form. Oat flakes or oatmeal is most familiar for its use as a cooked cereal, in granola, and casseroles. Cooking with the other grain flakes, barley, rye, rice, and wheat can provide interesting variety. Beyond its traditional uses, the grain flakes offer a nutritious, quick alternative if you are pressed for time but want a cooked grain at your meal. For instance, instead of the 45 minutes for cooking brown rice, rice flakes need only 15 minutes to cook. Barley flakes cook in 25 minutes instead of 75 minutes for pearled barley.

Most flakes are processed by steaming the grain followed by rolling. Oat flakes definitely require the steaming process, but the other grains can go through a dry radiant heat process that produces a better tasting, more nutritious product that cooks up like the original whole grain. In this method, the grain is quickly cooked for 15-20 seconds under dry heat and then sent through the rollers. Read your labels for flaked grain which undergoes this process.

Flakes, especially oat flakes, are the basis for **granola**. Even though people tend to think of granola as a recent "back to nature" phenomena, a prototype was invented during the Civil War by none other that J.H. Kellogg. His version was a cereal of baked oatmeal and whole grain dough that he envisioned as a good staple food for vegetarians. Granola is a nutritious cereal high in fiber and is available in dozens of versions depending on what sweeteners, dried fruits, nuts, spices, and other grains are used. However, since granola tends to be high in fat and sweeteners, it should be eaten in moderation. Besides combining with milk, granola can be eaten out of hand or made into a delicious cooked cereal.

Other **cooked cereals** include coarsely ground 7-grain or 4-grain combinations and "cream of " type cereals made from wheat, rice, rye, or buckwheat. These can be made with milk or water and are delicious when combined with dried fruit or nuts. Five-20 minutes is all that is needed to cook these cereals in the morning. To wake up to a prepared breakfast, put the cereal in a "slow cooker" pot on low overnight, or use the thermos bottle and hot water cooking method. Another alternative is to warm up leftover rice, barley, or buckwheat for a breakfast cereal and add dried fruit, honey, or maple syrup.

Cereals from whole, flaked, cracked, or ground grains are the most nutritious but do require some preparation time. **Ready to eat cereals** attempt to close the time gap. But, many commercial ready to eat cereals are a combination of over-processed grains, little fiber, preservatives, artificial colors, artificial flavors, sprayed-on vitamins and minerals, and loads of sugar. Kellogg's Frosted Rice had so much iron added to it at one point that a man from Seattle found that he could move the flakes around his bowl with a magnet! Some cereals are more than half sugar with others close behind in the 30-47% range. The recent analysis of the 1976-80 Health and Nutrition Examination Survey conducted by the Department of Health and Human Service revealed that cold cereals contribute 4.6% for the entire population's sugar intake. For children age 1-10 years old, the figure rose to 9%.

Good, nutritious ready to eat cereals are available, however. Many look and taste similar to the old standards such as Raisin Bran, Wheaties, Cheerios, and Rice Krispies, with the exception that they are contain no questionable additives and are much lower in sugar and salt. Instead of corn syrup or white sugar, some alternative cereals use barley malt syrup or, occasionally, honey or fruit juice as sweeteners.

Puffed cereals are produced by heating moist grains and then suddenly dropping the pressure in the cooking unit. This causes steam to expand rapidly, exploding the grains. Puffed cereals are lower in nutritional content than cooked whole grain cereals, nonetheless, they often seem to "hit the spot" for breakfast or snacks. Read your labels with this item. Look for puffed cereals with minimal sweeteners and salt and no artificial flavors or colors.

Finely ground whole grain **baby cereals**, free of sugar, salt, and preservatives, are available to provide delicious, proper nourishment for children. Besides "cream of" cereals (brown rice, barley, rye, wheat, and oatmeal), sprouted cereals are a good alternative. Sprouting the grain converts some of the starch into maltose which, besides providing natural sweetness, facilitates digestion of the grain. Sprouting also increases the protein content and vitamins A, B, C, and E. After sprouting, the grains are toasted and finely ground. Another popular baby cereal, Kokoh, is a mixture of finely ground brown rice, sweet brown rice, oats, and sesame seeds which requires 20 minutes of cooking. Just because labels declare a cereal to be a baby cereal, don't let that stop you or any other adult from eating it. The delicious, smooth textures are appropriate for all ages.

NOTE: The rapid growth and metabolism of infants requires a higher amount of nutrients as a percentage of body weight than adults (although the actual total amount needed is lower than adults since the infants are obviously smaller than adults). Iron is the most difficult nutrient to obtain from food after a child is weaned from breast milk or formula until the age of 1 1/2 years. This is one instance where a baby cereal enriched in iron is generally recommended for children 6 months up to 3 years old. These cereals contain a specially prepared iron source that is extremely bioavailable. At the present time fortification with this type of iron is available only in refined baby cereals. Combining the whole grain with some of the enriched, refined cereal may be a reasonable alternative.

Wheat germ, the embryo of the grain, often is added to cereals during manufacture or at the table by the consumer. Its popularity stems from the fact that it is high in the entire B complex except B_{12} and high in vitamin E, protein, and iron. Since the major component of wheat germ is oil, it goes rancid quickly and should be eaten only while fresh. Therefore, wheat germ should never be purchased in bulk. The best way to buy wheat germ is in nitrogen flushed packages. Nitrogen gas is a natural component of air that displaces the oxygen which initiates rancidity. Once opened, it should be refrigerated and used within a week. Toasted wheat germ when refrigerated or frozen, will retain its freshness somewhat longer than raw, but the toasting process also reduces the nutritional content somewhat. Fresh wheat germ should never taste bitter.

Corn germ is now available in nitrogen flushed packages. It has a sweet nutty flavor and is higher in vitamins and mineral content than wheat germ. Once open, store in the refrigerator and use within 1 week.

Bran, the outside protective shell of any grain, is well known for its fiber content. Wheat bran is the most popular and is also referred to as "Miller's bran" or "unprocessed bran". The more processed foods one eats, the less fiber one gets.   Therefore, eating minimally processed foods from whole grains, fresh fruits, and vegetables will provide generous amounts of fiber for the average person. If more is needed, using bran will facilitate proper digestion and elimination. Only a small amount of bran is needed, ranging from 1/2 teaspoon to 2 tablespoons. However, it must be taken with plenty of liquid, otherwise it can prove to be too harsh. Eating too much bran can have a negative effect of binding up minerals such as copper, iron, and zinc and preventing their absorption.

For those allergic to wheat who still need added fiber, bran from rice or oats is a good alternative. As mentioned previously concerning oats, lately, **oat bran** has been getting better reviews than wheat bran for its superior ability in reducing blood cholesterol. It belongs to a group called soluble fibers which absorb water and change the fiber into a soft mass to act as a gentle bulking agent. Wheat bran, in comparison, belongs to the family of insoluble fibers whose laxative effect derives from simply irritating the intestines. Oat bran can be used as a cooked cereal or in baking. See FIBER for more details.

Unless eaten within two weeks, most ground or whole grain cereals should be refrigerated to protect from rancidity, especially during the summer. Except for granola type cereals, puffed cereals or ready to eat cereals should be stored in tightly sealed containers in a cool place and used quickly.

Recipes

GREAT HOMEMADE GRANOLA   *makes about 8 cups*
With homemade granola you can determine the sweetness and complexity. Plus, you get that incredible aroma as it bakes!

6 cups oat flakes or substitute 2 cups with rye or wheat flakes
1/2 cup chopped almonds, pecans, cashews, or sunflower seeds
1/4 cup shredded dried coconut
1/3 cup safflower or corn oil
1 teaspoon vanilla extract
1/2 cup honey, maple syrup, or rice syrup
1/4 teaspoon salt (opt.)

1. Preheat oven to 325°.
2. Mix all ingredients together and spread mixture on 2 cookie sheets making a thin layer.
3. Place in oven and bake about 20 minutes or until golden brown and fragrant. Stir frequently while in oven to prevent burning.
4. Granola will crisp up as it cools.

OIL-FREE GRANOLA   *makes about 6 cups*
Granola is even delicious when it is made without the oil! The secret is to warm the sweetener before adding to the mixture before baking the granola at a low temperature.

4 cups rolled oats
1 cup rye or wheat flakes
1/3 cup coconut (opt.)
1/2 cup total: favorite nuts or seeds combination
pinch of salt (opt.)
1 teaspoon vanilla extract
1/3 - 1/2 cup warmed honey, maple syrup, or rice syrup
raisins (opt.)

1. Preheat oven to 300°.
2. In a large bowl, combine oats, rye flakes, coconut, nuts, and salt.
3. Warm sweetener and vanilla over a low heat and mix in thoroughly with oat mixture.
4. Spread thinly on a cookie sheet.
5. Place in oven for 20-25 minutes, stirring every 5 minutes to prevent burning. Granola is done when it smells fragrant and flakes *begin* to turn golden.
6. If adding raisins, stir in after granola bakes.
7. Let granola cool before serving. Store in a tightly sealed container in the refrigerator.

Recipes

FLAKED GRAIN FLAT BREAD   *makes 13 X 9 inch pan*

Flat breads are good bases for spreads and accompaniments to soups. This recipe uses no leavening and gets its good flavor from flaked grain. Use a single grain or a combination to equal the 4 cups.

4 cups oat, rye, barley or wheat flakes
1/4 tsp. salt
4 cups boiling water

1. Preheat oven to 350°.
2. Using a blender or food processor, grind 2 cups flakes until coarse flour texture is obtained.
3. Repeat with remaining flakes.
4. Add salt to ground flakes and lightly toast the mixture over medium low heat in a dry skillet. (Be careful—it burns easily.)
5. Transfer ingredients to a large mixing bowl. Gradually add water to obtain a thick "cookie batter" consistency. You will use about 3 cups of water.
6. Let batter sit 5-10 minutes and pat into an oiled 13 X 9 baking dish 1/2-3/4" thick.
7. Bake at 350° for 30-40 minutes. Bread should be browned and somewhat hard.
8. Slice and serve.

WHOLE GRAIN BREAKFAST CEREAL   *serves 3*

Breakfast can be quick to fix when leftovers are used.

2 cups cooked rice, barley, millet, buckwheat
1 1/2 cups water
1/4 cup raisins (optional)
1/2 tsp. cinnamon powder (optional)
roasted walnuts or pecans

1. Add water to grain in a medium sized saucepan.
2. Break up lumps with a fork.
3. Stir in raisins and cinnamon.
4. Bring mixture to a boil, reduce heat to low.
5. Cover and simmer 15 minutes. Stir frequently to prevent burning.
6. When cereal is creamy, serve and garnish each portion with roasted walnuts or pecans.

Recipes

JUICY CEREAL　　　　　　　　　　*serves 2-3*

If you're alert enough in the morning to be in a creative mood, try this trick. It's too easy to be true!

1 cup oats, rye, rice, barley, or wheat flakes
1 1/2 cup apple juice or your favorite flavor (Pina colada?? Why not?)
1 1/2 cup water
pinch of salt (opt.)

1. Bring apple juice and water to a boil.
2. Add salt and grain flakes.
3. Stir, reduce heat, and simmer 15-20 minutes until liquid is absorbed and serve.

WHEAT GERM BREADSTICKS　　　*makes about 2 dozen*

No words can describe the delicious flavor of these non-yeasted breadsticks! They can be mixed and baked within 45 minutes.

2 1/4 cups whole wheat flour
2 1/4 cups raw wheat germ
1 teaspoon salt
2 TB. roasted sesame seeds
1 1/2 cup milk, soy milk, or nut milk
1/3 cup safflower oil
2 TB. honey or rice syrup

1. Preheat oven to 350°.
2. Combine flour, wheat germ, salt, and sesame seeds together in a medium sized bowl.
3. Blend milk, oil, and syrup in blender or food processor.
4. Add wet mixture with the dry ingredients in the bowl.
5. Knead on a floured surface until it holds together quite well (about 3 minutes).
6. Roll dough to 1/4 - 1/2" thickness.
7. Cut into sticks 5" long.
8. Place on an oiled cookie sheet and bake until golden brown. (Check at 20 minutes. They may go as long as 30 minutes.)
9. Serve with soup, dips, spaghetti, or eat as a snack.

Recipes

OAT BRAN MUFFINS   *makes 1 dozen*

These delicious muffins contain no flour, only oat bran. Quick to make, they are a perfect snack or breakfast bread.

2 1/2 cups oat bran
1/4 cup raisins
1 TB. baking powder
1/4 teaspoon salt
3/4 cup milk, soy milk,
or 3/4 cup water blended with 1 TB. of sesame tahini
2 eggs or 1/3 cup fresh tofu
2 TB. honey, maple syrup, or brown rice syrup
2 TB. sesame, safflower, or corn oil

1. Preheat oven to 425°.
2. Combine all dry ingredients, mixing well.
3. Beat liquids and eggs together. (If using tofu instead of eggs, process with liquids until smooth in a blender or food processor.)
4. Add liquids to dry ingredients, stirring only until moistened.
5. Fill oiled muffin cups almost full.
6. Bake for 12-15 minutes or until done.

FLOUR

Years ago it used to be so easy to go to the store to buy flour since, generally, the choice was between all purpose refined white flour or refined white cake flour. But now the shelves and bins are lined with flour ranging from the familiar all purpose white to the more obscure amaranth flour! What flour should be used when?

All whole grains can be ground into flour, but each has its own characteristics. Flour made from wheat is what most people envision when the word "flour" is mentioned. There are, however, different types of flour even within the wheat division.

Whole wheat flour is made by grinding the entire hard variety of wheat berry. It includes the outside bran layer, the starchy endosperm, and the germ of the kernel, ie. wheat germ. Hard wheat is high in gluten, the protein that stretches to form an elastic framework that forms in response to yeast or natural leavening and the action of kneading bread. It is the gluten which yields light, airy loaves. If regular whole wheat flour is used in unyeasted baked goods, the results are somewhat dense and heavy. Although these qualities are enjoyed by many, others prefer to combine whole wheat flour with white flour or substitute with whole wheat pastry flour for a lighter texture. (See WHOLE WHEAT PASTRY FLOUR below)

White flour is made from wheat which has had both the bran layer and the wheat germ removed. Unlike whole wheat flour, white flour needs to be aged to improve its workability as a dough. Use only unbleached white flour that is aged naturally to avoid the chemical bleaching agents that are often added to white flour to quicken the natural aging process.   One company enriches their organic whole wheat pastry flour with soy flour to improve nutrient value and baking quality.

Whole wheat pastry flour is a good alternative to white flour. It is ground from the soft variety of wheat which is lower in gluten.   Use pastry flour for pie crusts, cakes, cookies, and pancakes whenever yeast is not used. When making breads or anything that you want to rise, use regular whole wheat flour.

Durum wheat is used in making whole wheat pasta since its high levels of protein and cellulose help keep cooked pasta firm.

Semolina is durum flour with the bran and germ removed. "White" pasta is made from semolina flour.

Gluten flour is made from hard wheat flour that has had much of its starch removed to concentrate the gluten. Since this process yields up to 80% protein, it is an effective booster of protein in baked goods. Gluten flour added to bread doughs helps the yeast work even better to make the dough rise faster, higher, and more evenly. Gluten flour also compensates for the lower gluten contents of other flours.

Graham flour is a coarse type of whole wheat flour ground from hard wheat. Although most famous for its use in graham crackers, it adds a pleasant texture and chewiness to all baked goods.

Non-wheat flours include the following:

Amaranth flour is a gluten-free, nutty flavored flour high in protein, calcium, and fiber. Amaranth is also high in lysine, the amino acid typically low in grains with the exception of quinoa. Use it to boost the protein quality and nutritional content of other grains by substituting 1/4 amaranth flour to 3/4 of another flour.

Corn flour is a more finely textured cornmeal that is good in breads, pancakes, and muffins.

Rye flour is most familiar for its use in breads and crackers. It is lower in gluten than whole wheat and therefore, is often combined with whole wheat to improve its rising ability. Rye flour is difficult to use because of its sticky consistency which tends to yield a moist, compact product. 100% rye products are delicious and can be made, but it is advisable to use recipes which specify using exclusively rye flour.

Soy flour is flour made from ground soybeans lightly toasted to heighten flavor and improve digestability. It is high in protein (35%) and high in fat (20%), and it is used as a nutrition booster. Since it has no gluten it cannot replace whole wheat flour. Because of its high fat content, soy flour is especially prone to rancidity. If it smells "off", throw the soy flour away before ruining your favorite recipe.

The rest of the grains can also be ground into flour. **Rice, corn, millet,** and **quinoa** are gluten-free while **buckwheat, oat,** and **barley** have low amounts of gluten. When making something that requires rising, combine these flours with whole wheat flour for best results. Each grain has its own unique flavor and texture to offer to a bread or baked product so experimentation can be fun. Start by substituting for each cup of whole wheat flour used in a recipe with 3/4 cup whole wheat flour and 1/4 cup flour of your choice and see how many variations from your basic recipe you can invent.

As with rye flour, initially it is advisable to use recipes which specify a certain flour other than whole wheat rather than substituting another type of flour for all of the wheat flour in a recipe. The number of recipes on packages of alternative flours and from many cookbooks proves that it can work, but textures and degree of heaviness probably will vary from what one may be accustomed. Flat breads, muffins, cookies, and pancakes can be made successfully with single non-wheat flours. Use actual recipes or have fun and experiment!

After using recipes specifying a flour other than wheat, the properties of the flours become apparent.

PROPERTIES OF VARIOUS FLOURS

TYPE OF FLOUR	FLAVOR	BAKED TEXTURE
amaranth	sweet	smooth, crisp crust moist, fine crumb
barley	malt-like after taste	firm, chewy crust cakelike crumb
brown rice	sweet	dry, fine crumb
buckwheat	musty, robust	moist, fine crumb
cornmeal	slightly sweet	grainy, slightly dry
millet	buttery, slightly sweet	moist, dense crumb smooth, thin crust
oat	sweet, nutty	coarse, large crumb firm crust
quinoa	sweet, nutty	delicate, cakelike crumb
rye	tangy, slightly sour	moist, supple crumb smooth, hard crust
soy	slightly bitter	moist, fine crumb spongy crust
wheat	sweet, nutty	supple crust coarse, large crumb (whole wheat) fine crumb (pastry flour)

When a non wheat flour is used without wheat, the baked textures listed above are accentuated. For instance, a product made solely with brown rice flour will yield a dry, crisp, grainy texture quite different from the texture and taste of a baked whole wheat product. 100% brown rice flour could be used in a cookie or flat bread recipe, but would be unsatisfactory in a cake. To remedy the situation without resorting to wheat, compensate for the dry, grainy texture of brown rice flour with a grain flour that yields a moist texture such as buckwheat, millet, rye, or soy. The converse also applies: when using a flour which may yield a product with too moist or gummy a texture, add a dry textured flour. To make a 100% buckwheat product, buckwheat groats which have been ground into a flour can be added to regular buckwheat flour to balance the gummy texture.

Whole grain flour should be stored in moisture proof bags or containers in the refrigerator or freezer and used within three months to avoid rancidity. Warm to room temperature before using to ensure better baking.

Treat your family, friends, and yourself (!) to these quick and easy holiday cookies and quick breads. Try the flours listed or experiment with your own combinations.

Recipes

WHOLE WHEAT PASTRY CRUST   *makes one 9" double crust or two 9" single crusts*
A delicious pastry is possible with whole wheat pastry flour. A lighter, easier to manage version replaces half of the flour with unbleached white flour.

3 cups whole wheat pastry flour (or 1 1/2 cups whole wheat pastry flour and 1 1/2 cups unbleached white flour)
Pinch of salt
1/2 cup unrefined oil (sesame, safflower, corn)
Approx. 1/4 cup water

1. Mix salt with flour.
2. Cut in oil with fork or your fingers until mixture has pebble-like consistency.
3. Gradually add water until dough forms into a damp, but smooth ball. (To avoid a tough crust, handle dough as little as possible.)
4. Let dough sit a few minutes.
5. Roll out on a floured pastry cloth or cutting board to desired size, flipping dough twice to prevent sticking.
6. Transfer to pie plate and prebake or add filling and then bake.

GINGERBREAD PEOPLE   *makes about 3 dozen*
This popular cookie can easily be made wheat-free.

2 cups rye flour
1 cup oat flour
1/2 teaspoon salt
2 teaspoons ground cinnamon
1 teaspoon ground ginger
1/2 teaspoon ground cloves
1/4 cup safflower oil
1 teaspoon vanilla extract
1/2 cup barley malt
1/4 cup water

1. Preheat oven to 325°.
2. Mix the dry ingredients in a medium sized bowl.
3. Mix liquid ingredients in a separate bowl and then add to the dry.
4. Mix liquid and dry ingredients well and form dough into 4 balls. Chill dough for at least 1 hour.
5. Roll dough on a floured surface to about 1/3" thickness.
6. Cut dough with gingerbread person cookie cutter and place the cookies on a lightly oiled cookie sheet.
7. Bake for about 15 minutes until firm but not browned. (If desired, brush diluted sweetener on cookies after 8 minutes baking time and then return to the oven.) Cookies will crisp as they cool.
8. Store in an airtight container.

Recipes

PECAN CRISPIES   *makes 3 dozen*

The crunchy, grainy rice flour is complemented with the soft textured oat flour for a light, delicious cookie.

1 1/2 cups brown rice flour
2 cups oat flour
1/2 teaspoon salt
1 1/2 cup chopped pecans
1/4 cup safflower oil
1/2 cup rice syrup or maple syrup
1/3 cup apple juice
1 teaspoon vanilla extract (omit if using maple syrup)

1. Preheat oven to 350°.
2. Mix dry ingredients and liquid ingredients separately.
3. Combine the two together to form a very thick dough.
4. Divide into 4 balls and chill 2 hours.
5. Form into flat, 3" cookies, smooth out edges and place on an oiled cookie sheet.
6. Bake for 25 minutes until firm but not browned. They will crisp as they cool.
Variation: Make a small indentation in the center of each cookie and fill with an unsweetened jam or jelly. Bake as usual.

WHOLE WHEAT-BUCKWHEAT MUFFINS   *makes 1 dozen*

Perfect with butter or your favorite nut butter for breakfast or with winter soups for a satisfying lunch.

1/4 cup safflower or corn oil
1/3 cup honey or rice syrup
1 egg, lightly beaten
1 1/2 cups water
2 cups whole wheat pastry flour
1/3 cup buckwheat flour
1/2 teaspoon salt
2 1/2 teaspoons baking powder

1. Preheat oven to 400°.
2. Combine oil and sweetener and beat well.
3. Add the egg and water and beat vigorously for 1-2 minutes.
4. Mix dry ingredients in a separate bowl.
5. Add dry ingredients to wet, stirring just to moisten. Avoid overmixing.
6. Fill oiled muffin cups to within 1/4" of the top and bake 20-25 minutes.
7. Cool the muffin pan on a wire rack for 10 minutes before removing muffins.

Recipes

CRANBERRY NUT MUFFINS   *makes 1 dozen*

Perfect for the holidays! You may want to freeze cranberries just so you can make this recipe throughout the entire year!

2 eggs, beaten
1/2 cup safflower or corn oil
1/2 cup rice syrup or honey
1 teaspoon vanilla extract
1 1/4 cup whole wheat pastry flour
1/4 cup flour of your choice: amaranth, barley, oat, millet
OR 2 TB. wheat germ plus 2 TB. wheat or oat bran
1 1/2 teaspoon baking powder
1 1/2 cups chopped fresh cranberries
1/2 cup chopped walnuts

1. Preheat oven to 350°.
2. In a small bowl combine eggs, oil, rice syrup, and vanilla.
3. In a larger bowl combine flours and baking powder.
4. Stir in liquid ingredients until just mixed. (Do not overmix.)
5. Add cranberries and walnuts and mix thoroughly.
6. Pour batter into an oiled 12 cup muffin tin.
7. Bake for 25 minutes. Remove from pan and cool on a wire rack.

BREADS

The best breads are simple. Besides using yeast or sourdough for leavening, bread consists basically of flour and a liquid. Optional ingredients include herbs, a sweetener (honey, molasses, barley malt, or whey powder) to help feed the yeast, oil or butter, bran, and nutrition boosters (powdered milk, soy flour, or eggs). Similar to the Orient depending upon rice as a staple food, Western societies depended upon their ability to transform wheat, rye, and barley into dense, moist, rich, satisfying loaves of bread. Unfortunately, during the past 50 years, many people were raised on white bread whose optional ingredients read like a chemistry book. Preservatives, dough conditioners, wood cellulose, hydrogenated oils, multiple types of sweeteners, artificial flavorings, and artificial colors were added to give bread textures and keeping properties not normally found in breads. As Julia Child, the famous cook and author, so aptly put it, "How can a society be so great, when its bread tastes like kleenex?"

Luckily, traditional breads are making a comeback. Not only are quality, whole wheat breads available, wheat-free and other specialty breads are being made to supply even more variety.

Sourdough breads are made with a special sourdough culture which is responsible for the characteristic tangy, pleasantly sour flavor. Sourdough breads have been made all over the world. The most famous legends about their origin concern the California Gold Rush miners who became so excited about a new gold claim that they got up and simply left their bread dough sitting out at the campsite. Upon returning, even though they noticed that the bread dough had soured, they baked it anyway. The result? Sourdough bread!

Most sourdough cultures are made from wheat flour and depend heavily upon the natural wild yeast in the environment. Because these yeasts vary according to the vicinity in which the breads are made, each bakery and household will make a uniquely flavored sourdough bread. Constant, careful maintenance of the culture is needed to ensure that proper combination of time, temperature, acidity, and dough consistency will yield a bread with good texture and flavor.

Recently, a new sourdough culturing technique was introduced in West Germany in order to provide sourdough breads with more consistent results. With rye flour as the sourdough medium instead of wheat, a special pure monoculture is used that does not require the presence of the wild yeasts. Less critical maintenance of the culture is needed since, once the sourdough reaches a certain pH level, the fermentation stops. Nutritionally, there is no difference between the "wild yeast" or the monoculture method. 10-15% of the sourdough breads sold in Germany are now made with the monoculture method. Currently in the United States, only "The Sourdough Bakery", whose original bakeries were located in Austin, Texas and presently at many of the Whole Foods Markets and other locations throughout the country, uses this special technique.

It is interesting to note that because of the general chemical makeup of rye flour, breads made from 100% rye flour must be made with sourdough culture in order to avoid the moist, sticky texture that is characteristic of the flour. Usually, most rye breads are made with white rye flour (removing the bran and wheat germ eliminates factors which contribute to its stickiness) or are made from a combination of wheat and rye flours.

Many sourdough breads also contain yeast in order to make a lighter, less dense bread. Read your labels if seeking one containing only the sourdough culture.

The majority of breads use yeast as the leavener instead of sourdough. Examples include English muffins, bagels, dinner rolls, hamburger and hot dog buns, pizza crusts, and pita bread.

Pita bread is the only one that may need some explanation. Often called pocket bread or Bible bread, pita bread is a round, flat bread usually made from whole wheat flour that can be opened to form a pocket to stuff with a sandwich filling or salad. Traditionally, it is filled with falafel or hummus.

Unless used within 2 days, refrigerate chemical free breads. Breads such as French breads dry out within a day but, like all breads, can be revived by cutting into pieces and steaming in a vegetable steamer for 3 minutes. To reheat bread in the oven, wrap bread in foil, sprinkle with water, and bake 10-15 minutes at 350°.

The fermentation time needed for yeasted and sourdough breads allows for the breakdown of an enzyme called phytase. This enzyme is used by new plants in order to gain access to the nutrients within the seed or whole grain kernel. Until that need arises, the nutrients are locked up by a substance called phytic acid. As bread ferments, iron, calcium, zinc, magnesium, and copper are unbound by the phytic acid and, consequently, are more available to the body.

In contrast, quick breads and unleavened breads are a category of breads which do not depend upon yeast or sourdough culture for leavening. Quick breads are generally used for snacks and desserts. Unleavened breads are often used for open-faced sandwiches or, if thin, rolled around a filling. Quick and unleavened breads lack the fermentation time required to deactivate the phytic acid, but, usually this presents no problem if the rest of the diet contains good food sources of the bound minerals.

Quickbreads use baking powder or baking soda as a leavener. These breads do not require kneading or rising time, so very little time is needed to prepare them. Baking powder is a combination of baking soda, an alkaline substance, with an acid such as creme of tartar, monocalcium phosphate, sodium acid pyrophosphate, or aluminum sulphate. Baking powders containing sodium aluminum sulphate should be avoided since excessive amounts of aluminum may contribute to aluminum toxicity. Aluminum-free baking powders are commonly sold. Also, numerous cookbooks have easy recipes for homemade baking powder using baking soda, creme of tartar, and arrowroot.

Unleavened breads are made from whole grains and water with no yeast, baking powder, or baking soda. As their alternative name, flatbread, implies these breads do not rise. Tortillas, chapatis, Essene bread, and mochi are popular flatbreads.

Tortillas made from corn or wheat are the most familiar flatbreads. Corn tortillas are made from cornmeal, water, and lime. The type of lime used is limestone, the mineral from the ground, and not the fruit. Wheat tortillas are made from white or whole wheat flour, water, and a source of fat. Choose tortillas made with vegetable oil to avoid the high amounts of saturated fats and cholesterol found in lard. The best varieties of tortillas specify on the package the particular type of unrefined oil that was used instead of the non-descript "vegetable oil" whose quality and source is undetermined.

Chapatis are similar to whole wheat tortillas except larger in size. They are the traditional accompaniment to curries and other vegetable dishes all over India.

Look for corn, whole wheat tortillas, and chapatis that are made from organically grown flour. Often these will be located in the frozen food section.

Another flatbread found in the frozen food area is **Essene bread**. This bread contains no flour, oil, sweetener, salt, or leavener. Wheat or rye berries are sprouted and ground, formed into a loaf, and baked at a very low temperature. What emerges is a chewy, dense, filling bread. Its natural sweetness is a result of the sprouting and is retained with low, slow heat. Essene bread can be eaten alone or with a salad, spread with butter, nut butter, or sandwich filling. Besides plain wheat and plain rye, Essene bread is available in other varieties: wheat with raisin, rye or wheat with seeds (sunflower, sesame, flax), wheat fruit-cake (dried fruits and nuts added), multigrain, and wheat with dates and cinnamon.

Mochi is an unleavened bread which at first glance looks like a slab of cement scored into 6 pieces! However, when it is placed in a 450° oven for 10 minutes, the pieces puff up and transform into delicious, chewy biscuits. Mochi is made from sweet brown rice that is soaked, steamed, and pounded to crush to cooked grain. The mochi is then rolled out to an even thickness and dried.

Mochi can be prepared in numerous ways. Split mochi in half after cooking and use it as a breakfast bread or dessert with butter or nut butter and honey, maple syrup, or fruit spread. At lunch and dinner, fill mochi with sandwich spreads, use like biscuits and cover with stew or sauce, or use like dumplings by adding to soup 15 minutes before serving.

Mochi can also be panfried over a low flame in a dry or oiled skillet. Cover the skillet and flip the mochi occasionally to prevent burning. Cook until the mochi puffs up.

Mochi comes in various flavors such as plain, sesame/garlic, cinnamon/raisin, and mugwort. (Mugwort is a plant with high calcium and iron content which has a flavor similar to spinach.) A vacuum packed mochi which requires no refrigeration for 2 months is available in addition to a brand which must be refrigerated until used. The vacuum packed mochi generally is made with the more traditional pounding methods and has a more gooey texture after cooking. The refrigerated mochi has undergone more modern mechanical extruding methods instead of the pounding and is more crisp when cooked. Both are good; personal preference of texture is the deciding factor. The vacuum packed variety is perfect for travelling and camping, although it must be refrigerated or kept very cool after opening the package.

Crackers, both leavened or unleavened, are made from wheat, rye, or rice flour. Look for crackers free of artificial colors, preservatives, and lard. Like bread, flavors and textures vary according to the type of flour, the addition of fat, the type of liquid used, the presence of a sweetener, seasonings, and the use of salt. Crackers made with white flour tend to be lighter but less flavorful than those made with whole wheat flour.

Whole wheat crackers are a delicious all-purpose type of cracker since they enable the flavor of the cheese, soup, dip, or spread to come through. Some whole wheat crackers are very simple and subtle while others are quite rich and reminiscent of cookies.

Rye crackers have a very distinct, full-bodied flavor. Many varieties use only rye flour, salt, and occasionally yeast as ingredients. Rye crackers are a heavier, more filling cracker that go well with soups, cheeses, and butter.

Brown rice crackers are very light, somewhat sweet, and very crunchy. The brown rice flour is lightly steamed, kneaded, shaped, and oven baked without the addition of oil. Seasonings such as tamari, sesame, garlic, onion, and sea vegetables provide variety. Brown rice crackers are a good accompaniment to soups, salads, and dips.

In general, fat added to any cracker will produce more of a rich-flavored product and reduce crunchiness. Crackers made with water as the liquid will be crisper than ones made with milk or yogurt. Consider what will be eaten with the cracker to decide what to buy. A sweet cracker may not compliment a salty cheese, and an herb cracker might conflict with an herb brie. Determine what flavor you want to dominate— the cracker or the accompaniment.

Rice cakes are unique, delicious, handy while travelling, and very versatile. They are unleavened and free of oil. To make rice cakes, whole grain brown rice is placed in a heated cooking mold. The cover is then vacuum sealed. When the mixture has cooked for the proper amount of time, the cover is opened and the vacuum broken. The decrease in pressure explodes the grains which then press into each other to form the rice cake.

Depending upon the manufacturer, rice cakes vary according to ingredients and texture. Thin, light rice cakes are available salted or unsalted made from rice or combinations of rice with sesame, millet, or buckwheat.

Thick and hearty rice cakes are also available which use approximately twice the amount of brown rice per cake. Salted and salt-free varieties include premium and organically grown brown rice, wehani (the Basmati hybrid rice with a nutty flavor) and mochi sweet brown rice (using the same type of rice used to make mochi to yield a thicker, more dense and filling rice cake).

Use rice cakes like crackers or bread for meals or snacks. A simple dessert can be made by spreading the rice cake with butter or nut butter and topping with raisins, honey, maple syrup, or malt syrup.

Recipes

QUICK MOCHI BREAKFAST BISCUITS   *serves 3-6*
Pop them in the oven, get dressed, and eat!

1 package raisin-cinnamon mochi (or plain mochi)
almond butter, sesame butter (tahini), or butter
apple butter or unsweetened apple jelly

1. Preheat oven to 450°.
2. Separate the mochi into 6 squares and place on an unoiled cookie sheet.
3. Put in oven and bake 10 minutes or until mochi has "puffed up".
4. Remove from oven, slice open and top with your favorite nut butter or butter and apple butter or jelly.

MOCHI MELT   *serves 4*
This easy stove top casserole satisfies the urge for melted cheese without dairy and its accompanying fat.

1 TB. sesame oil
1 large onion, diced
3 carrots, thinly sliced
1/2 red cabbage shredded
2 cups kale, 1 inch diagonal strips
4 squares of mochi cut in 1 inch squares
1 TB. tamari shoyu
1/4 cup water

1. Sauté onion in oil in dutch oven or large pot for 5 minutes.
2. Layer carrots, cabbage, and kale in that order on top of onions.
3. Distribute cut mochi squares on kale.
4. Pour shoyu and water over top. When steam rises from pot, lower heat to medium, cover and cook 15 minutes.
5. When done, mochi will have "melted" over tender-crisp vegetables. Sprinkle with gomasio, if desired.

Recipes

RYEBERRY BREAD   *makes 1 loaf*
This is a delicious sourdough bread made without yeast and without much effort.

1 cup whole rye berries (or use wheat)
5 cups water
1/4 teaspoon sea salt
whole wheat flour
sesame oil

1. Rinse rye to remove any surface dirt.
2. Combine rye and water in a pressure cooker.
3. Bring to pressure and cook 1 1/2 hours (or bring to a boil in a regular pot, cover, and simmer 3 hours, adding more water to equal original level).
4. After pressure comes down, add salt and enough whole wheat flour to make a kneadable dough.
5. Knead on a floured surface 300 times, adding more flour if needed.
6. Form into a loaf and put in oiled bread pan.
7. Cover with a damp cloth and set in a warm place for 8-12 hours.
8. Preheat oven to 300°.
9. Bake bread for 30 minutes.
10. Increase heat to 350° and bake bread 1 more hour.
11. After removing bread from oven, remove from bread pan and let cool on a cooling rack before cutting.

BLUE CORN TORTILLAS   *makes 12-15*
Purple tortillas, anyone? Try this easy recipe which combines blue cornmeal with whole wheat flour for delicious tortillas that anyone can make.

1 cup blue cornmeal
1 cup boiling water
2-2 1/2 cups whole wheat flour
1/2 teaspoon sea salt

1. Pour the boiling water over the cornmeal. Let sit 10 minutes or more.
2. Mix salt and whole wheat flour. Add enough flour to the cornmeal mixture to make a kneadable dough.
3. Knead 5-10 minutes and then let sit 5 minutes.
4. Pinch off a piece of dough the size of a golf ball.
5. Roll it out on a floured board to a 4" circle.
6. Heat a griddle or skillet over high heat. No oil is necessary.
7. Add a tortilla and cook over high heat for 2 minutes on each side.
8. Repeat until all dough is used up.

Recipes_____

HONEY-WHOLE WHEAT BREAD   *makes 2 loaves*
In 1975, this recipe and the help of Marion Commack, a family friend, made my
very first loaf of yeast bread a success!   Try it out!

1/4 cup warm water (105°-115°). Test it with your knuckle—not too
hot, slightly more than lukewarm.
1 package or 2 teaspoons active dry yeast
1 1/2 cups scalded milk, cooled to 105°. Or use lukewarm water for heavier, crisper
crust and full-bodied wheat flavor.
2 TB. melted butter or oil (corn or safflower)
2 teaspoons salt
2 TB.-1/2 cup honey (how sweet do you want it???)
6-6 1/2 cups whole wheat flour (not pastry flour)

1. Pour water in a large bowl, add yeast and stir until dissolved.
2. Stir in the scalded and cooled milk or water and add butter, salt, and honey.
    Stir until well blended.
3. Stir in 3 cups of flour, 1 cup at a time.
4. Add 4th cup of flour and beat until dough is smooth and elastic.
5. Mix in 5th cup of flour to make a stiff dough.
6. Measure 6th cup of flour, sprinkle half of it on your kneading surface.
7. Turn out dough on floured surface. Flour your hands and start to knead: Fold
    dough toward you with your fingers and push firmly away with the heel of your
    hands.
8. Add more flour to board as it is kneaded in until the dough no longer sticks.
9. When dough is smooth and non-sticky, place in a greased bowl and lightly
    grease top of dough.
10. Cover with a dish towel and set in a warm place to rise: about 80°.
11. Let dough rise until almost doubled (about 1 1/2 hours). Insert 2 fingers 1/2"
    into the dough. It is ready for the next step if the indentations remain.
12. Punch dough down to squeeze the air bubbles. Shape into a ball and divide
    in half to form 2 loaves.
13. Press out air bubbles and shape into a smooth oval. Pinch seams in the center
    and on the ends.
14. Put loaves in greased bread pans, seams down.
15. Cover; let rise in warm place until almost doubled (about 45 minutes).
16. Put in preheated 375° oven (350° for glass pans) for about 45 minutes. Bread
    will be browned and start to pull away from the sides.
17. Cool before slicing.

PASTAS

One of the quickest ways to serve grains without sacrificing nutrition is to use whole grain pastas. **Whole wheat pasta** is made from durum wheat, a hard wheat known for its ability to keep the pasta from disintegrating while being cooked. Traditional **white pasta** is made from semolina flour (durum wheat stripped of its bran and wheatgerm). Nutritionally, the differences between them are similar to those between whole wheat and white flour. Whole wheat pasta has a rich, nutty flavor, and because no fiber is removed, it is more filling than white pasta even though the calorie count is the same.

Shapes of pasta range from the more familiar elbows, spaghetti, and lasagna to the more exotic spirals, stuffing shells, and tubular shaped ziti. Each manufacturer has its own unique recipe which accounts for the differences in flavors despite the similarity in shape.

The basic ingredients for pasta are flour and water. Flavor and color differences stem from the addition of dried vegetables, sesame, soy, brown rice, or Jerusalem artichoke flour. For those allergic to wheat or in the mood for a different flavor, pasta in all shapes is available in 100% corn.

Many delicious pastas are made in the United States, but semolina pasta imported from Italy is quite special when a particular shape such as riso, capellini, fusilli, ziti, and linguine is needed for an Italian recipe.

Most people are more familiar with the Americanized commercial version of Italian pasta than Japanese pasta. Both are delicious, and yet each has its own properties, flavors, and uses. The best Italian pasta is freshly made with hand cranked kitchen pasta machines, but economies of scale require a different process for large amounts. Commercial **Italian pastas** are made from high gluten durum wheat and extruded under high pressure in a machine which kneads the dough and forces it through a die for a specific shape. The resulting pasta is dried quickly in hot drying rooms. The hardiness of Italian pasta is appropriate with cheeses, tomato sauce, and heavy creams.

Japanese pasta is made from a combination of both hard and soft wheat instead of the high gluten durum wheat in order to produce a pasta that is less dense and more appropriate for soups, cold dishes, fish, and light sauces. Because of the roll and cut manufacturing method and the lower gluten content of the wheat, the pastas cannot be made with100% whole wheat flour although it is not completely refined. The whole wheat flour is sifted to remove a small portion of the bran and wheat germ because both tend to cut through the gluten "glue strands" during the kneading process. However, as much bran and germ is retained as possible. The addition of salt helps to strengthen the gluten and bind the dough. Once the dough is made, it is allowed to sit for several hours to develop the gluten before being rolled into a long continuous sheet and then cut. The noodles are then naturally air dried without heat over a 30-hour period in rooms that have fans to keep the air circulating.

Japanese noodles can be cooked in the same method as other pastas or according to the more traditional "shock method". The "shock method" involves adding the noodles to boiling water and "shocking" them with a cup of cold water each time the water returns to a boil. This is done for 3 times after which the pasta should be perfectly done. (Save the cooking water as a delicious broth for soups or sauces. The noodle broth also gives vegetables an exceptional flavor when used as the cooking liquid.)

Like Italian pastas, oriental pastas have different names for the different shapes and ingredients used in each type.

Soba are buckwheat noodles made of 100% buckwheat (great for those allergic to wheat!) or with proportions of 40-60% buckwheat flour with the remainder as unbleached white flour. Jinenjo flour (a Japanese wild mountain yam traditionally used to promote strength and vitality) or dried mugwort (a plant rich in iron with a spinach-like flavor) can also be added. Although the 100% soba is delicious, the buckwheat-wheat flour combinations are easier to work with and are lighter in texture. Serve soba chilled in summer and hot in winter.

Udon are flat thin noodles made from sifted whole wheat flour sometimes combined with unbleached flour or brown rice flour (genmai udon) for a more delicate texture. Udon have a unique, lighter flavor than other whole wheat pastas. Besides being delicious hot, udon's texture and flavor when cold is superior to other chilled whole wheat pastas.

Somen are very thin, delicate noodles that are even lighter tasting than udon. They are always served chilled during the summer months.

Bifun are clear Chinese-style rice noodles made from rice flour and potato starch. **Saifun** are clear noodles made from mung bean starch. Both varieties are light and well suited for soups and vegetable medleys. Steep in hot water 3-5 minutes.

Kuzu kiri are light colored noodles made from kuzu powder and potato starch which are traditionally used in sukiyaki and salads. Unlike bifun and saifun, kuzu kiri are more substantial and require 20 minutes cooking.

Ramen are thin, spiral noodles that are primarily wheat but occasionally combined with buckwheat or rice flours. Most frequently, ramen is sold in a package along with an instant broth packet. Boiling water and 5 minutes rehydrate the precooked noodles and instant broth into a delicious soup or noodle dish. Unlike the common white flour ramen which is precooked in boiling refined oil, quality whole grain ramen is precooked with steam and free of preservatives.

Fresh pasta is a delight! As an alternative to dry pastas and when there is no time to make it on one's own, delicious **fresh pasta** made from semolina flour, eggs, and water can be purchased. All you need is boiling water and three minutes for a quick meal of fettucini or spaghetti. The flavor is incredible!

With over fifty types of pasta from which to choose, it would be possible to eat a different kind of pasta each week of the year. Experiment and enjoy!

Recipes

GARLIC FRIED NOODLES   *serves 3*
Words cannot begin to describe the flavor!

8 oz. whole wheat ribbons, udon, or soba
2TB. sesame or olive oil
4 cloves garlic, minced
tamari shoyu
sunflower seeds

1. Cook noodles, drain, and rinse under cold water.
2. Heat oil in a large skillet or wok. Add garlic and sauté 2 minutes being careful not to burn.
3. Add cooked noodles. Stir to coat with oil and garlic.
4. Add shoyu to taste.
5. Stir over medium/low heat until noodles are warmed through.
6. Garnish with sunflower seeds for crunch.

SUMMER NOODLE SALAD   *serves 4*
A noodle salad is perfect for hot weather. Little cooking is needed and it can be prepared ahead of time so you can relax instead of cook when your friends arrive.

8 oz. whole wheat macaroni, shells, udon, or soba
3 TB. sesame oil
2 tsp. prepared mustard
1 tsp. brown rice vinegar or lemon juice
1 TB. tamari shoyu
2 cloves garlic, minced
4 green onions thinly sliced on the diagonal
1/4 cup parsley, coarsely chopped
2 ribs celery, diced
2 large carrots, grated
1 1/2 cups cooked garbanzo beans or 1 lb. tofu (opt.)

1. Cook pasta and drain.
2. Mix together oil, mustard, vinegar, and shoyu.   Stir into pasta, coating well.
3. Add remaining ingredients and mix thoroughly.
4. Refrigerate at least 2 hours before serving.

Recipes

SUZETTE GREENLEE'S
COLLEGE ROOMMATE'S BEST FRIEND'S MOTHER'S LASAGNA   *serves 8-12*
Every Italian family has its own unique lasagna. This recipe, "handed down" to a friend, Suzette Greenley, will make anyone want to marry into an Italian family for even more delights.

Notes from Suzette: "I got this recipe from a college roommate from Pittsburg. She got it from the mother of her best friend, who was Italian. It is the best lasagna I have ever had. I recommend that you use tomato paste from Italian plum tomatoes, as the taste is superior for this dish."

8 oz. lasagna noodles
1 lb. ground beef (opt.)
1 large onion, chopped
2 cloves garlic, minced
2 cans (6 oz. each) tomato paste
1 1/2 cups water
1 TB. parsley
1 tsp. salt
1/2 tsp. basil
8 oz. ricotta
2 eggs, beaten
1 lb. mozzarella or 1/2 lb. mozzarella and 1/2 lb. provolone
1/4 cup grated parmesan

1. Shred mozzarella or combination of mozzarella and provolone.
2. In large skillet, brown meat with onion and garlic. Drain off fat.
   (NOTE: If omitting meat, brown onion and garlic in small amount of oil.)
3. Stir in paste, water, parsley, salt, and basil. Simmer 10 minutes.
4. Meanwhile, cook noodles and drain.
5. Blend ricotta and eggs.
6. In a 13 X 9 X 2 inch baking dish spread a thin layer of sauce.
7. Top with half of the noodles, all of the ricotta, half of the shredded cheese.
8. Cover with half of the remaining sauce and all remaining noodles.
9. Top with remaining sauce and shredded cheese.
10. Sprinkle with parmesan.
11. Bake at 350° F. for 30 minutes.
12. Let stand 10 minutes before cutting.
13. Serve with salad and French bread.

Recipes

SUZETTE'S FETTUCINE ALFREDO   *serves 4*
Suzette couldn't stop with the lasagna!

More notes from Suzette: "This is very easy, very quick, and very good. The only thing that takes more than 3 minutes is boiling the water. You may wish to add some fresh parsley or a little pepper to the sauce, but do not add any salt or use salted butter, as the cheese makes it salty enough. For truly superior results, I substitute for the cream with a few tablespoons of creme fraiche thinned with milk to pouring consistency. Hang the calories—this is heaven!"

1 lb. fresh fettucine noodles
1/2 cup unsalted (sweet) butter
1/2 cup light cream
1 cup freshly grated parmesan
pinch of nutmeg

1. Put water on to boil for noodles.
2. In separate pan, melt butter over very low heat; do not let it brown.
3. When water boils and noodles have started cooking, stir in cream and parmesan in pan with butter.
4. Season sauce with nutmeg.
5. When noodles are cooked al dente, drain and toss gently with sauce.
6. Serve immediately.

ALANA'S SOBA SALAD W/ TAHINI-MISO DRESSING   *serves 3-4*
Another friend, Alana Sugar, is the inspiration for this incredible noodle dish which features her favorite type of Japanese pasta, mugwort soba. It is delicious hot or cold.

1 pkg. soba (mugwort or plain)
3 TB. mellow miso
3 TB. tahini
1/3 cup water
2 TB. lemon juice
1 TB. mirin (sweet rice cooking wine)
1/2 tsp. garlic granules or ginger powder
OR 1 tsp. each if using fresh herbs
sesame seeds for garnish

1. Cook noodles, drain, and rinse under cold water.
2. Combine other ingredients. Pour over noodles and toss.
3. Garnish with sesame seeds. Add cubed tofu or lightly steamed vegetables if desired.

3

LEGUMES, NUTS,
& SEEDS

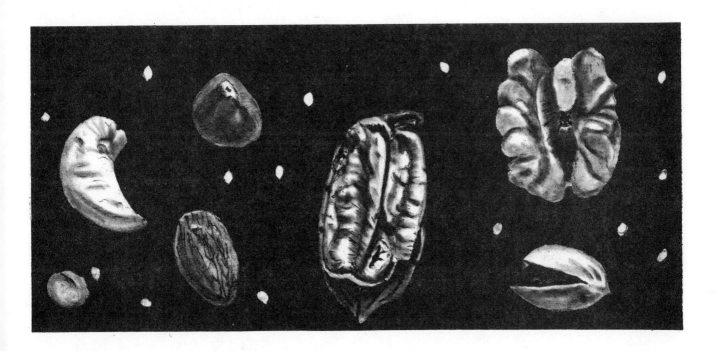

LEGUMES

When combined with grains, seeds, or dairy products, beans are an excellent protein source low in fat and calories, while high in fiber. They are easy to store, inexpensive, and best of all, delicious. Besides soups, beans are used in dips, spreads, and as meat replacements in loaves and casseroles.

There are a number of cooking methods for beans. All suggest soaking the beans overnight or 8 hours. There are two schools of thought as to what should be done with the soaking water. Some say that the beans should be drained and rinsed to remove the naturally occuring starch in the bean which contributes to the flatulence some people experience after eating beans. Others say that the beans should be cooked directly in the soaking water since it contains many nutrients which have leached into the water. Either way, thorough cooking is most important for best digestion. If there seems to be no difference in the digestion of the beans, cook the beans in the soaking water for optimum nutrition.

Lentils and split peas do not need pre-soaking. Azuki beans can also be cooked without pre-soaking, but if time allows, soak for even better digestion.

If necessary, pre-soaking time can be reduced to 2 hours by first bringing rinsed beans to a boil in 3 times their volume in water for 3 minutes. Cover the pot, remove from the heat, and let sit for 2 hours before cooking as usual. Discard the soaking water, add fresh water (or use soaking water), and cook as usual.

The addition of a bay leaf, cumin, or a two-inch piece of kombu, a sea vegetable, may also help digestion of the beans as well as impart a delicious flavor.

Cooking methods vary. Beans can be boiled, pressure cooked, baked, or cooked in an electric slow cooker. When beans are boiled, it is necessary to be present during the cooking in order to monitor an adequate water level. Use 4 cups of cold water per cup of dried beans (the amount used prior to soaking). Bring to a boil, cover and simmer until done. Another boiling method is called the "shock method." Use 2 1/2 cups of cold water per cup of dried beans. Bring to a boil, cover, and decrease heat to a simmer. When the water level reduces, add enough cold water to stop the boiling. This alternating "shocking" of cold water with the boiling water and long, slow, low heat cooking brings out the best flavor of the beans. Continue "shocking" the beans until done.

Pressure cooking is handy when time is limited but avoid pressure cooking lima beans, lentils, split peas, and soybeans, which tend to foam up and clog the pressure cooker vent. When pressure cooking, use 2 cups of water per cup of dried beans. Add more if a more soupy consistency is desired. Start gauging the time when at full pressure. Reduce the heat to medium low and put a flame deflector under the pressure cooker to distribute the heat evenly and prevent burning. After approximately 45 minutes, allow the pressure to come down naturally, if possible, or run cold water over the lid until the pressure comes down.

Oven baked beans are boiled first with 4-5 times the amount of water for 15-20 minutes to loosen the skins. Then the beans and the water are poured into a bean pot or baking dish, covered, and baked at 350° for about 3-4 hours.

To cook beans in a slow cooker, adjust the cooker to the high setting for 1 hour and then on low for 8-10 hours. The advantage of slow cookers is that the beans can cook all day without requiring your presence to watch the water level.

Do not add salt, miso, tamari shoyu (soy sauce), sweeteners, fats, tomatoes, or vinegar until the beans are cooked since these lengthen the cooking process and harden the bean's skin.

The addition of onion, garlic, and/or chunks of winter squash or root vegetables to beans at the onset of cooking imparts a delicious sweet flavor without the need for concentrated sweeteners which may cause some digestive discomfort when combined with beans.

Cooking times listed may vary due to the age of the beans and the amount of heat used. When thoroughly cooked, beans should be easily mashed with a fork.

A description and common use of each of the beans is listed below. Despite the fact that certain beans are used for specific recipes, experiment with the other beans for variety.

Aduki beans are burgundy colored beans native of Japan which are now grown in the United States. Their low fat content make them more easily digested than other beans. Add cubes of winter squash the last half hour of cooking for an exceptional dish. Season with sea salt or tamari shoyu.

Boiling time— 1 1/2 hours. Pressure cook 45 minutes.

Anasazi beans are true native American unhybridized beans that look like white speckled pinto beans. They have been cultivated in America since 1100 A.D. The very name, "anasazi", is translated from the Navaho Indian language as "ancient ones" or "predecessor". Anasazi beans have a sweet, pinto bean-like flavor and can be used accordingly.

Boiling time— 1 1/2-2 hours. Pressure cook 45 minutes.

Black beans or **black turtle beans** are a Mexican and South American staple often accompanied by rice and/or tomatoes, cooked in a soup, or used in enchiladas, burritos, or chapatis. Cook with bay leaf, garlic, cumin, or Mexican blend of spice to bring out the flavor.

Boiling time— 1 1/2-2 hours. Pressure cook 45 minutes.

Black-eyed peas are a familiar bean to southern regions of the United States and Latin America traditionally cooked with rice. This bean can be identified by its creamy white oval shape and black "eye." A "must" in Texas New Year's celebrations, it is often marinated and transformed into "Texas Caviar."

Boiling time— 1 hour. Pressure cook 40 minutes.

Chickpeas or **garbanzo beans** resemble, upon close scrutiny (and with a good imagination!), the head and beak of a chicken. Chickpeas, a common bean in Middle Eastern,

South American, and Mediterranean cooking, are now popular in the United States especially in the form of marinated chickpeas, hommus (a dip made from chickpeas and sesame tahini), and falafel (a spicy garbanzo mixture formed into meatball shapes or patties). This hearty but mild flavored bean requires longer cooking time than other beans.

Boiling time— 3 1/2 hours. Pressure cook 1 hour.

Kidney beans are red beans named after their shape. They are often used in chili, soups, and salads since they keep their shape so well.

Boiling time— 1-1 1/2 hours. Pressure cook 45 minutes.

Lentils come in two varieties— red and green, neither of which need pre-soaking. **Red lentils,** extremely quick to cook, lose their red color during cooking and begin to resemble green split peas. When washing red lentils, they will tend to clump together and look "soapy" when moistened. As this occurs, most new "red lentil cooks" worry whether they forgot to rinse the cooking pot thoroughly after it had been washed. Be assured you probably did; the soapy film occurs normally as starch is released. Since red lentils also like to foam while cooking, it may be advisable to cook them uncovered or with the lid slightly ajar. Red lentils may be substituted for green lentils in any recipe.

Boiling time— 20 minutes. Pressure cooking not advised.

Green lentils also cook quickly compared to most beans and are a favorite for making casseroles, soups, and burgers.

Boiling time— 40 minutes. Pressure cook 30 minutes.

Lima beans are flat white beans native to South and Central America. Their buttery flavor and starchy texture are good in soups, stews, and casseroles.

Boiling time— 1 1/2 hours. Pressure cooking not advised.

Mung beans are commonly sprouted for use in Chinese cooking but are an important part of Indian curries and dahls when cooked.

Boiling time— 1 1/2 hours. Pressure cook 30 minutes.

Peanuts are, contrary to popular belief, beans and not nuts. Although some people enjoy the flavor of boiled peanuts, peanuts are generally eaten out of hand either roasted or unroasted or ground into peanut butter. (More information about peanuts can be found in the section concerning peanut butter.)

Split peas are dried green or yellow peas split for quicker cooking. Although both varieties are cooked in the same way and are nutritionally similar, the yellow split peas are somewhat milder in flavor. Use in soups or spreads.

Boiling time— 1-1 1/2 hour. Pressure cooking not advised.

Pinto beans are pale pink and brown speckled oblong shaped beans that are a staple in the Southwest for refried beans, burritos, and chilis.

Boiling time— 1 1/2-2 hours. Pressure cook 45 minutes.

Red beans are another Mexican food staple that are related to kidney and pinto beans and can be substituted for them.

Boiling time— 1 1/2-2 hours. Pressure cook 45 minutes.

White beans include great northern and navy beans and are distinguished mainly by size since their flavor is so similar. Use in soups, stews, and casseroles.

Boiling time— 1 1/2-2 hours. Pressure cook 40 minutes.

SOYFOODS

Soybeans have a high protein and oil content which makes them very versatile but also harder to digest. Traditional methods of preparing soybeans into tofu, miso, tempeh, soy milk, and soy sauce make them easier to digest. When cooked in its whole bean form, they should be cooked very thoroughly.

Boiling time— 4 - 5 hours. Pressure cook 1 1/2-2 hours.

Black soybeans are related to the yellow variety but are more tasty and easier to digest.

Boiling time— 4 hours. Pressure cook 1 1/2 hours.

Soyflakes are whole soybeans that are toasted for 30 seconds and then flaked in a roller mill. In this form the cooking time is reduced to 45-60 minutes.

Tofu has gone from relative obscurity to being one of the most celebrated foods due to its versatility and nutritional content.

Even though it is highly digestible, low in calories, high in protein, inexpensive, and free of cholesterol, as recently as 10 years ago, tofu was little known as anything beyond "that bean curd stuff" served in Chinese and Japanese restaurants.

Tofu is made by washing, soaking, grinding, and boiling soybeans. The resulting soymilk is strained to remove the fiber and then reheated. A coagulant is added, either the preferred, traditionally used nigari (an alkaline mineral coagulant derived from the refining of natural sea salt), nigari-style coagulants (magnesium chloride or calcium chloride) or calcium sulphate to curdle the soymilk. The curds are separated from the whey and put under pressure to harden. A four ounce serving of tofu contains approximately 80 calories, 9 mg. of protein, 5 grams of fat, and 8 mg. of sodium.

Oddly enough, tofu keeps fresh when stored in water. Once made, it will keep fresh under refrigeration for 1 week if the container it is stored in is drained and replenished with fresh water daily. Some tofu is sold in sealed water-filled tubs. Its shelf life is usually 7-14 days, but once opened, it should be stored in fresh water and changed daily as with bulk tofu. Spoiled tofu has a sour flavor, yellowing water, discolored appearance, and a slimy film. Really fresh tofu is creamy white and virtually has no flavor.

Admittedly, the flavor of plain tofu is quite bland, but this bland quality of tofu is partially what is responsible for its versatility. It was never meant to be eaten without the benefits of marinating, simmering, baking, or sautéeing with other foods and seasonings. Depending upon what it is cooked with and how it is cooked, tofu could be eaten at every meal and yet have an entirely different flavor.

The other factor contributing to its versatility is its texture. Basically a soft, custard-like consistency, tofu's texture can be altered by the way it is initially made, cooked, and how it is stored. Tofu is sold as either **"soft" tofu** or "hard" tofu depending upon how long the curds are pressed. Soft tofu works well in dips, sauces, salad dressings, and for soft non-dairy cheese substitutes for ricotta cheese and cottage cheese.

Since it holds its shape better, **"hard" tofu** is preferred when using tofu in cubed or sliced form. However, alterations can be made to make soft tofu harder and hard tofu softer. Soft tofu can be firmed by draining some of the liquid from the tofu. Place the tofu in a strainer or colander until the desired texture is reached. Another method is to lay the tofu in a cloth or between paper towels on a hard surface. Place a plate or cutting board on top, weighted down with a heavy object (try a bottle of juice or a heavy book) for a couple minutes to expel the liquid. Conversely, if your recipe calls for soft tofu and you have hard tofu on hand, simply add more liquid or soak in water.

Locally made soft tofu is sold in bulk. Both soft and hard tofu are sold in vacuum packed containers. You can be assured of packaged tofu's freshness by noting the expiration date on the side of the package.

Tofu's texture can also be changed by freezing the tofu in a container or plastic bag without water for at least 48 hours. Its naturally white color will turn yellow while in its frozen state but, once thawed, tofu will return to its original color. Use frozen tofu within 6 months. Thawed **frozen tofu** has a chewy, meaty texture which, when crumbled, is perfect as a substitute for ground beef in casseroles, pizza, stews, or spaghetti sauces. Sliced or cubed frozen tofu has a texture similar to chicken or veal, great for mock chicken salads and mock veal cutlets. Freezing tofu also increases its ability to absorb flavors.

Freeze dried tofu further expands on the versatility of frozen tofu with a product that has a finer, firm grained texture and is more absorbent and soft when reconstituted. It serves as a concentrated energy source containing up to 7 times more nutrients than an equal weight of fresh tofu. Since it has only 1/6 the weight of fresh tofu and needs no refrigeration, it is an ideal backpacking food. Once the package is open, store in an air tight plastic bag or container and use within 4 months. To reconstitute, soak the cakes in warm water for 3-5 minutes. Press between towels or the palms of your hands to squeeze out excess liquid. Then cook with soups, stews, vegetables, or alone with your choice of seasonings to absorb flavors. Freeze dried tofu will swell to only 7% of its original volume and since it is so concentrated, one cake is usually enough per person.

People who choose to or need to avoid dairy products, eggs, or animal proteins find tofu a perfect alternative. Although preparing tofu is quick and easy, many prepared tofu foods can be purchased from both the dairy case and frozen food areas including such items as tofu 'no egg' salad, cottage tofu, dips, frozen dinners, tofu burgers, tofu 'hot dogs', tofu 'bologna', and tofu mayonnaise and tofu salad dressings. With the help of a special seasoning mix, fresh tofu can be transformed into mock scrambled eggs. Many flavors of other 'tofu-helper' type mixes are now available to make burgers, stir-fries, and casseroles.

Tempeh is a traditional Indonesian soyfood whose wonderful flavor, meaty texture, and excellent nutritional value is due to the process of fermentation with *Rhizopus oligosporus* mold culture. This fermentation process is similar to that used in making cheese, yogurt, wines, beer, miso, and tamari shoyu.

Tempeh's taste and texture are often compared to that of chicken or beef. But let's face it, although tempeh has a meaty texture, tempeh is tempeh; it tastes like tempeh and it tastes great! Nonetheless, use it as a meat substitute in some of your favorite recipes.

Tempeh's flavor comes to life with the appropriate seasonings, marinades, and cooking methods.

Unlike tofu, tempeh is made from whole soybeans and so contains all its nutrients, including the fiber. It has the highest quality protein of any soyfood containing 19 1/2 % complete protein with all the essential amino acids, about the same as beef or chicken.

Tempeh has often been considered a significant source of B_{12}, but generally this is not true of tempeh that is processed in the United States.   The source of B_{12} in tempeh is neither the soybeans nor the Rhizopus mold, but a bacteria of the genus Klebsiella which develop during pre-fermentation "accidental" inoculation. In traditional Indonesian preparation, the bacteria are also introduced via the mixed starter culture which is grown on hibiscus leaves. Since most U.S. shops use a pure Rhizopus oligosporus culture, any B_{12} that would be present would come from unreliable environmental sources.

But B_{12} is just part of the story. As a result from the culturing process, levels of many vitamins are significantly increased. Enzymes from the mold help break down the proteins, fats, and complex carbohydrates, improving digestibility.

Tempeh is often found in the frozen food department since the mold continues to grow even when refrigerated. Black spore formation is not indicative of spoilage although tempeh's flavor is milder when the cottony mycelium is white and the aroma is a clean, mushroom-like smell. However, some people prefer the stronger flavor that develops through lengthier aging. But, if it turns green, throw the tempeh away! Refrigerated, tempeh will keep 7 days and up to 6 months when frozen.

There are many varieties of tempeh; some require cooking while others simply need to be warmed. Plain soy, 5-grain, or quinoa-soy tempeh are easy to prepare. Just thoroughly cook: marinate and panfry or bake, deep fry, or simmer in herbs and broil or stir fry. Pre-seasoned, pre-cooked burgers and cutlets are more convenient— simply warm in the oven or lightly fry.

Soy grits are coarsely ground, uncooked soybeans that are added to grains and other dishes to boost nutritive value. Use twice the amount of water to grits and cook 20-30 minutes alone or along with a stew. When cooking with a grain, add more water than usually needed to allow for the grits' absorption.

TVP is the abbreviation for textured vegetable protein which is used as a meat analog, a product that tastes and feels like meat but is made from a vegetable source. TVP only has the texture, not the flavor of meat. The production of TVP is a highly processed, sophisticated method which uses heat, pressure, and chemicals to extract the protein which is then spun into fibers for use in foods. Herbs and spices are used for the flavoring but, unfortunately, artificial flavors are commonly used in prepared products that taste similar to beef, chicken, and pork. Use TVP and products which contain it only if no artificial flavors or colors are used.

Recipes

BEST BEANS   *serves 4*
Cooking the beans with vegetables creates an incredibly flavored bean dish which requires no additional sweetener.

1 1/2 cups beans (pinto, black, garbanzo, blackeyed peas, or kidneys)
4 inch piece kombu
1 large onion, thinly sliced
2 large carrots, 1 inch chunks
3 ribs celery
2 cloves garlic
water
salt, shoyu, or miso to taste
1 TB. mustard (opt.)
2 TB. barley malt or rice syrup (opt.)

1. Soak beans 8 hours or do quick soak method.
2. Combine beans, kombu, vegetables and cover with water in pressure cooker or pot.
3. Pressure cook 45 minutes or simmer 4 hours (watch water level).
4. Season with salt, mustard, and sweetener and cook 15 minutes more.

TERRY'S LENTILS and RICE   *serves 2-3*
No wonder the menu is no surprise when my husband cooks dinner. This recipe is easy, quick, and delicious!

4 cups water
1 cup brown rice
2/3 cup green lentils
1/2 tsp. celery seed, dill, or curry
salt or shoyu to taste

1. Bring all ingredients except salt to a boil.
2. Reduce heat and simmer, covered 30 minutes.
3. Add salt or shoyu and cook an additional 10-15 minutes.
4. Serve with steamed or sautéed vegetables.

Recipes _____

CURRIED SPLIT PEAS   *serves 3-4*

This yields a somewhat dry split pea side dish often called "dahl". If a soup or sauce is desired, add more water.

1 cup yellow split peas
1 tsp. sesame oil
1 red onion, thinly sliced
3 cloves garlic, minced
1 tsp. curry powder
2 1/2-3 cups water
1 tsp. tamari shoyu

1. Rinse the split peas in cold water.
2. In a medium saucepan, sauté the onion in sesame oil for 3 minutes.
3. Add the garlic and sauté 2 minutes and then add the curry powder and sauté 1 more minute.
4. Combine the beans and water with the onions, garlic, and curry. Bring to a boil and simmer 1 1/2 hours or until split peas are very soft. Check periodically while cooking to insure adequate water level.
5. Add tamari shoyu when the peas are done.
6. Let sit 10 minutes before serving.

TASTY TOFU   *serves 4*

Tofu comes to life when simmered a long time with other vegetables, sauces, or soups. Try this recipe with the dried tofu for a special treat.

1 tsp. sesame oil
1 large onion, thinly sliced
2 cups water
1 lb. tofu, cut in cubes or in slices OR 4 squares dried tofu
4 large carrots, cut in 1 inch chunks
4 ribs celery, cut in 1 inch slices
2 medium beets, cut in bite sized pieces
1 TB. tamari shoyu OR 2 TB. white miso
2 TB. sesame tahini

1. In a large saucepan, sauté the onion until translucent.
2. Add the water, dried tofu, vegetables, and the shoyu or miso.
3. Bring to a boil, cover and reduce heat to medium.
4. Cook 30 minutes or until vegetables are soft.
5. Dilute the tahini in broth.
6. Add tahini mixture to the dried tofu and vegetables. Mix thoroughly.
7. Turn off heat and let sit 5-10 minutes to blend flavors.
8. Serve with a whole grain, bread, or mochi.

Recipes

TEMPEH SPAGHETTI　　　　　*serves 3-4*

This recipe is a great way to introduce your family (and yourself) to the flavor and texture of tempeh. A perfect flavor combination that is quick and easy!

1 pkg. pre-seasoned tempeh burgers
1 quart favorite spaghetti sauce
1 onion, chopped
1/4 lb. mushrooms, quartered
1 medium zucchini, sliced
whole wheat spaghetti
parmesan cheese (opt.)
black olives (opt.)

1. Cube tempeh burgers into bite sized pieces.
2. Sauté in olive oil for 3 minutes or warm in an oven or broiler if no extra fat is desired.
3. Remove tempeh, add an extra tablespoon of olive oil, and sauté vegetables for 5 minutes.
4. Add spaghetti sauce and tempeh.
5. Simmer 20-30 minutes.
6. Serve over spaghetti and top with parmesan cheese and/or black olives.

SWEET AND SOUR TEMPEH　　　　　*serves 6-8*

Serve this marinated tempeh over whole grains, noodles, or in a sandwich. Long simmering is the secret to bringing out the full flavor.

two 8 oz. packages uncooked tempeh
2 TB. fresh lemon juice
2 TB. tamari shoyu (naturally aged soy sauce)
1 1/2 cup water
1/4 cup tomato sauce
1 TB. honey or rice syrup
1 tsp. freshly minced ginger
4 medium cloves of garlic, crushed

1. If planning to serve over a whole grain or noodles, cut tempeh into cubes or small triangles. If tempeh is going to be used in sandwiches, cut into bars.
2. Combine sauce ingredients in a large saucepan.
3. Bring to a boil and add tempeh.
4. Reduce heat, cover, and simmer 45 minutes to 1 hour. Add more water if necessary.
5. Serve with sauce or cook until the sauce is completely absorbed. (Don't let it burn!)
   Delicious hot or cold.

Recipes

ITALIAN TOFU   *serves 2-3*

I especially like the texture and flavor absorbability of frozen tofu. This recipe developed while I was in an Italian mood. Fennel seeds are essential to its success!

2 cups water
pinch of salt
2 carrots, thinly sliced
3 ribs celery, thinly sliced
1/2 onion, thinly sliced
1/4 head cabbage, thinly sliced
(Red cabbage is particularly attractive, even though it does make the cooking water and, consequently, the tofu, purple!)
1 lb. frozen tofu, thawed, squeezed dry, and cubed
1 teaspoon Italian seasoning
1/2 teaspoon fennel seeds

1. Boil water. Add a pinch of salt and add carrots. Return to a boil and simmer for 2 minutes.
2. Remove carrots, place in a large bowl, and add celery. Repeat above process with the celery.
3. Continue with the onion and cabbage as above.
4. Mix the vegetables together.
5. Add the tofu and seasonings to the vegetable cooking water.
6. Simmer, uncovered, until the tofu absorbs all the liquid.
7. Serve with the vegetables, noodles, or grain of your choice. Delicious as a filling for tortillas.

NUTS AND SEEDS

Nuts and seeds are very concentrated foods high in vitamins and minerals which provide good protein when combined with beans, dairy products, and rice. However, they are also high in fat and calories and therefore should be eaten in moderation.

Nuts and seeds are most often available shelled or hulled for convenience. Unfortunately, this eliminates the protective coating which retards rancidity. Some manufacturers compensate for this by coating the nuts and the packaging inself with preservatives, so it is important to buy shelled nuts and seeds from reputable stores and manufacturers.

Nuts in the shell will keep 1 year if stored in a cool, dry place. Buy twice the quantity of nuts in the shell for the amount needed shelled. Shelled nuts will keep 4 months if refrigerated and up to 1 year if stored in an airtight container in the freezer. Unrefrigerated shelled nuts and seeds kept in tightly covered glass jars, preferably tinted, could last up to 2 months, depending on the condition of the nut when first stored and the temperature of the room. For best results, refrigerate when possible. If traveling or keeping nuts and seeds at work or school, buy small amounts and replenish with a fresh batch frequently to prevent rancidity from occuring.

Are roasted or raw nuts and seeds more nutritious? The answer depends upon whom you ask. Some say that heat denatures the protein and fat in the nuts, while others say that roasting counterbalances the expansive nature of the fat in the nuts. The most important point to remember is that whether the nut is raw or roasted, it should be fresh, free of rancidity. Rancidity can cause damage to the cells in the body as well as undermine the flavor of the otherwise delicious nut or seed. The inside portion of the nut or seed should be of uniform color. Dark patches indicate that rancidity is starting to occur.

Roasted nuts tend to turn rancid quicker since roasting forces the natural oils to the surface. Some commercially roasted nuts are laden with preservatives, sugar, monosodium glutamate (MSG), vegetable gums, salt, and seasonings to mask any "off" rancid flavors which can also be caused from roasting nuts in rancid oil that has been used repeatedly. Look for roasted nuts that are dry roasted plain or roasted with tamari shoyu (soy sauce) to give a full-bodied, salty flavor.

Raw nuts can be roasted at home in the oven or pan roasted. To oven roast, spread nuts or seeds on a baking sheet and place in a pre-heated 300° oven for 20 minutes, stirring occasionally. To pan roast, put a thin layer of nuts in a skillet over low heat for 10-15 minutes, stirring frequently. Not only will you have fresh roasted nuts/seeds, but an incredible aroma will permeate the house!

Whole nuts are preferable to pre-chopped or ground nuts since broken nuts are more susceptible to rancidity. Chop your own at home or grind nuts in a blender, food processor, or electric nut, seed, or coffee mill just prior to use.

Besides using nuts and seeds as snacks, use nuts in baked goods, vegetable dishes, salads, casseroles, grain dishes, and sandwich spreads. They add texture as well as nutrition.

Almonds are related to peaches, nectarines, and other members of the rose family. Sweet almonds are the edible variety while bitter almonds are used to make almond extract and as an ingredient in cosmetics. Almonds retain a tough brown skin after shelling that not only is edible and high in fiber but serves to protect the nuts from oxidizing and turning rancid. Broken or split almonds tend to spoil more quickly. If blanched nuts are desired, best flavor results from blanching them at home. Simply pour boiling water over the almonds and let them cool. Then drain them and slip the skins off with your fingers. Dry the blanched almonds on a paper towel before using in recipes. Blanched almonds are a favorite for making nut milks.

Brazil nuts grow wild in Venezuela and, oddly enough, in Brazil. Since they are rich and creamy, brazil nuts are perfect in smoothies— if you can afford the calories! Brazil nuts are also high in dietary fiber.

Cashews are never sold with their outer shell because of a powerful toxin that lies between the outer shell and the shell that surrounds the nut itself. The cashew is heated, causing the outer shell to burst while eliminating the poisonous properties. Botanically, the cashew is related to poison oak, poison sumac, and mangoes, and, therefore, can cause allergic reactions in sensitive individuals. Because of its sweet flavor and creamy texture, cashews are a favorite ingredient in sauces and nut milks.

Dried **coconut** is from the fruit of the tropical nut. Its fat is primarily saturated unlike the predominance of monosaturated and polyunsaturated fats in other nuts and seeds. Often found sweetened, unsweetened coconut is delicious on its own and perfect for baking. Coconut is usually added to foods that already contain a sweetener, so there really is not much reason to buy it sweetened. Refrigerate after purchase.

Hazelnuts (filberts) purchased in the United States generally come from Oregon and Washington. Its flavor is unique and delicious, especially when the nuts are roasted. Hazelnut butter is considered a gourmet delight in Europe.

Macadamia nuts are also available only in the shelled form. Primarily grown in Hawaii and Australia, they are sweet and buttery. Because of their high fat content and price, macadamia nuts are considered a "decadent delicacy"!

Peanuts are considered nuts by most people although in reality, peanuts are a member of the legume family. 50% of the peanut crop is made into peanut butter. Peanut butter is ground from Virginia peanuts, Valencia peanuts, or Spanish peanuts. Most people prefer the flavor of the Valencia peanut. Since the peanut is susceptible to a carcinogenic mold called aflatoxin, it is advisable to buy peanut butter from a reputable company who takes care in storing whole, undamaged peanuts in a dry, temperature controlled environment. Peanut butter ground from certified organic peanuts goes that extra step in insuring a chemical free food whose flavor is hard to beat.
Federal law bars artificial sweeteners, colors, flavors, synthetic preservatives, and vitamin fortifiers from all brands of peanut butter. However, manufacturers are free to add

sugar, salt, and hydrogenated oils which degrade the nutrition of an otherwise good food. When bought in jars, 100% "natural" peanut butter often has a layer of oil at the top because stabilizers have not been added to keep the oil from separating out. Just stir the oil back into the nut butter before use.

Most brands of 100% peanut butter are available both salted and unsalted. Initially those used to traditional commercial brands of peanut butter may prefer salted, but after salt is decreased in all facets of the diet, the salted may seem much too salty.

Pecans are one of the few real native American nuts mostly grown in south and southwestern United States. Since they are high in fat, pecans should be purchased whole and not ground or broken in order to buy nuts as rancid-free as possible. The soft texture of pecans enables them to be ground or broken at home very easily in a blender.

Pine nuts (pignolias), famous for their use in pesto and poultry stuffings, are harvested from pinecones from trees grown around the Mediterranean although a similar variety is grown on a limited scale in the United States. Pine nuts have a sweet taste that can only be described as "pine-like"!

Pistachios are the seed of an evergreen grown in California and in the Middle East that is a necessary ingredient in pistachio ice cream! The pale-green nutmeat is naturally (and preferably) encased in a greyish-beige outer shell. Avoid pistachios that are dyed red for cosmetic purposes. Since the outer shell is hard to crack, pistachios are sold pre-cracked. Even though salted pistachios are more common, they are available unsalted.

Pumpkin seeds that are available commercially come from a special type of pumpkin that yields long, flat, dark green seeds instead of the pale, fibrous seeds from jack-o-lantern pumpkins or pie pumpkins. Also called "pepitas", these seeds are known for their high concentrations of protein and zinc.

When is the last time you used **sesame seeds** without the bun? Although sprinkling them on hamburger buns is a popular use for sesame seeds, many people are becoming familiar with other uses of both hulled and unhulled sesame seeds.

Sesame seeds are primarily grown in Latin America, an area sometimes suspect for its use of pesticides. However, sesame seeds grow very well in Arizona and northern Mexico without the use of pesticides.

From importer to consumer, sesame seeds can be purchased in either hulled or unhulled form. How sesame seeds are hulled is just as important as whether or not they are organic. The most common method of removing the shells from other seeds or nuts is by machine but, until recently, removing the hull from sesame seeds was commonly done by dissolving the hulls in a chemical solvent containing lye, acids, and enzyme solutions. Traces of these solvents may remain, even though the seeds are washed after treatment. Companies concerned with quality are now using a method of mechanical hulling without chemicals.

One of the most delicious products that can be made from hulled sesame seeds is **sesame tahini**, a peanut butter-like spread made by grinding the hulled seeds into a smooth consistency. Tahini is even more delicious when made from **mechanically hulled** sesame seeds because it is sweet and smooth with no cloying, chemical aftertaste. It also has a lighter flavor and texture than sesame butter which is made from unhulled seeds.

Sesame's nutritional profile can raise the quantity and quality of protein in foods. For example, because it is high in the sulphur containing amino acids such as methionine and low in lysine, it complements the protein profile of legumes which has just the opposite. This bean/sesame combination can also be added to grains to make a "complete" meal.

Although an important asset to vegetarian diets, it's not only for vegetarians. So how do you use it? Tahini is very versatile, suitable at any meal. For breakfast, try it on your toast, add to smoothies, combine with applesauce, jams, or syrups for a pancake topper, or use it as a fruit dip. At lunch or dinner, it can be a main ingredient for garbanzo bean based hommus or combined with other beans for sandwich spreads, fillings, or dips. Use it to make salad dressings or non-dairy "cream of" soups. And don't forget desserts. Possibilities are endless.

Tahini is available in both raw and toasted. The lighter flavor of raw tahini is more versatile than the toasted tahini which is more suitable as a spread by itself.

Sunflower seeds, another native American seed, are delicious as a high protein snack and as an addition to breads, and also as a crunchy substitute for bacon bits and croutons on cooked vegetables and salads! Roast for best flavor. Sunflower seeds still in the hull can be sprouted.

What would life be without **walnuts**? No doubt, Christmas and Thanksgiving would need to be cancelled! No other nut is so revered in cooking and baking. Walnuts found in most stores are of the English walnut variety. Because of their extremely high oil content, like pecans, they are more susceptible to rancidity. Buy walnut halves instead of walnut pieces. If pieces or chopped walnuts are required, crush them at home before using in cooking and in desserts for fresher, more tasty results.

Recipes

CHILI ROASTED NUTS

Peanuts, cashews, or pumpkin seeds are great snacks, especially when roasted with chili powder. Great also as an accompaniment to Mexican dinners.

2 cups nuts
pinch of sea salt or 2 teaspoons tamari shoyu
1 TB. oil (if using sea salt)
1 teaspoon chili powder

1. Preheat oven to 300°.
2. Place nuts on ungreased cookie sheet, put in oven, and roast 10-15 minutes or until the nuts turn golden brown. Stir occasionally to prevent burning.
3. Meanwhile, heat oil in a small skillet and cook chili powder and salt for 3 minutes over low heat. If using tamari shoyu, simply add the chili powder to the tamari.
4. When nuts are golden brown, add sea salt or tamari mixture to nuts and return to the oven for 2 minutes.
5. Cool before storing.

"YOUR OWN" NUT MIX

Combine all your favorites into a new snack sensation!

1/2 cup almonds (raw or tamari roasted)
1/2 cup cashews (raw or tamari roasted)
1/2 cup sunflower or pumpkin seeds (raw or tamari roasted)
1/2 cup peanuts or pecans (raw or roasted)
1/4 cup coconut
1/2 cup raisins, pitted dates, apricots, or other unsulphured dried fruit

1. Mix together.
2. Eat!!

Recipes

CASHEW GRAVY   *yields 1 1/4 cup*

Ground cashews become very creamy when blended with a liquid. Take advantage of the stock remaining in the vegetable cooking pot and make an amazing sauce.

1/4 cup roasted cashews
1 cup hot vegetable stock or water
1/2 tsp. tamari shoyu or 2 tsp. white miso (opt.)
1 tsp. arrowroot or kuzu (opt.)

1. Grind cashews in a blender or electric nut/coffee grinder.
2. Using a blender, Japanese suribachi, or whisk, gradually add the stock until desired consistency is obtained.
3. Blend in optional seasonings.
4. If sauce becomes too thin or if less concentration of nuts is desired, dilute arrowroot or kuzu with cold water. Return gravy to a boil, add thickener and simmer until thick, stirring constantly.
5. Serve over vegetables, beans, casseroles, or vegetarian "burgers".

TAHINI MISO SAUCE   *yields 1 1/2 cups*

So easy! This sauce is incredible over steamed vegetables (try using the cooking water as stock), grain dishes, tofu, or salads.

5 TB. sesame tahini
1 TB. miso
1/2 tsp. dried herb or spice (garlic, curry, parsley, chives, etc.)
1 cup water or stock, hot or cold

1. Soak herb or spice in water or stock for 5 minutes.
2. Mix tahini and miso with a fork or suribachi (Japanese grooved mortar and pestle).
3. Gradually blend in seasoning liquid to desired consistency with a whisk or continue using the suribachi.
4. Pour into gravy boat or over entrée.
   (**NOTE:** if reheating the sauce, use very low heat and stir continiously to prevent curdling of the tahini.)

4

FATS & VEGETABLE OILS

Oils used in cooking and salad dressings are processed from nuts, seeds, and beans. Despite all the emphasis on low fat cooking, *small* amounts of vegetable oils are necessary since they are carriers of the fat soluble vitamins A, D, E, and K and rich sources of vitamin E and linoleic acid.

Linoleic acid cannot be synthesized by the body and therefore must be obtained from the diet. (Other sources of linoleic acid besides oils include fish, nuts, seeds, and beans.) Linoleic acid is so essential to the body because it helps strengthen cell walls and capillaries, reduces blood clotting, and lubricates hair and skin. Body cells need two other fatty acids, **arachidonic acid** and **linolenic acid.** Although all three: linoleic acid, arachidonic acid, and linolenic acid are known as the **essential fatty acids,** both arachidonic and linolenic acids can be synthesized in the body if linoleic acid is supplied in the diet.

SATURATED VS. UNSATURATED FATS

"Saturated fat" and "unsaturated fat" are two terms used quite frequently. Basically, the differences lie in the molecular structure. Fats consist of carbon atoms linked in a row. Each carbon atom is capable of forming bonds on all four sides, primarily with hydrogen and other carbon atoms. Sometimes a carbon atom will not link with a hydrogen atom but will instead form a double bond with the carbon atom next to it. If a fat molecule lacks a hydrogen atom at an available location, it is called an **unsaturated** fat. If it has more than one double bond, the link between two carbon atoms, and thus, more open spaces, it is called **polyunsaturated**. ("Poly" means many.) If only one space is open (one double bond), it is called a **mono-unsaturated** fat. ("Mono" means one.) If all available spaces are filled with hydrogen atoms, it is called a **saturated** fat.

All foods contain saturated and unsaturated fats but in varying proportions. Vegetable oils are no exception, but generally animal foods are higher in saturated fat and vegetable foods are higher in unsaturated fat. Exceptions in the vegetable category include coconut oil and palm oil, both of which are highly saturated.

Saturated fats are solid at room temperature such as butter and fat from meat. Too high a proportion of saturated fats in the diet tend to clog the arteries and may lead to heart disease or other degenerative disease.

Unsaturated fats, such as vegetable oils, are liquid at room temperature. Just because a fat is unsaturated does not mean that it can be used in any amount without harm. Some researchers believe that polyunsaturated oils can help reduce serum cholesterol but altering the type of fat consumed without trying to increase fiber intake and better the diet is no

improvement. A diet high in soluble fiber can help move the cholesterol out of your body.
Taking polyunsaturated oils to reduce cholesterol without fiber to move that cholesterol out
can over-burden the gall bladder and colon, possibly producing gallstones or colon cancer.

Animal studies show that diets too high in polyunsaturated fats may lead to cancer
because of the high oxidation of the polyunsaturated fats. The emphasis is moderation.
Moderation in consumption of both saturated and unsaturated fats, coupled with a high
fiber diet from whole foods will benefit most people.

Omega 3 and Omega 6 fatty acids have received much attention recently in regard to
their role in coronary heart disease. For years people have been advised to eat more polyunsaturated fats than saturated fats to lower blood cholesterol and thus reduce the risk of
heart and artery disease. Recent research has concentrated on a fatty acid-derived class of
substances called prostaglandins. Prostaglandins are produced by every cell in the body
and control such things as reproduction, fertility, inflammation, immunity, and intracellu-
lar communication. Initially thought that linoleic acid was primarily responsible for producing prostaglandins, it was discovered that arachidonic acid, dihomogammalinolenic
acid (DHA) and eicosapentaenoic acid (EPA) all had the ability to alter prostaglandin levels.
In response to the famous study of the Eskimos in Greenland who had extremely low incidences of heart attacks in comparison with the average same aged person consuming a
typical American diet, an extensive study found that EPA stimulated the production of a
certain group of prostaglandins and blocked the production of thromboxane which promotes clotting of the blood. (Most heart attacks in the United States occur when a blood
clot gets stuck in an already-narrowed coronary artery.) In comparison, linoleic acid stimulates the synthesis of another group of prostaglandins and thromboxane, and, in effect,
promotes clotting.

The family of fatty acids high in EPA, DHA, and gamma linolenic acids are called
"Omega 3" fatty acids and include fish oils, walnut oil, evening primrose oil, and linseed
oils. (The name "Omega" is used to refer to the position of the terminal double bond found
in the unsaturated fatty acid side chain.) The group of fatty acids high in linoleic and
arachadonic acids are called "Omega 6" fatty acids and include sesame oil, safflower oil,
sunflower oil, and corn oil. Research indicates that a higher intake of Omega 3 fatty acids
than is currently consumed in the United States may be beneficial in treatment and prevention of coronary artery disease as well as premenstrual syndrome, hypertension, and
rheumatoid arthritis.

Good news for those who love to use **olive oil**! Olive oil is a mono-unsaturated fat
(oleic acid) that seems to reduce the amount of LDL (low density lipoproteins) which carry
cholesterol through the body's system for cell building needs but leave any excess cholesterol in arterial walls and other tissues. Therefore, reducing the amounts of LDL reduces
cholesterol buildup. Like the studies concerning the Greenland Eskimos using a higher
ratio of foods high in Omega 3 fatty acids, cultures using olive oil as the predominant fat
tend to have lower incidences of heart disease. Lower rates of cancer may also be attributed to diets using olive oil in cooking.

Again, moderate amounts of the different fatty acids in certain ratios are the keys, not
complete isolation of a certain type of fatty acids. The latest recommendations from the
American Heart Association and the American Cancer Society recommend no more than
30% of all calories consumed in one day come from fat. Of that 30%, they suggest that less
than 10% come from saturated fat, up to 10% from polyunsaturated fat, with the remainder
from monounsaturated fats.

HYDROGENATION

"Hydrogenation" is the process of taking a polyunsaturated oil and bubbling hydrogen through it in order to break the original double bonds and attach additional hydrogen molecules. This, in effect, makes the polyunsaturated fat a saturated one—with all its negative properties. **Margarine** is a hydrogenated, artificially saturated fat, despite the fact that it *originated* from a polyunsaturated source such as corn oil. Depending upon the degree of hydrogenation, margarine may be no better for you than comparably saturated animal fats and perhaps even worse. Not all the evidence is in as of yet, but concerns about how the chemical nature of the fats is changed and how usable these altered fats are in the body should be considered. As an alternative, combine warm butter with vegetable oil in equal amounts for a spread lower in saturated fats that is also free of questionable processing.

Nonetheless, some vegetarians or people allergic to dairy products prefer to use margarine instead of butter. If margarine is used, avoid products that contain cottonseed oil and artificial additives. Oil from cottonseed may contain harmful residues and is best avoided since cotton is heavily sprayed while being grown. When no preservatives are used in margarines, the salt content must be over 2%.

Partially hydrogenated oil is no better than fully hydrogenated oil. Oils are partially hydrogenated in order to produce a product that is easy to work with but less dense than fully hydrogenated fats. Partial hydrogenation also delays rancidity. Filling the double bonds with hydrogen prevents oxygen molecules from attaching to the unattached molecules. When oxygen molecules so attach, the process of oxidation (rancidity) begins.

All vegetable oils are free of cholesterol regardless of the brand, but the similarity stops there. Some oils contain synthetic preservatives and are heavily refined, bleached, and deodorized after extraction with chemical solvents, while others are simply mechanically pressed, filtered, and bottled.

HOW OILS ARE MADE

The manufacturing of oils is somewhat more complicated than crushing a nut, seed, or bean in a food processor. First, the raw material is cleaned, hulled, and then steamed to increase the availability of the oil. The steaming temperature varies depending on the raw material but generally ranges from 110°-250° F.

After cooking, the oil is extracted either mechanically or with a solvent. Oils labeled as **"mechanically pressed"** or **"expeller pressed"** are produced by continuously driven screws that crush the seed into a pulp, producing the oil. (Despite the term "cold pressed", the machines actually generate heat between 140°-160° so the term is actually meaningless.)

Once the oil is extracted, an oil destined to be "unrefined" is filtered to remove any large particles and then bottled. This type of oil appears dark with some sediment and has a taste and odor identical to the raw material used.

Solvent extracted oil continues with the process after the expeller pressing in order to extract the rest of the oil left in the residue. Hexane, a highly flammable, colorless, volatile, and *toxic* petroleum derivative, is used as the solvent to extract all but 1/2-1% of the oil in the residue. In order to remove the hexane after extraction, temperatures up to 300° are used to ignite and evaporate the hexane out of the oils. Large amounts are not left but some residue may linger. If the oil is bottled at this point, it can still be considered an unrefined oil.

Many oils, however, including some which are expeller pressed, continue through the refining stages. They are degummed to separate the gummy substances. This process removes the natually occuring lecithin from the oils which causes oils to smoke at high temperatures. (Lecithin removed from soy oil is sold as food supplements and used in food processing.)

After degumming, the oil is refined in an alkali solution containing lye or caustic soda and heated at temperatures between 140°-160°. This removes free fatty acids (including some of the vitamin E) which can oxidize and cause the oil to go rancid. Oils that undergo this process do not go rancid as quickly as an unrefined oil, but many nutrients are lost in the process.

The oil is then mixed with clay or activated charcoal to remove any pigments or soap left from the refining process and filtered to clarify the oil. Further clarification is accomplished through deodorizing. In this process, steam is blown through the oil under a high vacuum at temperatures up to 475° for 10-12 hours. After deodorizing, preservatives can be added. In some brands, methyl silicone is added to prevent bubbling over while deep frying.

In the final stage of refinement, the oil is clear and light in color with no odor or taste. At this point it will be bottled unless the oil needs to be hydrogenated to further process the oil into vegetable shortening, margarine, or special deep-frying oils.

Contrast the mechanically pressed versus solvent extraction processes used in extracting the oil. Then consider the stages of refinement that are possible. The degree of processing is a clue as to how much nutrient value is present in the oil. The least amount of processing and the fewer chemicals added to an oil, the more nutritious the end product.

CHOOSING A GOOD VEGETABLE OIL

Choosing a good vegetable oil is easy. Read your labels and look closely at the oil itself. A good vegetable oil will be labeled "expeller pressed", "mechanically pressed", or "unrefined". It should appear somewhat dark and possibly contain some sediment on the bottom. Upon opening the bottle at home, the oil should have an odor and taste similar to the raw material used.

Buy only the amount that can be used within a month. Unrefined oils go rancid quickly and, consequently, should be stored in the refrigerator after opening. Soy, peanut, and olive oils can solidify in the refrigerator, but this does not harm the oil. Simply bring the bottle out about 10 minutes before you use it in order to let the oil return to its liquid state. Rancidity can also occur even before a bottle of vegetable oil is opened. For the freshest oil possible, buy oils which have undergone a nitrogen flushing process. Nitrogen, a harmless component of the air we breathe, is forced in after the oil is bottled and immediately capped. This displaces the oxygen and thus prevents rancidity, at least until it is opened by the consumer.

There are many oils available, each having its own distinctive flavor and purpose.

Canola oil is made from rapeseed plants. It has about 1/2 the amount of saturated fat found in vegetable oils, is high in mono-unsaturated fats, and contains about 10% of the Omega-3 fatty acids.

Corn oil has a rich, buttery flavor which makes it a favorite for baking, sautéeing, and popping corn while still being suitable for salad dressings. Because of its tendency to foam and smoke at high heats, corn oil is not suitable for deep frying.

Olive oil has a fruity, rich, delicate flavor superior for salad dressings and Italian cooking. It has a low smoking point of 375° which makes it less desirable for stir frying and even less for deep frying.

Olive oil is the only oil that can truly be called cold pressed since olives do not need to be heated in order to extract the oil.   Olives can be pressed with a hydraulic press with the expressed oil still at room temperature. The oils extracted from the first pressing are called virgin olive oil. There are three grades of virgin olive oil.

Extra virgin has the best flavor and aroma. It comes from a low yield, first pressing of the olive with no added preservatives or additives.

Fine virgin has a good flavor but has a higher acid content with no added preservatives or additives.

Plain virgin has a slightly off flavor and the highest acidity.

Pure olive oil, even though the term "pure" connotes something better, actually comes from a second pressing. The oil extracted during this second pressing contains more of the pulp, skin, and particles of pit than the first pressings. This gives a bitter taste to the oil, so it is then washed with hot water or given a chemical treatment to neutralize the bitterness.

Why ruin your salad or cooking with an inferior tasting oil? Extra virgin olive oil may cost more but the quality and flavor is worth it. Experiment with the various brands of olive oil. Each is unique depending upon the area, season of harvest, and type of olive used.

Peanut oil has a strong flavor and is used frequently for stir frying, baking, and fondues. It has good stability and a long shelf life due to its high level (20%) of saturated fat.

Safflower oil is one of the most popular oils due to its mild flavor, high smoking point of 515°, and because it has the highest ratio of polyunsaturated fats. However, since it is so high in polyunsaturated fats, it is the least stable oil and is more prone to rancidity. Deep frying with safflower oil might not be advisable since the rate of oxidation increases even more dramatically with the high temperature. Safflower oil is primarily used in sautéeing and baking. Many people also use safflower oil in salad dressings, but because of its greasy texture, some prefer to combine it with other oils.

Sesame oil is the most stable of all the oils and because of this is most appropriate for deep frying. It has a delicious, nutty flavor that is a favorite for salads, sautéeing, stir frying, and baking. **Toasted sesame oil** is also available. The sesame seeds are toasted first before pressing to extract the oil. Toasted sesame oil has an even richer taste and aroma than regular sesame oil. It is generally used as a condiment rather than as a cooking agent.

Soy oil has a strong, domineering flavor. Commercially, it is the most widely used oil in the United States, but much of it is refined in order to improve the flavor.

Sunflower oil is second only to safflower oil in terms of its high amount of polyunsaturated fats. It has a pleasant, somewhat stronger flavor than safflower and serves as an all-purpose oil. However, unrefined sunflower oil quite often tastes rancid, probably originating from using rancid nuts as the source of oil. Refined sunflower oil will have no pronounced flavor due to extensive processing.

Coconut oil and **palm kernal oil** are used primarily in candies, cakes, and cookies. They are very high in saturated fats, containing twice as much as lard.

Exotic oils such as avocado, almond, hazelnut, pumpkin seed, and walnut oils are generally used for special effects in cooking. They are also used as alternatives for those allergic to the sources of other oils. Walnut oil contains Omega-3 fatty acids.

Wheat germ oil is not used in cooking but as a supplement because of its high vitamin E and octacosonal content. It goes rancid very quickly, so buy small bottles and keep it refrigerated.

Recipes

VEGETABLE/BEAN MARINADE
Bay leaves and black peppercorns are perfect seasoning partners to enhance the flavors of cooked beans and raw or cooked vegetables.

3/4 cup vinegar (wine, apple cider, rice, or balsamic vinegar)
1/2 cup olive oil
1 small bay leaf
5 whole black peppercorns
1/2 teaspoon sea salt

1. Mix above ingredients together in a small saucepan.
2. Warm over medium heat for 5 minutes.
3. Pour over vegetables or beans and let marinate for at least 1 hour.

MARINADE FOR MEATS
Less tender cuts of meat become succulent when soaked in oil, vinegar, and herbs before roasting, broiling, or grilling.

1/2 cup safflower or olive oil
1/4 cup vinegar or lemon juice
2 cloves garlic, minced
1/4 teaspoon salt (opt.) or 1 TB. tamari shoyu
1 TB. fresh parsley, finely chopped or 1 teaspoon dried parsley
1 teaspoon dried chives
(**HINT:** dried mustard, chili powder, curry powder, or any other favorite seasoning can be used. Try a new one each time.)
1-1 1/2 lb. round steak, chuck steak, fajita (skirt steaks), ribs, london broil, lamb shoulder roast or chops

1. Combine marinade ingredients and pour over meat. Make sure meat is covered by the liquid. If not, make more marinade.
2. Cover meat and marinade. Refrigerate 3-12 hours.
3. Remove meat from marinade (save marinade) and roast, broil, or grill as normal.
4. Marinade can be used to baste meat during cooking, if desired.

SESAME SALAD DRESSING   *makes 1 cup*
A good quality oil tastes like its source. The flavor of sesame oil is particularly good with any salad.

2/3 cup sesame oil (regular or toasted sesame oil)
1/3 cup lemon juice, lime juice, or vinegar
1/8 teaspoon cumin
1/2 teaspoon dried parsley or 1 TB. fresh parsley
salt or tamari shoyu to taste

1. Mix together thoroughly.
2. Pour over salad or use as a marinade.

5

DAIRY, CHEESE, & EGGS

MILK

Milk products are most noted as a source of highly absorbed calcium. Pasteurization of milk came about as an answer to controlling the spread of communicable diseases such as diphtheria and scarlet fever and bacteria such as salmonella. In modern day pasteurization methods, milk is heated to 161° for 15 seconds to kill all pathogenic micro-organisms. After this short time span, the nutritive value of pasteurized milk is only slightly lower than raw milk in terms of thiamine (B_1), B_{12} and vitamin C. Pasteurization does not make the milk sterile. Sterilization kills all organisms and is generally used for fluid milk products that are packaged in asceptic containers that need no refrigeration. Controversy concerning the benefits vs. safety of raw milk and pasteurized milk continues. As of September 1987, 27 states ban the sale of raw and/or certified raw milk in retail outlets (except raw milk cheese).

Alabama	Minnesota
Colorado	Mississippi
Delaware	Nevada
District of Columbia	North Carolina
(Washington, D.C.)	North Dakota
Florida	Ohio
Hawaii	Rhode Island
Illinois	South Dakota
Indiana	Tennessee
Iowa	Texas
Kentucky	Virginia
Louisiana	West Virginia
Maryland	Wisconsin
Michigan	Wyoming

After milk is pasteurized, the cream is separated and then recombined with skim milk in varying amounts.

- **skim milk** contains less than 0.5% milk fat
- **lowfat** 0.5-2.0% milk fat
- **whole milk** 3.25-4.0% milk fat
- **half and half** at least 10.5% milk fat
- **light cream** at least 18% milk fat
- **whipping cream** 30-35.9% milk fat
- **heavy cream** at least 36% milk fat

Homogenization distributes the fat particles evenly throughout the milk. The process involves sending the milk at high pressure through a small nozzle onto a hard surface to break the fat globules into very small particles. Homogenization decreases the flavor, sensitivity to light, stability to heat, and whipping properties of milk. Some studies suggest that homogenization could be related to coronary heart disease. According to Kurt Oster, M.D. of Bridgeport, Connecticut, breaking the fat into smaller pieces allows xanthine oxidase, an enzyme which helps in the breakdown of protein, to pass unchanged through the intestinal wall. This allows the xanthine oxidase to go through the lymphatic system and into the bloodstream where it can cause damage to the inside of the arterial wall. It is theorized that in response, the body tries to repair the damage by depositing fibrin and cholesterol inside the blood vessel, thus setting up a situation of possible arteriosclerosis. The data is still controversial. Nonetheless, pasteurized, unhomogenized milk is available for that "old-fashioned, straight-from-the-farm" type flavor. Many people prefer it simply because of the cream that floats to the top. The cream can be skimmed and eaten immediately (before someone else gets it!), whipped, made into butter, discarded, or stirred to disperse it through the milk.

Acidophilus milk was developed to provide a way to promote the proliferation of beneficial bacteria in the intestines without the sour flavor of yogurt, the usual medium for *Lactobacillus acidophilus* (see yogurt for details on fermented dairy products). The sweet flavor of the acidophilus milk is obtained by adding acidophilus that has already been cultured on a different medium directly to the milk with no further fermentation procedures. Further cultivating the acidophilus in the milk would produce a sour flavor as a result of the *Lactobacillus acidophilus* culture feeding on the lactose. Because acidophilus milk is not cultured, it will have the same amount of lactose as regular cow's milk. Therefore, unlike yogurt, acidophilus milk is not more beneficial for those with a lactose intolerance.

Goat's milk is sold when available.   People allergic to cow's milk sometimes find they can tolerate goat's milk, but this is not always so. Others use goat's milk because its smaller fat globules make it easier to digest. Its calcium content at 326 mg. per cup is higher than whole cow's milk calcium value of 291 mg. per cup. On the other hand, goat's milk is low in folacin (folic acid), containing only 2 mg. versus the 12 mg. available in cow's milk. Individuals who drink goat's milk should make sure they obtain adequate folacin from another source.

Non-fat dry milk can be reconstituted or used in its powdered form to enrich sauces, cereals, or baked goods. Look for non-fat, non-instant spray dried powdered milk. Full fat dry milk decomposes easily. Non-instant, even though more work to reconstitute, is superior than instant in cooking or making yogurt. Reconstituted instant dry milk is often lumpy with a chalky consistency. Spray-dried milk is processed at lower temperatures than dry milk processed in the old roller drying methods. Therefore, more nutrients are preserved with spray-dried milk.

Store powdered milk in an airtight container in the refrigerator. To reconstitute, use 2/3 cup powdered milk to 1 quart water. First add a small amount of water to the dry milk to make a paste. Then gradually add the remainder of the water and blend. Chill at least 2 hours for best flavor.

Powdered milk is handy when you want milk with your granola while travelling, camping, or going someplace without fresh milk. Just mix a couple of tablespoons with your granola, package tightly to prevent moisture, and add water when you are ready to eat.

CREAM & BUTTER

The best **cream** is free of additives or preservatives. However, because it is high in fat and could go rancid, preservative-free cream must be used quickly. Here is a chance to use the cream from unhomogenized milk. Skim the top for "free" delicious cream ready to be whipped or used plain over cereal, desserts, or fruit.

According to Federal regulations, **butter** must contain 80% butterfat. Both salted and unsalted varieties are available. Salted butter keeps longer but is more likely to stick to pans and skillets. Unsalted butter, also called sweet butter, has a more delicate flavor and since it doesn't keep as long, requires the use of even fresher cream by the manufacturer.

CULTURED MILK PRODUCTS

Buttermilk has a tangy distinctive yogurt-like flavor from the bacteria that is added to skim milk to ferment the milk sugar. It is thicker than regular milk and lower in fat. Its calcium content is just slightly less than cow's milk.

Cottage cheese has the reputation as having an ingredients listing that reads like a chemistry book. A few dairies produce good clean products containing basically milk inoculated with lactic acid bacteria, cream, and salt. Read your labels. **Lowfat** cottage cheese contains 2% fat while the creamy **farmer style** contains 4%. The **dry curd** cottage cheese, made from low fat milk and non-fat milk, is very low in fat and sodium. Since it lacks the cream and salt found in regular cottage cheese, it is dry, crumbly, and bland. Most people use it as an ingredient in recipes or season it before eating plain to give it flavor. Due to the action of the lactic acid bacteria in cottage cheese, some of the lactose is broken down. Individuals with a lactose intolerance may find better results with cottage cheese than with milk. **NOTE:** 2 cups of cottage cheese has the same amount of calcium as 1 cup of milk.

The best **yogurt** contains active cultures that are added *after* the milk is pasteurized after the yogurt is made. Some yogurts are little more than a sweet creamy snack but the presence of active cultures brings yogurt to its full potential. Besides providing protein and calcium, yogurt is used to introduce beneficial bacteria into the digestive tract and inhibit harmful bacteria in order to promote better digestion and elimination.

Yogurts vary according to the type of culture and complexity of ingredients. The bacteria which turn milk into yogurt are ***Lactobacillus bulgaricus*** and ***Streptococcus thermophilus***. Occasionally a brand of yogurt will include ***Lactobacillus acidophilus***. Acidophilus is a more potent and permanent promoter of beneficial bacteria. Yogurt that contains acidophilus is often suggested to be used during yeast infections, after bouts of diarrhea, and after a course of antibiotics.

Individuals who are allergic to milk because of the inability to digest lactose, the carbohydrate in milk, may have better results with yogurt since it contains 75% of the amount found in a comparable serving of milk. *Streptococcus thermophilus* contributes about 3 times the amount of lactase (the enzyme responsible for digesting the milk sugar) than *Lactobacillus bulgaricus*. Buy a yogurt that contains *Streptococcus thermophilus* if milk digestion is a problem. Yogurts made with nonfat dry milk may not work as well for a lactose intolerant person since the nonfat dry milk adds high amounts of lactose.

Yogurt can be made with whole milk, part skim, or skim milk Some plain yogurts are quite similar to a medium thick creamy homemade product while others are as thick as custard. Yogurt made from part skim or skim milk always contain nonfat dry milk to make up for the creamy fat that would be present in whole milk. Besides nonfat dry milk, gelatin, carrageenan, stabilizers, pH modifiers, or other thickeners may be added to yogurts to reach a certain thickness characteristic of the brand.

Some yogurts are made from unhomogenized milk. With them you have the option of stirring the cream into the rest of the yogurt for a thick consistency or eating the cream immediately for a moment of real pleasure!

Calcium is slightly lower per cup (274 mg.) in whole milk yogurt as compared to a cup of whole milk (290 mg.) Low fat yogurt contains about 415 mg. of calcium, thanks to the nonfat dry milk solids.

Fruit flavored yogurts are sweetened with honey, maple syrup, sugar, corn syrup, or fructose. Nutritionally, your best bet is to buy fresh fruit and add it to plain yogurt; it tastes just as good and you'll eliminate a large amount of sugar. But for convenience and as a better alternative to ice cream, ready-made fruit flavored yogurts often "hit the spot."

Any colors added to yogurt should be derived only from vegetable coloring agents such as beet juice, or annatto seeds, grape skins, or tumeric. Read your labels.

Substitute yogurt for milk, cream, buttermilk, mayonnaise, or sour cream in recipes. Add to smoothies, on top of baked potatoes, or to crown that pumpkin pie!

Kefir is a type of liquid yogurt made by adding kefir grains, (naturally formed organisms made of milk proteins) to milk and letting it incubate over night at room temperature. It tastes like a thick, tangy milkshake. Plain kefir is unsweetened and fruit flavors are sweetened with fructose. Plain kefir has a significant amount of calcium: 350 mg. per cup!

Recipes

KEFIR CHEESE DIP   *makes 1/2 cup*

Low calorie kefir cheese allows you the opportunity to use a dip without feeling guilty. Combine with a packaged dip seasoning mix or invent your own.

8 oz. kefir cheese
1 TB. chives, fresh and finely chopped
1 teaspoon dill, fresh and finely chopped
1 clove garlic, minced

1. Mix all ingredients together.
2. Refrigerate 1 hour to combine flavors.
3. Serve with fresh vegetables, crackers, or chips.

YOGURT RICE   *makes 2 cups*

A great, unique way to use up leftover rice...make it tangy!

2 cups cooked brown rice
1 TB. fresh dill, finely chopped or 1 teaspoon dried dillweed
1/2 cucumber, seeded and chopped (opt.)
1 small carrot, grated (opt.)
1 cup yogurt
1. Combine all ingredients.
2. Marinate at least 2 hours before serving.

YOGURT "SOUR CREAM"   *makes 1 1/2 cups*

OK, so this is simple, but it's a classic!

1 cup plain yogurt
1/2 cup chopped fresh chives

1. Mix and chill.
2. Serve over baked potatoes.

HERBED CHEESE DIP   *makes 1 1/2 cups*

Puréed cottage cheese makes a low calorie base for this creamy dip.

8 oz. cottage cheese
1/2 cup kefir cheese or sour cream
2 TB. chopped fresh parsley
2 TB. olive oil
1 TB. lemon juice
1 TB. chives fresh or dried
1/2 teaspoon garlic powder
pinch of salt
pinch of ground pepper

1. Purée cottage cheese in a blender or food processor until smooth.
2. Add rest of ingredients and, again, blend until smooth.
3. Turn into a small bowl. Chill at least 1 hour for best flavor.

CHEESE

"Cheese, please." But what type?

Pasteurized process cheese is made by mixing several natural cheeses with an emulsifier to keep the different cheeses from separating out. **Pasteurized process cheese food** is made from combining pasteurized process cheese with whey, cream, or milk.

Those used to processed cheeses have a real treat in store for them with cheeses that are free of artificial colors, artificial flavors, preservatives, stabilizers, and emulsifiers. Unlike processed cheeses, natural cheeses taste so good there is no need for any chemical to mask or enhance flavors. A large variety of the highest quality cheeses are available, both domestic and imported.

Natural cheese is made "from scratch." Whole or part-skim milk, a bacterial culture, and an enzyme transforms the milk into curds and whey. The whey is removed and the curd is ripened or cured with the help of bacteria or yeast.

The unique flavor and texture of the cheeses is determined by the kind of milk used (cow's, goat's, sheep), the amount and type of salt and spices, and the ripening conditions— temperature, humidity, and length of time.

Cheese can be divided into three main categories: soft, semi hard, and hard.

Soft cheeses can be unripened, mold ripened, or bacteria ripened. Unripened cheeses include cottage cheese, ricotta cheese, cream cheese, neufchatel, kefir cheese, and feta. These types of cheeses are more perishable than other cheeses and because of this are often laden with preservatives and stabilizers in standard commercial brands. Vegetable stabilizers such as guar gum present no apparent health problem.

Neufchatel, yogurt cheese, and kefir cheese are good lower fat alternatives to cream cheese. Kefir cheese, like the liquid kefir, has a somewhat tart taste that is great in sandwiches and dips. Yogurt cheese is yogurt whose moisture content has been greatly reduced. All can be used as regular full fat cream cheese.

Mold ripened soft cheeses ripen from the outside-in and have cheese rinds which are edible. Camembert and brie fit this category. Bacteria ripened soft cheeses such as limburger also ripen from the outside-in.

Semi hard cheeses ripen from the inside-out. Bleu, gorgonzola, and stilton are examples of mold ripened crumbly cheeses. Monterey jack and bel paese are bacteria ripened semi hard cheeses.

Hard cheeses include firm ripened and hard ripened cheeses. These cheeses are cured for a longer period of time and are able to be stored for a longer period of time. Swiss, cheddar, jarlsberg, gruyere, sap sago, edam, gjetost, and provolone are firm ripened. Sharpness is relative to the length of curing. Cheddar cheeses usually range in age from 90 days to 4 years.

Parmesan and romano are hard ripened cheeses which are cured slowly for a long time. Of the two basic varieties of parmesan cheese—Italian and Argentine, Italian parmesan is aged longer, has less moisture, a more intense flavor, and is more expensive. Both Argentine and Italian parmesan are delicious and unique in their own way.

Parmesan should be grated just before using for best results. For convenience, buy freshly grated parmesan that is stored in the dairy case free of preservatives. Many commercially packed grated parmesans lack flavor and contain preservatives.

Romano cheese is made from sheep's milk. Look for Pecorino Romano as well as Locatelli, the highest grade Romano.

Cheese made from raw milk has a more superior flavor than a similar cheese made from pasteurized milk. **Raw milk cheese** is aged more slowly and requires more production skill than pasteurized cheese. Federal law requires that raw milk cheese be aged at least 60 days to insure that any problems from harmful bacteria are eliminated by the naturally occuring acidity of the cheese. Therefore it is impossible to offer, for example, an imported raw milk brie. Cheese production does require some heat, but since the temperature never goes above 120°, it is still considered a raw milk cheese.

Some cheeses are labeled as **rennet free cheeses**. To make cheese, the protein in milk must coagulate in order to separate the curds and whey. Often rennet is used, an enzyme extracted from the lining of the fourth stomach of calves. People who object to an animal-based rennet can buy cheeses made with a bacteria culture. Neither affects the taste nor nutritive value of the cheese.

Most cheeses are pale yellow or white in color. The color varies as to the milk and the presence of molds, bacteria, or coloring agents. No cheese has a natural orange color. If it looks as if a cheese is colored, read the label to make sure the coloring is vegetable based from natural carotene or annatto seed extract.

Not all cheese is made with cow's milk. Unique and tasty cheeses are also made with goat or sheep's milk. Some people who are allergic to cow's milk may find that they can use cheese from goat or sheep's milk with less difficulty.

However, those same people who are allergic to liquid milk may find that *cheeses* from cow's milk, especially the longer aged cheeses, are tolerated. Allergies can arise when undigested proteins enter the bloodstream. The cheese making process "predigests" the proteins. Those who are lactose intolerant may be able to eat cheese since most of the lactose is drained from the milk when the whey is separated from the curd. The least amount of lactose will remain in hard cheeses that are longer aged. Swiss cheese and extra sharp cheddar cheeses, for example, have only a trace of lactose, much less than a mild cheddar.

Soy cheeses are imitation cheeses based upon soymilk. In addition to soymilk, its ingredients include soy oil, calcium caseinate, tofu, salt, lecithin, citric acid, guar gum, and annatto seed. Be advised that soy cheese is **not** non-dairy. Calcium caseinate, a milk derived protein, is added as a binder which also enables the "cheese" to melt. Individuals allergic to the protein in milk will more than likely have difficulty digesting the soy cheese. However, soy cheese **is** free of lactose and cholesterol, so those who must avoid dairy for these reasons may find it a good substitute.

As a manufactured imitation cheese, it is does not replicate the nutrients found in real cheese. Soy cheese contains 85 mg. calcium per ounce in comparison with 204 mg. of calcium in cheddar cheese. One ounce of Swiss cheese contains 272 mg. of calcium. The less moisture a cheese contains, the more concentrated it is in nutrients.

Low fat cheeses— Low fat cheeses are a good alternative for those who like cheese but need to limit its high fat content. Fat makes cheese creamy and its texture smooth. The average fat content of hard cheeses is approximately 9 grams per ounce. Some cheeses are naturally low in fat such as part skim and regular mozzarella, feta, kefir cheese, neufchatel, and camembert. Specially made low fat cheeses include Swiss lace, lattost, New Holland, garden vegetable, farmers, and hoop cheese. Although not as rich in flavor as those with a higher fat content, they are very good.

Salt is a necessary ingredient in the processing of cheese in that it helps control the bacteria. During aging some cheeses are rubbed in salt while others are soaked in brine. Swiss, gruyere, mozzarella, and neufchatel tend to be lower in sodium. The cheeses highest in sodium include roquefort, parmesan, romano, and bleu. Some specially made low sodium cheeses are available such as no salt raw milk cheddar and low sodium raw milk muenster. The low fat cheeses previously mentioned also tend to be low in sodium.

Many commercial **cheese spreads** are up to 60% water, gums, and gelatins and may have cheese curds but no cheese! In contrast, natural cheese spreads are made from cheddar cheese, cream, whey solids, herbs and/or spices, and annatto bean for color.

Storing cheese properly will save money and frustration. Hard cheeses store longer because of their low moisture content, while the soft cheeses have a greater tendency to mold. Store cheese in the refrigerator snugly wrapped in foil or plastic wrap to keep it from drying out or from picking up unwanted moisture. Bleu cheeses should be loosely wrapped or placed in a covered container to prevent other foods from picking up the odor. If mold appears on your cheese, simply cut it off. If a strange odor accompanies the mold, toss it.

Some cheeses can be frozen but the texture will be crumbly when thawed. Cheddar, edam, gouda, mozzarella, muenster, provolone and Swiss freeze best. Hoop cheese freezes exceptionally well with no change in texture.

People are most familiar with cheddar, Swiss, and monterey jack cheeses. Experiment with those less familiar to discover what you've been missing. A few suggestions are mentioned below:

FONDUE— combine Gruyere with Emmenthaler Swiss.

MEXICAN COOKING— Jack, Colby, Muenster, Hoop Cheese.

OMELETS— Havarti with dill, Swiss, Muenster, Cheddar, Parmesan, Jarlsberg.

ITALIAN— Bel Paese, Fontina, Parmesan, Romano, Ricotta, Mozzarella, Provolone.

SANDWICHES— Swiss, Muenster, Cheddar, Colby, Jack, Provolone, Havarti, Jarlsberg, Edam, Gouda.

APPETIZERS/DESSERTS—Bleu, Roquefort, Brie, Bel Paese, Fontina, Swiss, Gouda, Edam, Havarti, Camembert, Stilton, Gorgonzola, Colby.

WITH CRACKERS—Bel Paese, Bleu, Brie, Camembert, Cheddar, Colby, Edam, Gjetost, Gruyere, Havarti, Jack, Roquefort, Stilton, Swiss, Rondole.

WITH FRUIT—Brie, Camembert, Cheddar, Colby, Cottage Cheese, Edam, Havarti, Ricotta, Rondole, Bel Paese, Fontina.

Recipes

CHEESE FONDUE

The perfect party food for creating a relaxed atmosphere while stimulating conversation. Chunks of crusty French bread are a must!

1 lb. gruyere or emmenthaler cheese, grated (or 1/2 lb. of each)
1 clove garlic
1 1/2 cup dry white wine (or apple juice!)
1 TB. lemon juice
1 TB. arrowroot diluted in 2 TB. water
1/4 tsp. ground nutmeg
dash of black pepper

1. Slice garlic in half and rub inside of heavy saucepan.
2. Remove garlic and add wine and lemon juice.
3. Heat until air bubbles rise and cover the surface but do not boil.
4. Reduce heat to low and add cheese gradually.
5. When cheese is melted, add remaining ingredients.
6. Stir until thickened.
7. Transfer to a fondue pot, crock pot, or electric skillet.
8. Keep fondue on low heat while serving.

STOVETOP MACARONI AND CHEESE   *serves 4*

An easy recipe that requires no baking and no cheese sauce preparation is great for those days you want to eat NOW!

3 quarts water
1/4 teaspoon salt
2 cups whole wheat macaroni, dry
1/2 cup dried arame (a sea vegetable-opt.)
1 TB. safflower or corn oil
1 large onion, thinly sliced
1 cup grated cheddar, monterey jack, colby, or muenster
1 TB. tamari shoyu (naturally aged soy sauce)
parsley

1. Bring water to a boil and add salt.
2. Add macaroni and cook until done, about 8 minutes.
3. Drain and rinse.
4. If using arame, soak in water 15 minutes and drain.
5. Heat oil in a large skillet.
6. Add onion and arame and saute 10 minutes.
7. Stir in macaroni and heat thoroughly.
8. Add cheese and shoyu.
9. Cover and cook over low heat until cheese melts.
10. Serve and garnish with parsley.

Recipes

BASIC CHEESE SAUCE   *makes 1 1/2 cups*
Sauce up vegetables, whole grains, meats, fish, beans, or pasta for a treat.

2 TB. butter
2 TB. whole wheat pastry flour
1 1/2 cups milk
1/4 teaspoon white pepper
1 teaspoon grated onion
1 clove garlic, minced (opt.)
1/4 teaspoon dried mustard (opt.)
pinch of sea salt (opt.)
1/3-1/2 cup grated cheddar or Swiss cheese

1. Melt butter in a saucepan.
2. Add flour and cook over low heat 5 minutes, stirring constantly.
3. Slowly add the milk and, using a wire whisk, continue to stir until thickened.
4. Stir in pepper, onions, dried mustard, and salt.
5. Add grated cheese and cook over low heat until cheese melts.
6. Indulge.

TEXAS CHEESE BALL
Roasted pecans from Texas make this a special treat.

1 lb. cream cheese
1/4 lb. crumbled bleu cheese
1/4 lb. sharp cheddar cheese, grated
2 cloves garlic, minced
1 teaspoon chili powder
1/2 cup roasted pecans, finely chopped

1. Soften cream cheese.
2. Combine all ingredients except pecans in a food processor or mixer.
3. When thoroughly mixed, shape into a ball and roll in pecans.
4. Chill until firm and serve with crackers.

EGGS

Despite all of the negative publicity the egg gets because of its high cholesterol content, it still is a good food in *moderation*. Eggs are high in protein, iron, zinc, vitamins A, B$_2$, D, E, and K and, best of all, convenient. According to the U.S. Dietary Guidelines, egg consumption should be limited, especially for those with elevated serum cholesterol. A moderate amount is considered to be 4 per person per week. Individual conditions and needs will vary from this general guide. Since most of the cholesterol is in the egg yolk, try separating the egg yolks from the egg whites. When buying eggs, you have a choice among standard, yard or fertile eggs.

"Standard" eggs are non-fertile, mass produced eggs laid by hens confined 3-6 per small cage with little room for movement.

Yard eggs are produced from free range chickens who generally eat whatever they choose, from food scraps or grain based feeds without additives. Eggs resulting from the mating of a chicken and a rooster are considered **fertile eggs**. In flocks in which hens and roosters are kept together, 80-95% of the eggs will be fertile. Cooking the eggs shortly after they are laid prevents the natural hatching progression.

Caging the hens is the most efficient way to produce eggs. Hens raised uncaged in floor houses which allow at least 2 square feet per bird are more costly to maintain. More labor is needed in general and the eggs need to be hand-gathered. Although hens can lay eggs without a rooster, adding a rooster to a flock in order to produce fertile eggs increases feed costs considerably.

At least partially as a result of the hen's living conditions, mass produced eggs tend to have thin shells, pale yolks, and bland flavor. Because yard and fertile eggs are generally raised in better conditions which includes natural sunlight, they tend to have thick shells, bright yellow yolks, and a richer flavor.

Some people prefer to use fertile eggs since, similar to the potential for whole grain wheat to sprout, all the aspects necessary for the generation of life are present. Advocates for fertile eggs also claim that the good living conditions and better feed are transmitted into better nutrient levels in the egg. In response, opponents claim that the basic nutritional values are the same for mass produced eggs and fertile eggs.

Several factors influence the size and quality of an egg: the age, weight and breed of the hen, environmental temperature, quality of feed, as well as stress and overcrowding.

Young hens lay small eggs; older hens lay large-jumbo eggs. Double yolked eggs occur in fresh batches of young hens whose cycles are just getting regulated. Layers are bred to be tall and thin, while broilers are bred to be meaty and big. The color of the shell is no indication of nutritional value. The white leghorn chicken which dominates the egg industry lays white eggs. Brown eggs are laid by other, larger breeds of hens, such as the Rhode Island Reds. Brown eggs tend to cost more because of increased production costs. The larger hens eat more and take up more room in a cage or floor house.

As with beef and poultry bred for consumption, some layers may also be fed antibiotics, hormones, and other drugs to compensate for crowded living quarters that can adversely affect the condition and health of the birds. Even the deep yellow color of the yolk is more often an indication of the type of feed rather than evidence that the hen had access to fresh air and sunshine.

Egg grading standards are based only on size and appearance, not nutrititional quality or freshness. Eggs are sized according to the minimum weight per dozen. Most recipes are based upon medium or large eggs.

Grading for quality depends upon the interior quality of the egg and the condition and appearance of the shell. Quality grading separates the eggs into Grades AA, A, B, C, and inedibles.

The space between the egg white and the shell at the large end of the egg is called the "air cell." The air cell starts to form when the freshly laid, warm egg is cooled. The contents of the egg and the membrane surrounding it contract, causing them to separate from the outer membrane. In a very fresh egg, the air cell is about the size of a dime and approximately 1/8 inch deep. As the egg ages, carbon dioxide escapes through the shell and the white becomes clearer. The air cell also becomes larger.

GRADE AA eggs are the best in quality and freshness since their AA properties will keep up to 10 days under proper conditions. The height of the egg, as well as the firm centering of the yolk, give the egg a superior appearance. The clear, firm, thick egg white is best for poaching, frying, and cooking in the shell when the appearance of the egg is important. Its shell is clean and unbroken, while its air cell is 1/8 inch or less in depth.

GRADE A eggs are not satisfactory for poaching but still excellent for frying and cooking purposes. After 10 days, a Grade AA egg will become a Grade A egg. Most egg packers list their eggs Grade A to give themselves flexibility in the length of time they can sell their eggs, even though it may have been Grade AA at the time of packing. Grade A eggs will keep up to 30 days under proper conditions. The air cell in a Grade A egg is 3/16 inch or less in depth. Its shell is clean, unbroken, and practically normal. Its egg white is clear and may be reasonably firm.

GRADE B eggs can be used when the appearance of the egg doesn't matter, such as in scrambled eggs or blended, cooked foods. Its shell is unbroken, slightly abnormal, and ranges from clean to very slightly stained. Its air cell is 3/8 inch or less in depth and can be bubbly. The egg white is clear but may be slightly weak.

After purchase, eggs should be refrigerated in their carton since egg shells are porous and can pick up odors and flavors. Store eggs point side down (rounded side up) to prevent movement of the egg cell toward the yolk. This keeps eggs fresher and keeps the yolk more centered. Additionally, the rounded side is stonger and will resist breakage.

Even though eggs can be stored up to one month, use eggs as soon as possible for best flavor and nutrition.

Recipes

EGG SALAD - VARIATIONS ON A THEME *serves 3-4*
I can't remember the last time I actually used mayonnaise in egg salad. Experimentations have led me to some great combinations. The amount of vegetables you use will determine whether you call it egg salad or a salad with eggs. Go with your mood.

4 hard boiled eggs

Moisten with 1 or more:	**Season with:**
avocado	dill
prepared mustard	tamari shoyu
cottage cheese	salt
yogurt	chives
olive oil and vinegar	basil
bottled salad dressing	cilantro
	cayenne or black pepper

Vegetables:
Choose as many as desired
celery, finely chopped
scallions, thinly sliced
grated cabbage
radishes, thinly sliced
peas
pea pods
green pepper, chopped
red onion, minced
sprouts
cucumbers, quartered and thinly sliced
pickles
potatoes, cooked and cubed
tomatoes, sliced or use whole cherry tomatoes
broccoli, steamed

1. Combine eggs with choices from moisteners, vegetables, and seasonings.
2. If time, refrigerate 10 minutes or even overnight to let flavors blend.
3. Serve with bread, tortillas, pita bread, vegetables, or with crackers.

Recipes

EGG and OLIVE ENCHILADAS   *serves 6-8*
Obviously not diet fare, but try using some low-fat substitutions: Use only 1/2 of the yolks from the hard boiled eggs and add cheese that is lower in fat. If you have the courage, maybe you could use less black olives (??!?).

1 large onion, chopped
2 bell peppers, chopped
4 cloves garlic, chopped
2 TB. olive oil
24 oz. tomato sauce
3 bay leaves
1 TB. ground cumin
1/4 teaspoon ground cloves
1/4 teaspoon salt (opt.)
8 hard boiled eggs
1 cup black olives, chopped
1 cup green onions, chopped
1 lb. monterey jack cheese, grated
garlic powder, cayenne, chili powder, to taste
12 tortillas, corn or flour

1. Preheat oven to 350°.
2. Sauté onion, bell peppers, and garlic in olive oil.
3. Add tomato sauce and seasonings. Bring to a boil, reduce heat, and simmer, covered, for 30 minutes.
4. Combine eggs, olives, green onions, and 3 cups of grated cheese.
5. When sauce is ready, heat a tortilla in an ungreased skillet over medium-hot heat until soft (a few seconds on each side).
6. Dip the tortilla in the sauce.
7. Fill each tortilla with 1/2 cup filling and roll the tortilla around the filling.
8. When all the tortillas have been filled, place them close together, seam side down in a large baking dish.
9. Cover with the rest of the sauce and top with the remaining grated cheese.
10. Bake, covered, for 30 minutes.
11. Serve with a salad.

Recipes

SCRAMBLED SAGES   *serves 2-3*

Just when you thought you've done everything possible with an egg....try this one for fun!

1 TB. safflower oil
1 onion, minced
6 mushrooms, quartered
1/2 green pepper, chopped
4 eggs, beaten with 4 TB. water
1/8 teaspoon dried sage
1 teaspoon tamari shoyu (naturally aged soy sauce)

1. Heat oil in a skillet over medium heat.
2. Add onion and sauté 5 minutes.
3. Add mushrooms and sauté 2 more minutes.
4. Add green pepper and continue to sauté 3 more minutes.
5. Add egg-water mixture and seasonings.
6. Stir frequently, scraping the cooked eggs off the sides and bottom of the skillet.
7. Cook until desired consistency.
8. Serve with toast, tortillas, rice, noodles, or grain flake flat bread (see recipe under CEREALS).

6

MEAT, POULTRY, FISH & SEAFOOD

MEAT

Cattle allowed the normal maturation time and fed chemical-free feed produce a nutritionally superior meat that is leaner, more tender, and better tasting.

In contrast, some meat producers rely upon growth hormones, antibiotics, and other drugs in order to achieve the greatest weight gain with the least amount of feed in the shortest period of time. Rather than contributing to an increase in protein-rich muscle tissue, most often these agents lead only to an increase in fat.

Antibiotics, initially used to curtail the spread of infectious disease in penned animals, have also proved to be effective growth enhancers when used in subtherapeutic doses. However, increased use has led to the development of antibiotic-resistant bacteria, most notably, an antibiotic-resistant strain of salmonella. It is even more critical for meat from animals given antibiotics to be handled with utmost care and cooked thoroughly since the super-salmonella strains can make people extremely ill. The danger increases if a person has been taking antibiotics before consuming the meat. Much of the "good bacteria" that normally inhabits the intestine will be depleted, setting the stage for the super-salmonella to multiply and cause trouble.

Antibiotic residues in meat may also lead to a development of resistant germs in the intestinal tracts in humans, rendering the use of antibiotics for certain illnesses ineffective. After numerous cases had been investigated, in 1987 the Center for Disease Control reported that there is a conclusive link between food poisoning and meat from animals given antibiotic drugs in feed.

Other drugs besides antibiotics and hormones are administered to livestock. The Office of Technology Assessment of 1986 estimated that 60% of beef cattle raised for food are routinely fed medicated feed. Although there are withdrawal regulations for approved drugs before slaughter, abuses do occur. Furthermore, FDA scientists estimate that 90% of all animal drugs have not been FDA approved.

Current U.S.D.A. guidelines for "natural" meat only require that the meat must be "minimally processed" and free of artificial coloring, flavoring and preservatives. Processing, not necessarily residue-free production is emphasized, leaving the word "natural" open to abuse and confusion.

However, future labeling for "natural" meat will become more meaningful as the U.S.D.A. implements their Verified Production Control (VPC) regulations within the year. Labels specifying a "natural" product will be allowed only with a residue-free certification from the U.S.D.A.

Certification requires that there be an "ownership relationship" between the feeder and the packer of the cattle so that feeding records can be accessed on each individual animal during the last 100 days prior to slaughter. This ensures that if a chemical residue problem did exist, the severity could be accurately gauged and controls implemented to stop the sale of the meat.

As of December 1987, five beef producers/packers were participating in production control procedures as outlined by the proposed verified production control regulations. In addition to certifying their meat as containing no chemical residues, these ranchers certify that no antibiotics, hormones, or steroids were ever administered or added to feed at any time of the steer's life. If an animal does get sick and needs medication, it is tagged and sold to commercial beef markets. Although individual attention and chemical-free feed is more costly and takes more time to produce, it ensures a higher quality, better tasting natural beef.

Liver is a very nutritious food but if obtained from an animal administered chemicals, it can be potentially toxic. The liver functions as the primary detoxification organ, therefore, any chemical ingested by the animal will ultimately be deposited in the animal's liver. Use liver only from animals naturally raised in a clean environment to ensure minimal contamination.

Sodium nitrite is a common food additive used in lunch meats, sausages, bacon, hot dogs, smoked meats, and ham. It is used to maintain the pink or red colors in meats, to enhance flavor by inhibiting rancidity, and to protect against bacterial growth— specifically the bacteria which produces botulism. Nitrates occur naturally in some vegetables and are made in the human body. However, a potentially carcinogenic situation occurs when *under certain cooking conditions*, nitrites are converted to nitrosamines. Vitamin C helps prevent this conversion and is now added to some cured meat containing sodium nitrite. Alternatives to sodium nitrite include freezing or selling freshly made meat products.

Red meat's reputation and sales have slipped during the last decade in response to the emphasis on reduced fat intake. But now the beef industry suggests that 3 oz. be considered an average serving size of meat instead of mammoth 8-12 oz. steaks as the norm. Ranchers are crossbreeding leaner cattle with traditional higher fat breeds for beef lower in fat, calories, and cholesterol. Nutritionists are also advising people to trim the fat before cooking.

New USDA guidelines define terms such as "extra lean", "lean", and "leaner, light, lite, or lower fat".

U.S.D.A. GUIDELINES FOR LABELING FAT CONTENT OF MEAT

CATEGORY	FAT IN RAW FLESH
Extra lean	less than 5%
Lean	less than 10%
Leaner, light, lite, or lower fat	at least 25% less than most comparable products

---

Lean meats have little marbling. Top round, eye round, London broil, filet mignon, and sirloin tip are the leanest cuts. Brisket, rib roast, and short ribs contain the most fat. Lean meats are best marinated (without added oil) and cooked slowly with moist heat.

Certain cooking methods also cut fat intake: Bake, broil, or roast on a rack so the meat remains above the drippings. Pan broil rather than panfry. Remove the layer of fat from stews or soups after cooling.

FRESH MEAT STORAGE TIME FOR MAXIMUM QUALITY

MEAT	REFRIGERATOR (36-40° F.)	FREEZER (0° F. or lower)
beef	3-5 days	6-12 months
pork, veal, lamb	3-5 days	6-9 months
ground beef, veal, lamb	1-2 days	3-4 months
ground pork	1-2 days	1-3 months
pork sausage	2-3 days	1-2 months
heart, liver, kidneys, brains, sweetbreads	1-2 days	3-4 months
tongue	6-7 days	3-4 months
leftover cooked meat	4-5 days	3-4 months

HOW MUCH MEAT TO BUY PER PERSON

Boneless cuts   1/4-1/3 lb.
(ground meats, boned roasts and steaks, stew meats)

Meat with some bone   1/3-1/2 lb.
(rib roasts, unboned steaks, chops)

Bony cuts   3/4-1 lb.
(ribs, shanks, brisket)

Recipes

LAMB KABOBS   *serves 4*

Don't wait until Easter to serve lamb. Try this recipe at your next barbeque.

1 lb. lamb shoulder, cut in 2" cubes
2 TB. lemon juice
1/4 cup olive oil
1 teaspoon salt
1/8 teaspoon pepper

8 large mushrooms
1 zucchini, cut into 1" slices
1 onion, cut into wedges
1 green pepper, cut into 1" squares
8 cherry tomatoes
4 skewers

1. Combine ingredients for marinade in a medium size bowl.
2. Add lamb, cover, and marinate at least 3 hours.
3. Preheat broiler.
4. Alternate meat with vegetables on 4 skewers.
5. Place skewers 4" from the heat source and broil, turning frequently.
6. Baste with olive oil while cooking.
7. Cook about 15 minutes or until done.
8. Serve with rice.

BEEF STROGANOFF   *serves 4*

An easy, elegant dish that uses yogurt instead of sour cream to reduce the calories but not the flavor.

1 lb. sirloin steak, thinly sliced and cut into strips 2" long
3 TB. butter or safflower oil
1/2 lb. mushroooms, sliced
1 onion, thinly sliced
salt and pepper to taste
3 TB. whole wheat flour
1 cup beef broth
1/2 teaspoon dry mustard
1 cup yogurt

1. Heat 1 TB. of butter in a large skillet and sauté onion and mushrooms 5 minutes.
2. Remove the mushrooms and onion from the skillet and add remaining 2 TB. of butter.
3. Sauté steak until it browns and season with salt and pepper.
4. Remove steak from skillet and add to mushrooms and onion that were set aside.
5. Add the flour to the oil remaining in the pan and stir until the flour becomes bubbly.
6. Add the beef stock to the flour mixture and cook until thickened.
7. Add dry mustard and return cooked steak, mushrooms, and onion to the thickened stock. Adjust seasonings.
8. Reheat mixture over low heat.
9. When heated through, stir in yogurt.
10. Serve with noodles or rice.

Recipes

Just because you feel you cannot afford steaks, you need not avoid buying meat, especially the good quality naturally raised beef and lamb. Long term cooking on the stove, in the oven, or in a crockpot brings out incredible flavor and tenderness in the less expensive cuts.

CHUNKY CURRIED BEEF "STEW"   *serves 4*

Seasoning with curry powder and using baked potatoes as a base for the topping instead of cooked in the stew transforms a traditional beef stew into an exciting new dish.

4 large baking potatoes
1 TB. safflower oil
1 1/4 lb. beef stew meat or chuck roast cut in 1/2" cubes
1 large onion cut in 1/2" slices
3 cloves garlic, minced
2 teaspoons curry powder
4 cups water
4 ribs celery, diced
2 rutabagas cut in 1" chunks or 4 carrots cut in 1" diagonals
1 cup peas, fresh or frozen
pinch of salt
2 TB. arrowroot
1/4 cup cold water

1. Preheat oven to 400° F.
2. Place potatoes in oven to bake for 1 hour or until done.
3. Heat oil in dutch oven.
4. Add meat and brown on all sides over medium heat.
5. Add onion and sauté until golden brown.
6. Add garlic and curry powder and sauté 1 more minute.
7. Add water, bring to a boil, cover and simmer 1 hour.
8. Combine celery and rutabagas with the stew and continue to simmer for 30 minutes.
9. Add peas and salt and simmer an additional 10 minutes.
10. Dilute arrowroot in cold water and add to stew.
11. Bring to a boil and stir constantly until thickened.
12. Serve over baked potatoes.

Recipes

CROCKPOT ROAST   *serves 6*

Crockpots enable you to cook meats slowly without them drying out or losing flavor. Experiment with herbs and spices to create new flavors, but remember crockpots use only half the amount of seasoning as normally used.

1 large onion, cut into quarters
3-4 lb. brisket, chuck roast, or arm roast
1/2 lb. mushrooms, left whole
3 cloves garlic, minced
pinch of salt
1/2 teaspoon parsley
1/4 teaspoon each: dillweed, basil, oregano
1/2 cup water

1. Put onion on bottom of crockpot.
2. Add meat and cover with mushrooms, garlic, and salt.
3. Mix dried herbs together and sprinkle over meat and vegetables.
4. Add 1/2 cup water.
5. Cover and cook on LOW for 10-12 hours or on HIGH for 4-5 hours.
6. When done, remove meat, cut, and serve with the cooked vegetables.

AMERICAN GOULASH   *serves 3-4*

Sometimes recipes are so simple, we forget about them. Serve this over baked potatoes, rice, noodles, or spaghetti squash.

1 lb. ground beef or chili meat
1 large onion, thinly sliced
4 cloves garlic, minced
2 medium zucchini, cubed
1 cup tomato sauce
1 TB. prepared mustard
1/2 cup water

1. Brown meat in a large skillet.
2. Remove meat and set aside.
3. Drain excess fat from the skillet, retaining approximately 1 teaspoon.
4. Sauté onion and garlic for 5 minutes.
5. Add zucchini and sauté another 2 minutes.
6. Add tomato sauce, mustard, water, and cooked meat.
7. Mix thoroughly, cover, and cook on low heat for 20 minutes.
8. Serve.

POULTRY

Like beef and lamb, chickens and turkeys can also be force-fed and confined. Poultry producers prefer crowded, enclosed conditions since it prevents the flocks from getting exercise and thus promotes bigger, fatter poultry. Unfortunately, these same crowded conditions create a breeding ground for disease. To prevent any major outbreaks which could wipe out the entire flock, chicken and turkeys are routinely fed antibiotics. The transmission of the antibiotics themselves is not the problem so much as the drug resistant, antibiotic altered bacteria which can breed in meat and possibly make people ill. The constant exposure to antibiotics can also cause one to become immune to them when antibiotics might be a necessity.

Commercial chickens are removed from antibiotics 7 days before slaughter. Butchers claim that the freshest commercial chickens are shipped to them placed in ice instead of pre-wrapped.

Look for **naturally raised, free range poultry** raised without antibiotics. Because they are allowed to exercise, the size of a natural chicken is often much smaller than a commercial variety. Poultry allowed to live in good conditions and to mature naturally are also much lower in fat and more delicious. Poultry dressed by hand is less susceptible to processing-induced salmonella contamination. (See SALMONELLA at end of chapter.) Although poultry producers such as Shelton and Pine Ridge were the pioneers in offering an alternative to the commercially raised variety, local naturally raised poultry may also be available. The higher prices sometimes reflected with natural poultry are due to increased production costs.

No longer are turkeys reserved for Thanksgiving and Christmas; now people include them in meals throughout the entire year. Insist upon naturally raised turkeys that are free of added chemicals or basting solutions.

GROUND TURKEY & CHICKEN

Don't be surprised if you start to find cows in the unemployment line. With all the excitement about ground poultry, many of our beefy friends may soon be looking for a job.

Ground turkey and chicken is lower in fat and calories than ground beef. Up to now there are no set standards for ground poultry that companies must meet. It can include all dark meat, a blend of dark and white meat, and the addition of skin. In general, raw ground poultry contains 15% or less fat as compared with 26.5% fat in regular ground beef, 20.7% in lean ground beef, and 17% in extra lean ground beef. Insist on all dark meat from skinless turkey or chicken thighs. Ground skinless turkey contains approximately 5% fat while ground, skinless chicken contains approximately 6% fat. If possible, buy ground poultry from naturally raised flocks.

Any discussion concerning heart disease and cholesterol should concern not only the amount of cholesterol but the amount of saturated fat present in the food. Even though the cholesterol content of ground poultry equals the amount found in ground beef, there is significantly less saturated fat in poultry than in beef. Saturated fat contributes about twice as much cholesterol to the bloodstream as does cholesterol in foods.

Recipes such as lasagna, spaghetti, chili, and casseroles that traditionally use ground beef can easily be substituted with ground poultry with little difference in flavor, appearance, or preparation. Although ground turkey can be used with no modifications necessary, recipes using ground chicken may benefit from a few minor alterations. The milder flavored ground chicken may need somewhat more seasoning than ground beef or ground turkey. Ground turkey is almost the same color as ground beef while the lighter color of ground chicken can be masked with a sauce or seasoning mix. Both ground turkey and chicken can also be made into patties or meat loaves. However, since they are so low in fat, pans and skillets need to be greased with extra oil or butter to prevent sticking.

Most sources of boneless, skinless turkey and chicken thighs arrive at the meat market frozen before being ground. If the frozen poultry is defrosted under refrigerated conditions before grinding, purchased ground poultry or dishes made with it can be safely refrozen, if desired.

Sausages and hot dogs are also made from turkey or chicken. These contain 30% less fat than regular beef hot dogs and can contain no nitrates, preservatives, cheap binders and fillers, or flavor enhancers such as MSG or sugar. What's next? Turkey lunch meats!

Salmonella bacteria in foods, including poultry, is not a new phenomenon. But increased consumer awareness can curtail any problems that could occur.

Salmonella, a bacteria that can produce food infections, is able to grow in a number of foods, including dairy products, meats, and meat products, poultry, eggs, and fish, if not handled properly both in processing plants and at home. Large poultry producers use machinery to "dress" their poultry. The potential for salmonella is reduced when the process is done by hand since machinery can puncture the intestines and spread contamination. Ask the counter clerks about the method used for the poultry being sold. The use of proper cooking, cleanliness, and storage can control the spread of contamination. Just follow these simple rules:

Keep foods refrigerated. Be sure the interim time from purchase to home refrigeration is minimal and consider transporting them in an ice chest during the hot weather.

Use meat, poultry, and fish within two days of purchase.

Wash hands before preparing and eating food.

Thoroughly wash your hands, kitchen counter tops, utensils, dishes, and cutting boards with soap and hot water after contact with raw proteins.

Do not allow foods to stand at room temperature after cooking for more than two hours. Bacteria thrive at temperatures between 45°-115°, so keep foods either below 40° or above 140°.

HOW MUCH POULTRY TO BUY PER PERSON

duck	1 lb.
goose	1 lb.
chicken	1/4-1/2 bird
if boneless	1/3-1/2 lb.
capon	1/2 lb.
roaster	1/2 lb.
stewing hen	1/2 lb.
cornish hen	1 bird
turkey/fryer-roaster	3/4-1 lb.
/hen or tom	1/2-3/4 lb.
ground poultry	1/4-1/3 lb.

HOW TO COOK DIFFERENT TYPES OF POULTRY

DUCK

how to cook: less than 3 lb.   - fry or broil
                 3-6 lb.   - roast or braise

special cooking instructions:
- remove excess fat from body cavity
- remove wing tips and first joint
- prick skin all over
- do not rub skin with oil
- place on a rack in a roasting pan
- roast at 400° for 15 minutes
- reduce heat to 325°, pour off fat
- stuff and roast until done

GOOSE

how to cook: 4-12 lb.   - roast
                 more than 14 lb.   - braise

special cooking instructions:
- remove excess fat from body cavity
- prick legs and wings
- spoon off fat several times

- place on a rack in a roasting pan
- roast at 450° for 30 minutes, turning every 10 minutes
- reduce heat to 325°, remove goose from rack, pour out fat
- stuff and place goose directly in roasting pan
- continue to roast until done

CHICKEN
broiler, fryer - young, tender, all-purpose bird
how to cook: 1 1/2-4 lb. - broil, fry, braise, roast, steam

capon - large amount of tender and flavorful white meat
how to cook: 4-7 lb.   - roast

roaster-large, plump young bird
how to cook: 3-5 lb.   - roast

stewing hen - large, mature bird, more fat, less meat
use for stocks, stews, soups, ground chicken
how to cook: 3- 6 1/2 lb.   - braise or stew

cornish hen - small, tender, meaty
crossbreed of Plymouth Rock chicken & Cornish gamecock
how to cook: 1-2 lb.   - roast, braise, broil, or fry

TURKEY
how to cook: 4-9 lb.   - broil, roast, oven-fry
                    10-19 lb.   - roast
                    more than 20 lb.   - roast or braise

POULTRY COOKING BASICS

- **steaming**

   Place young, tender poultry on a rack or steaming basket above 1" of steaming water. Cover the pot and steam parts for 45 minutes and whole birds for 1 1/2 hours. Add extra boiling water if necessary.

- **basic roasting**

   Place whole poultry breast side up or halves or parts skin-side up in a shallow pan or roasting pan. Prick the skin of a duck or goose with a fork to let fatty juices run out; on other poultry brush skin with a light coating of oil. Rub the body cavity with salt and herbs such as sage and thyme or basil. Stuff or place quartered onion and celery in cavity. Cover loosely with foil, removing foil 20 minutes before poultry is done to brown the meat. Roast at 325-350° for approx. 40 minutes per pound for poultry less than 8 lbs. and 20 minutes per pound for larger poultry.

- **broiling**

  Cut poultry into halves, quarters, or pieces, leaving the skin on to prevent excessive drying. Prick the skin on ducklings and parboil to allow fatty juices to escape and reduce the chance of flaring while broiling; brush other poultry with oil or butter. Place them skin-side down on a lightly oiled broiler rack several inches from the heat to permit slow cooking. During broiling, turn the pieces 2 or 3 times, brushing them with fat or barbeque sauce. Allow 20-30 minutes to broil chicken and 1-1 1/4 hours for turkey and duckling.

- **braising**

  Braise whole or cut-up poultry in a heavy pan in a 325° oven or over medium heat on the stove. Place the bird in the pan and cover with a tight-fitting lid to allow it to steam in the juices released during cooking. To brown: brown pieces in a small amount of oil before cooking on top of the stove or uncover the last 30 minutes if braising in the oven. For added flavor, add dried prunes or apricots and 1/2 cup water during cooking.

- **stewing or simmering**

  Place poultry in enough water to cover, season with onions, celery, and favorite herbs, cover, and bring water to a boil. Reduce the heat and simmer 1 1/2-3 hours until tender.

POULTRY STORAGE TIME FOR MAXIMUM QUALITY

TYPE	REFRIGERATOR	FREEZER
raw chicken, whole	1-2 days	12 months
cut up	1-2 days	9 months
livers	1-2 days	3 months
raw duck & goose, whole	1-2 days	6 months
raw turkey, whole	1-2 days	12 months
cut up	1-2 days	6 months
cooked poultry	2-4 days	4-6 months
cooked stuffing, broth, or gravy	1-2 days	stuffing may not freeze fast enough to prevent bacteria from multiplying rapidly

Recipes

ROAST CHICKEN OR TURKEY

Believe it or not, one of the easiest ways to prepare poultry is roasting. Although a stuffing is delicious, a chicken or turkey can be roasted with an onion and a few ribs of celery instead.

whole chicken or turkey
corn or safflower oil
pinch of salt
1 teaspoon sage
1/2 teaspoon thyme
1 onion, quartered
2 ribs celery, quartered

SUPPLIES:

heavy duty aluminum foil
darning needle, sterilized
unwaxed dental floss

1. Preheat oven to 325°.
2. Remove the neck and giblets from the neck or body cavity area.
3. Wash the chicken both inside and out. Dry with paper towel.
4. Remove excess fat.
5. Brush outside with a light coating of oil.
6. Rub the body cavity with salt, sage, and thyme. (Double the sage and thyme if using a turkey over 12 lbs.)
7. Place onion and celery inside the cavity.
8. Thread a darning needle with unwaxed dental floss and sew the edges of the cavity together.
9. Place it in a shallow roasting pan or baking dish, breast side up.
10. Using heavy duty aluminum foil, tear off a piece 10 inches longer than the chicken to make a cooking tent.
11. Crease foil crosswise down the center and place over chicken, crimping loosely onto the sides of the pan to secure it.
12. Place chicken in the oven.
13. NO BASTING IS NECESSARY!
14. To brown the chicken, remove the tent 20 minutes before the roasting is finished.
15. Allow 40 minutes roasting time per lb. for chicken and 20 minutes per lb. for turkey.
16. When chicken is done, remove from oven and allow 20 minutes before carving to retain juices and to make carving easier.

Recipes

MOM'S POULTRY GRAVY   *makes 2 cups*

I know everyone says that no one can cook as well as his/her own mother, but really, my mother *does* take the prize, especially for her incredible gravy. Her secret is using salted potato stock as the base.

neck and giblets from chicken or turkey
water
1/4 cup meat drippings
4 TB. whole wheat, barley, or brown rice flour
1/2 cup water
1 small potato
water or vegetable stock
salt to taste

1. Wash neck and giblets thoroughly. Set liver aside.
2. Cover neck and giblets with water and bring to a boil.
3. Cover pan with lid and simmer 1 1/2 hours. Add liver during the last 20 minutes.
4. Remove neck, giblets, and liver for use in preparing dressing or other dishes.
5. Time permitting, put drippings from roasting the meat into the refrigerator or freezer to remove excess fat. The fat will float to the top of the jar or container and harden. Simply remove the layer and proceed with making the gravy. (**NOTE:** Congealing the fat requires 30 minutes in the freezer. However, it is not necessary to wait until the turkey is completely done roasting to remove meat drippings. To save time, extract some of the drippings when the aluminum foil tent is removed.)
6. Cut a small potato into small pieces and bring to a boil with 2 cups water and 1/4 teaspoon salt. Reduce heat, cover, and simmer 20 minutes. Remove potato and use the broth.
7. In a saucepan, combine giblet cooking water and enough potato stock to make 2 cups total.
8. Add 1/4 cups of fat free drippings to the liquid and salt to taste. Bring to a boil.
9. Place 4 TB. of flour and 1/2 cup water in a jar. Shake to thoroughly mix the flour and water.
10. Turn off heat from boiling broth and add the flour and water thickening, stirring constantly to prevent gravy from becoming lumpy.
11. Bring to a boil again, stirring constantly until desired thickness is obtained.
12. Taste, correct seasonings, if needed, and serve.

Recipes

CHICKEN TERIYAKI   *serves 3-4*
Marinating for a long time transforms a "chicken again?" dish into a tender, succulent "why don't you make this more often?" dish.

2 1/2 - 3 lb. chicken (skin may be removed to reduce fat if desired)
1/4 cup tamari shoyu
1 inch ginger root, grated
1 TB. honey or rice syrup
2 TB. vinegar or lemon juice
1/3 cup water
2 cloves garlic, minced
2 teaspoons arrowroot
2 TB. cold water

1. Wash chicken and cut into serving pieces.
2. Combine shoyu, ginger, rice syrup, vinegar, water, and garlic.
3. Place chicken in a mixing bowl and cover with sauce.
4. Cover bowl and refrigerate overnight or at least 6 hours.
5. Preheat oven to 325°.
6. Remove chicken from bowl and place in a baking dish, skin side up.
7. Reserve marinade.
8. Bake uncovered for 1 1/2 hours. Baste with 1/4 of the marinade every 20 minutes until marinade is used.
9. To thicken marinade for a gravy, dissolve arrowroot in cold water.
10. Pour hot marinade into saucepan and add diluted arrowroot.
11. Bring to a boil, reduce heat, and stir constantly until thickened.
12. Place chicken on serving platter and pour thickened marinade into a gravy boat.

Experiment with the following recipes using ground poultry and then use it as a low fat alternative in your ground beef family favorites. They'll never know the difference unless you tell them!

BASIC TURKEY SAUSAGE   *makes 1 lb.*
Fresh sausage is extremely easy to make. Try the suggested variations or experiment to devise that special secret recipe.

1 lb. ground turkey
1/2 tsp. pepper
1/2 tsp. salt (opt.)
1 tsp. sage

1. Combine all ingredients and mix well.
2. Refrigerate for a few hours or overnight to let the flavors mingle and develop.
3. Shape into 8 patties.
4. Lightly oil a skillet and cook over medium heat until done.
Variations: Replace sage with Italian seasoning or any other favorite combination. Add 1/4 tsp. cayenne pepper to give it some zip! How about some garlic? Form patties, wrap individually without precooking, and freeze until needed. Shape into link shapes, wrap each in foil, and poach in water for 15 minutes. Refrigerate or freeze for "brown-and-serve" sausage links.

Recipes

LINDA MARLENA'S TEXAS TURKEY CHILI   *makes 10 cups*

I'm always impressed by the creative recipes that a friend, Linda Marlena, is able to devise. In this recipe, she uses ground turkey to transform an old favorite into an entrée that is much lower in fat but just as tasty.

2 lbs. ground turkey
2 cups dry pinto or kidney beans
2 TB. oil
1 1/2 cups onion, finely chopped
1 1/2 teaspoons garlic, finely chopped
2 large green peppers, diced
1 teaspoon ground cumin
4 teaspoons chili powder
pinch cayenne pepper
1 teaspoon oregano
4 cups chopped tomatoes, fresh or canned
2 cups water
1 bay leaf
1/4 cup red wine (opt.)
salt to taste
grated cheddar cheese for garnish

1. Cover beans with water and soak overnight. Drain.
2. Brown the ground turkey. Drain off excess fat.
3. Heat oil in a large saucepan or dutch oven. Add onion, garlic, green pepper, cumin, chili powder, cayenne pepper, and oregano.
4. Sauté, stirring occasionally, for 5 minutes.
5. Add browned meat, tomatoes, water, bay leaf, red wine, salt, and drained beans.
6. Bring to a boil, reduce heat, and simmer for 1 1/2- 2 hours, until beans are tender.
7. Taste for seasoning and garnish with grated cheese.

FISH AND SEAFOOD

Fish...delicious, easy to prepare, and quick...certainly the perfect food for busy lifestyles!

Its nutritional profile is equally impressive. Fish is high in protein and B vitamins, and, in saltwater varieties, a good source of iodine.

The sodium level of both freshwater and salt water fish is only slightly higher than meat.

Depending upon the type of fish and preparation method, fish is also low in calories and fat. However, recently, the benefits of fish high in fat have been making the headlines. Not only are they good sources of vitamin A, research has revealed that the presence of high amounts of Omega-3 fatty acids in fatty fish appear to lessen the chances of blood platelet cells sticking together, thus possibly lowering the incidence of heart attacks.

The flavor of quality, really **fresh fish** is hard to beat. Fish such as catfish, rainbow trout, and baby coho salmon are raised on "farms", however, the majority of fish are caught from large boats which go out from 1-7 days. Nets are thrown behind the boat and dragged for fish. After a load is caught, the fish are packed in large pens that are filled with alternating layers of ice and fish. Upon reaching shore, the fish are purchased, unloaded, evaluated as poor, fair, or good, and then priced. At the processing plant, the fish are iced down, filleted, candled for parasites, packed in 10-25# tins which conduct cold well, and flown or trucked encased in ice or dry ice. Special handling, limited availability, and air freight contribute to the higher costs of quality, fresh fish. The superior flavor difference is remarkable.

HOW TO BUY

Because of the extensive variety, sometimes it seems difficult to make a choice of what to buy. The best rule of thumb is to ask the fish department counter clerks what they would recommend as freshest and best tasting depending upon the type of dinner and cooking method you have in mind.

Fresh fish are moist, shiny, and translucent, free of any "fishy" odor. The flesh is firm & elastic when pressed with the fingers. After purchasing, refrigerate immediately or transport in an insulated ice chest if traveling time home is delayed or quite lengthy. Fish is one of the most perishable foods for two reasons: the enzymes that cause spoiling are continually active and the natural oils in fish can go rancid even at low temperatures. For best results, use fish within 24 hours or freeze.

The **fat content** varies from less than 1% to as high as 25% in some fish. Lean fish are good with sauces and preparations that retain or add moisture. Fatty fish are best baked, broiled, or grilled since they require little butter or oil to keep moist. In general, the more white a fish is in color, the more lean and mild in flavor.

Fish also vary in **thickness and density**. Flounder, including sole, is very thin and delicate, requiring only quick, brief cooking. Medium thick and firm fish include mahi-mahi, salmon, cod, lake trout, orange roughy, and tuna. Very thick, dense fish such as swordfish, shark, grouper, and halibut have a "meaty" texture. Both medium thick and very thick and dense fish are best poached, baked, broiled, or grilled.

So what about **frozen fish**? Fish that is frozen properly can be equal in quality to fresh seafood. Some fishing boats that are out for as long as 14 days process and freeze the fish immediately on board rather than waiting to have them processed and frozen on shore. New Zealand orange roughy is a prime example. Freshly frozen fish retains most of the fresh flavor. Old fish that is frozen has already deteriorated in flavor and often has a tough and rubbery texture. If buying packaged frozen fish, buy solidly frozen, tightly wrapped packages free of discoloration and excessive ice buildup. Moisture from the surface of the fish transfers to air pockets that result from loosely wrapped packages. This moisture forms into ice crystals that are deposited on the side of the package. Once thawed, fish from this type of situation will be extremely dry and tough.

When **freezing fish at home**, freeze the fish in its original wrapper made from specially coated paper designed to retain moisture. Lean steaks and fillets can be frozen up to 6 months. The optimum freezer storage life of fatty steaks and fillets is only up to 3 months since its fat can turn rancid if held longer. Frozen shrimp can be stored up to 12 months.

When **thawing frozen fish**, thaw in the refrigerator, *NOT AT ROOM TEMPERATURE*, allowing about 24 hours for a 1 lb. package. If a quick thaw is needed, place the fish in a "zipper-lock" plastic bag and place in a pan of cold water in the refrigerator. To retain more juices and moisture, do not thaw frozen fish completely. Use the semi-thawed fish immediately or within 24 hours after thawing.

Since water pollution is so prevalent, the question of fish and seafood contamination is asked frequently. Lean fish, deep sea water fish, and freshwater fish raised on fish "farms" are least affected.

COOKING FISH

Fish has little connective tissue so it is cooked to develop its flavor, not to tenderize as occurs with meat. Cook briefly at moderate temperatures to retain moistness. Overcooked fish falls apart into pieces and develops a tough texture, tasteless flavor, and fishy odor. A general time guide calls for 10 minutes at 350-400° when fish is 1 inch at its thickest point. Add or subtract 2 minutes for each 1/4 inch above or below 1 inch. When done, fish flakes when pierced with a fork in its thickest part while the original translucent appearance of fish becomes opaque.

Grilling, whether on charcoal, gas, or electric grills is always a treat. The fish develops a unique flavor and aroma as it is exposed to both heat and smoke. Oilier fish such as salmon, yellowfin tuna, lake trout, halibut, shark, and swordfish work best since they are somewhat self-basting and more firm.

A few basic tips will prevent overcooking, undercooking, and fish sticking to the grill:

•Use a fire that is moderately hot— enough to sear the surface of the flesh but not so hot that the outside is charred before the fish is cooked all the way through.

•Preheat the grill and keep the grill surface clean and well oiled.

•Place fish on grill perpendicular to the grill bars to minimize contact of the fish with the grill.

•Brush fish with melted butter, oil, or oily sauce to prevent fish from sticking to the grill. Baste frequently with a pastry brush while cooking to seal in the natural juices.

•Test with a small bamboo or metal skewer in the thickest part of the fish and feel the resistance of the flesh. Remove from the grill just before it flakes easily.

Certain types of cuts grill better than others. Steaks, the thick, crosscut sections of a large fish, work especially well. Marinate in lemon or lime juice 20-30 minutes before cooking to enhance flavor and firm the fish. When using fish that is not big or firm enough to be made into steaks, fillets can be used, however, they must have the skin attached to prevent falling apart while grilling. Small, whole, thick skinned, scaled and gutted fish can also be used. If weighing between 2-3 lbs, they should be scored diagonally across the thickest portion to permit uniform heat penetration. Whole, scaled and gutted fish over 3 lbs. require a grill cover and slow cooking over a low fire. Do not score as with smaller whole fish since the longer cooking time would result in a significant loss of natural juices.

Grilled fish is often marinated before cooking. **Marinades,** usually oil and acid combinations, can enhance mild flavored fish and mellow strong flavored fish while tenderizing. They can be as simple as a combination of lemon or lime juice with a small amount of oil or as complex as a recipe with 15 ingredients. Generally the more simple is your best bet not only time-wise, but flavor-wise as a simple marinade will allow the fish and not the marinade to be the main attraction. Mayonnaise, wine, mirin (rice wine), tomato sauce, vinegar, tamari shoyu soy sauce, prepared salad dressings, fresh herbs, or dried herbs can all be delicious ingredients in a good marinade. Thick, firm fish can be marinated as little as 30 minutes up to 8 hours. Thin and delicate fish should merely be brushed with the marinade before cooking since the acidity of the marinades will "cook" the fish even before it is cooked as with ceviche made with thicker textured fish.

Grilling can also be done in foil although, technically, this is a steaming process. Grilling in foil retains the natural juices with only a minimal amount of oil and, best of all, there is no grill to clean!

FISH: COMMON AND NOT SO COMMON

Most people are quite familiar with cod and ocean perch. Even though both are delicious, it is exciting to try the many flavors and textures available in other fish. Refer to the list below for a description of all those unusual fish you always wondered about and had seen other customers buy.

Baby coho salmon are small "farm raised" salmon that are somewhat milder in flavor than regular salmon steaks and fillets. They are a cross-breed between salmon and trout. Panfry, oven fry, bake, poach, broil, or steam.

Bluefish is a delicious, oily fish that is ideally broiled. The best recipes use neutralizing acids in tomatoes or onions and/or citrus fruits such as lemon or lime. Be sparing when using additional oil with bluefish. Also, because it one of the high oil, EPA-rich fish, buy only very fresh bluefish as it can go rancid quickly and become very strong in flavor.

Bluefish may also be oven fried or baked but do not poach or make into chowders since it will fall apart into fine pieces with these methods.

Catfish are most known for being dredged in cornmeal and then fried. Farm-raised catfish has a delicate flavor and flaky, white flesh. Broil or bake.

Hake is a member of the cod family with a coarser texture and less bland flavor than other cods. Although you can use your favorite cod recipes with hake, it is generally cooked in or served with a sauce based on tomato and onion.

Halibut is a type of flounder. Small halibut are thin and delicate, however, the more popular thick steaks from large halibut have a firm texture with white, delicate meat.

Mahi-mahi is a white meat, large flaked, moist, firm fish. More known for its place in Hawaiian cuisine, it is fast becoming a popular choice because of its sweet and delicate flavor. Mahi-mahi is a type of dolphin, not to be confused, however, with the mammal called "dolphin" which is a member of the porpoise family. Mahi-mahi is very versatile. Prepare with any cooking method.

Monkfish, known as the poor man's lobster, can be baked, broiled, or poached. Only the lean white meat of the tail is sold from this fish.

Orange roughy, a deep sea fish from New Zealand, is another versatile fish adapting to any cooking method. Its popularity stems from its very mild "is this really a fish?" flavor and boneless, all white meat. Orange roughy is quick-frozen right on the boat and shipped frozen to retail stores.

Salmon, according to the experience of many people, means canned salmon. Unfortunately, these people are missing out on one of the real pleasures in life: fresh salmon. Available in both steaks and fillets, fresh salmon is usually poached, broiled, or grilled. Known as the "filet mignon of the West Coast".

Scallops have a buttery texture and delicate flavor that demands very little cooking to be retained. **Bay scallops** grow in shallow water, are light tan in color, and measure about 1/2" in diameter. They are perfect for sauces and salads. **Sea scallops** are dredged up from deep waters, are creamy white in color, measure 2" in diameter and, according to many, better flavored. Use in main dish recipes to take advantage of their size.

Shark consumption in the U.S. has never been high in the past, perhaps because of movies such as "Jaws I and II". However, for those who have tried it, the blacktipped and mako varieties are prized for their firm texture, white meat, and delicious, mild flavor. Since shark are so similar in flavor and texture they can substitute for the more expensive swordfish.

Shrimp, although hardly a unique item, has been subject to common inquiries such as how much to buy per person and the differences among the sizes. In general, gauge on buying 1/4 lb. per person. **Jumbo shrimp** are very large shrimp ranging from 10-15 per lb. **Medium shrimp** range from 25-35 per lb. **Small shrimp** range from 36-50 or more. Unless stated otherwise, most shrimp displayed in fish cases is thawed from frozen fish.

Sole. Despite the names, the more popular types of sole, Dover sole and lemon sole, are in reality, flounders. Authentic sole is obtained only as an import from England or France at import prices. Sole's delicate texture and flavor is perfect for light meals.

Swordfish is in its prime during the summer and fall, just in time for barbeques. Its distinctly flavored meat is very firm. Marinate in herbs and olive oil and then grill or oven broil for an incredible meal. Known as the "filet mignon of the East Coast".

Whitefish, a popular fish in the Great Lakes region, is a large flaked, delicately flavored fish related to salmon and trout.

HOW MUCH FISH TO BUY PER PERSON
AND APPROPRIATE COOKING METHODS

TYPE	BUY PER PERSON	COOKING METHOD
whole fish (as it comes from the water)	3/4-1 lb	steam, poach, bake, (may be stuffed)
whole dressed (scaled & gutted, fins removed)	3/4-1 lb.	steam, poach, bake, (may be stuffed)
drawn (gutted, whole fish)	3/4-1 lb.	steam, poach, bake, (may be stuffed)
pan-dressed (small, gutted fish; heads, tail, & fins removed)	1/2-3/4 lb.	pan-fry or ovenfry, bake (may be stuffed)
steaks (crosscut sections of a large fish)	1/3-1/2 lb.	bake, broil, steam, poach, grill
fillets (boned, meaty sides of fish)	1/4-1/3 lb.	panfry, ovenfry, bake, poach, broil, steam
butterfly (2 fillets connected by a piece of skin)	1/4-1/3 lb.	panfry, ovenfry, bake, poach, broil, steam

Recipes

BASIC BAKED FISH   *serves 2*

Think you can't cook fish very well? Of course, you can! In fact, the hardest part is turning on the oven!

3/4 lb. fish fillet
safflower oil
1 teaspoon herbs and spices (garlic, dill, fish seasoning herbs, etc.)
salt or tamari shoyu

1. Preheat oven to 350°.
2. Rinse fillets under water and pat dry.
3. Place in oiled 8 X 8" baking dish.
4. Sprinkle with desired seasonings and salt or tamari shoyu.
5. Place in oven, uncovered, and bake 20-30 minutes depending upon variety and thickness of fish. Fish is done when it flakes easily when tested with a fork.

OVEN FRIED FISH   *serves 2*

Enjoy "fried fish" with much less oil. Potato flakes serve as an interesting breading alternative.

3/4 lb. firm fish fillet
pinch of sea salt
1 teaspoon garlic powder
1/2 cup mashed potato flakes, corn meal, or fine bread crumbs
2 TB. safflower oil

1. Preheat oven to 500°.
2. Rinse fish under cold water.
3. Mix together sea salt, garlic powder, and flakes or crumbs.
4. Dip fish into breading mixture, coating well.
5. Place fish in 8 X 8" baking dish.
6. Drizzle oil over fish.
7. Put in preheated oven on middle rack for 10-12 minutes.
8. Serve with noodles, whole grain, or potatoes.

Recipes

QUICK FISH CHOWDER   *serves 3-4*
A creamy, warming soup that hits the spot on cool days. Dairy-free and ready in less than 30 minutes!

1 TB. safflower or corn oil
1 large onion, chopped
5 medium sized potatoes, large cubes
4 cups water
1/2 teaspoon salt
1 bay leaf
3 ribs celery
1/2 pkg. frozen peas or 1 cup fresh peas
1/2 lb. firm fish (cod, snapper, orange roughy), cut in bite sized chunks
black pepper to taste

1. Heat oil in soup pot.
2. Add onion and saute until translucent.
3. Add potatoes, water, salt, bay leaf, and celery and bring to a boil.
4. Reduce heat to medium low and simmer 15 minutes.
5. For a creamy texture, blend some of the cooked potatoes and soup liquid in a blender and return to soup pot.
6. Add peas and fish and continue to simmer 10 more minutes.
7. Season with black pepper and serve.

GRILLED FISH FILLET IN FOIL   *serves 3-4*
What a treat! The grill keeps clean and the fish keeps moist by "cooking" the fish in foil!

1 lb. orange roughy
1 lemon, sliced
4 green onions, thinly sliced
1 teaspoon olive oil
1 teaspoon curry powder
2 garlic cloves, minced

1. Place the fish fillets in a square of heavy-duty aluminum foil.
2. Arrange the lemon and green onions over the fish, drizzle with the olive oil, and sprinkle with the seasonings.
3. Fold up the edges of the foil and seal to make an airtight package.
4. Place over hot coals and grill for 15-20 minutes or bake in 375° oven for 12-18 minutes.
5. Serve immediately.

Recipes

MARINATED FISH WITH UDON AND VEGETABLES *serves 2-3*
A complete dinner—elegant but easy.

3/4 lb. fish fillet (orange roughy, cod, red snapper)
1 TB. tamari shoyu
1 teaspoon fresh ginger juice (grate fresh ginger and squeeze gratings to extract juice)
1/4 cup water or stock
8 oz. udon noodles (whole wheat udon or genmai-brown rice udon are best. Use whole wheat ribbons as an alternative.)
3/4 lb. broccoli, coarsely chopped
1/2 head cauliflower, separated into flowerets
tamari shoyu (naturally aged soy sauce)
1 large or 2 small leeks, cut in 1/2" chunks

1. Marinate fish fillets in tamari shoyu, ginger juice, and water or stock for 30 minutes.
2. Meanwhile, boil water for the udon.
3. Fan udon into the boiling water, stir, and cook 8 minutes or until done. (Cut a noodle in half horizontally. If a white "core" is present, cook udon a few more minutes. If creamy white throughout, the noodles are done.)
4. Drain the udon over another pot in order to save the udon cooking stock.
5. Rinse the drained udon under cold water.
6. Return to original cooking pot and place on flame tamer over low heat.
7. Add 1/4 cup of the udon cooking water to a wok or skillet.
8. Bring to a boil, add the chopped broccoli and cauliflower flowerets and "stir fry" with the liquid.
9. Sprinkle with tamari shoyu and cover until crisp-tender.
10. After the fish marinates, add the fish, leeks, and 1 cup of the udon cooking liquid to a skillet and bring to a boil.
11. Reduce heat to medium, cover, and steam 7-8 minutes until fish flakes when touched with a fork.
12. Dissolve kuzu in a small amount of cold water.
13. Remove fish from skillet and add kuzu to fish cooking liquid and leeks.
14. Bring to a boil, stirring constantly until sauce thickens.
15. Serve fish over udon and cover with sauce. Arrange vegetables on the side. Mmmm!

Recipes

GRILLED SALMON STEAKS   *serves 4*

Lime juice and olive oil create a delicious marinade which gives grilled salmon a new twist in flavor.

4 salmon steaks
juice of 2 limes
1/3 cup olive oil
1 TB. fresh dill, minced or seasoning mixture with an emphasis on dill
2 TB. fresh parsley, minced
2 cloves garlic, minced
dill sprigs

1. Place the salmon steaks in a shallow bowl.
2. Combine lime juice, olive oil, dill, parsley, and garlic and pour over salmon steaks.
3. Cover bowl and marinate fish in the refrigerator 2-8 hours, turning the fish occasionally.
4. Remove fish from marinade; reserve the marinade.
5. Grill the fish on a barbeque or under the broiler, turning the steaks once and basting with the reserved marinade.
6. Grill just until the fish flakes easily with a fork, about 4-5 minutes on each side.
7. Transfer to plates. Garnish with dill sprigs and serve.

SNAPPY PASTA SALAD   *serves 3-4*

Tired of pasta salads with tuna? Baked snapper fillets are a good change of pace.

3/4 lb. red snapper or oregon snapper fillets
8 oz. whole wheat ribbons or whole wheat udon or somen noodles
3 TB. olive oil
2 TB. vinegar, lemon juice, or lime juice
1 TB. tamari shoyu soy sauce
1 teaspoon favorite seasoning mixture
(try an "all purpose" variety if you can't decide)
2 cloves, garlic, minced
1 cup fresh or frozen peas, cooked
4 green onions, minced
1 red bell pepper, chopped
1 small cucumber, thinly sliced
2 TB. chopped parsley
calamata black olives (opt.)
cherry tomatoes (opt.)

1. Preheat oven to 400°.
2. Arrange fish in a baking dish. Sprinkle with small amount of water.
3. Bake until fish is flaky and tender, about 8 minutes.
4. Meanwhile cook pasta al dente and drain.
5. Immediately toss with oil, vinegar, tamari shoyu, seasoning, and garlic.
6. Add vegetables and cooked fish. Adjust seasonings.
7. Chill for at least 1 hour and serve.

7

FRUITS & VEGETABLES

Fruits and vegetables are the main sources of vitamin A, vitamin C, thiamin (B_1), additional iron, riboflavin (B_2), fiber, and folacin. And, besides these technical aspects, they simply taste great! Nothing is more delicious than really fresh, high quality produce. The flavor of homegrown produce is best and ultimately fresh when picked and eaten or cooked immediately. Unfortunately, not many of us have the time, the facilities, and the knowledge to grow all our own food and so we depend upon a small group to provide our needs.

Transportation and technology have enabled us to experience foods grown far from our immediate vacinity. In fact, a walk through any produce section in a store will probably feature more products shipped from "far away places" than locally grown. Customers have come to expect the variety. Providing quality, freshness, and variety at the best price is a real challenge for the produce industry. These standards can only be achieved through careful buying skills and knowledge. Direct contact with farmers or with produce brokers whose quality standards are high is what differentiates a quality produce department from a mediocre one which does not get much attention.

ORGANICALLY GROWN PRODUCE

Quality produce departments will offer organically grown fruits and vegetables when possible. With the emphasis on maximum yields, produce tends to be more heavily sprayed with synthetic fertilizers and pesticides than most foods. High yields are worthy goals, but the use of synthetic chemicals ignores and disrupts our complex ecologic system. Soil vitality and fertility is depleted and chemical residues enter the food chain and ultimately our bodies. (See also WHAT IS ORGANIC)

Synthetic chemical fertilizers and pesticides are not the only chemicals routinely used in agriculture. Others include growth regulators, chemicals to prevent sprouting on root vegetables, herbicides, fumigants, and chemicals for artificial ripening, preservatives, waxes, and artificial colors. Most of these are being used regardless that tests have shown them to be harmful. Others are being used despite the fact that no testing has been done. Even once it is shown to be harmful, it takes years to remove a chemical from the market.

The availability of organic produce is limited for two major reasons. In the short term chemical fertilizers and pesticides are cheaper to use for maximum yields. Secondly, the number of farmers, wholesalers, and retailers committed to organic foods is so small that in the past, distribution and growing methods have been less efficient. The more organically grown produce people buy, the more farmers will be convinced that there is a market that will appreciate their efforts.

Although few states have a legal definition for "organically grown" foods, farmer owned associations have banded together to provide credibility and maintain standards. One major organization, the Organic Crop Improvement Association (OCIA), is a confederation of organic farmers and processors from all over the world. The OCIA is dedicated to provide organic crop improvement through professional development of organic farmers and processors, including technical assistance, education, information, publications, and research. An independent third party agent inspects the individual operations to be certified and verifies that production techniques are consistent with the association's strict standards.

Certified members have the right to use the OCIA trademark on their foods as well as on products made exclusively with certified organic foods. Similar to the REAL dairy products seal, the trademark is brand-neutral and attests to the fact that the products to which they are affixed are genuine, safe, or otherwise produced according to uniform and consistent high standards.

Independent third party agencies are also forming to regulate the organically grown produce industry. Whether by state law, self-regulation groups, or third party agencies, produce labeled as organically grown needs to have proper verification available to the store produce buyer. Local produce which cannot prove total organic standards is labeled as "locally grown" or possibly "pesticide free" if that claim can truly be made. When a product is labeled as "organically grown", you can be assured that it truly is of that quality.

Produce labeled **"IPM"** refers to foods grown according to the "Integrated Pest Management" method. Also considered an "intelligent person's method", IPM utilizes the most environmentally responsible, yet effective pest control methods. A farmer using IPM methods first determines the cause of the problem and then investigates the life cycles and particular characteristics of the pest. Then the treatment is chosen which is least likely to disturb the environment. Natural predators and biological agents are often used. Sometimes entirely different crops or farming techniques are used that better suit the environment and deter pests. Chemical pesticides and herbicides are applied only as a last resort.

Produce grown by farmers who are changing to organically growing methods is also labeled as "IPM" until they are able to comply with the time requirements and other standards as required.

The following constitute the Organic Crop Improvement Association certification standards:

ADMISSIBILITY

1. Certification may be on a whole farm or a field by field basis. If the latter, all fields of the farm unit must be committed to an ongoing program of organic crop improvement.

2. No crop shall be sold as "OCIA Certified Organic" if the same crop is also produced elsewhere on the farm using methods or materials that do not conform to these standards, unless the farmer can clearly demonstrate that there exist both the physical facilities and the organizational ability to ensure that there is no possibility of crop mixing. This criterion applies equally to situations when uncertified crop is produced by the same farmer on another farm unit, or is purchased for resale.

3. No field shall be certified for a harvest to occur less than three years after the most recent use of a non-acceptable pesticide (insecticide, herbicide, fungicide, etc.) or less than two years after the most recent application of a non-acceptable fertilizer.

4. In cases where an adjoining farm is growing heavily sprayed crops, or there is other possibility of contamination, there must exist adequate physical barriers to maintain the integrity of certified fields. When contamination is suspected, the certification agent shall require residue testing.

5. Complete information describing at least three (preferably five) most recent years' production methods and materials, as well as information about current production practices, must be provided. The applicant for certification must also furnish an outline of farm management strategies directed at achieving strict compliance with these standards.

6. To be certified, a farm or field must be managed in accordance with the required practices listed below, using authorized methods and materials.

7. The applicant must provide a notarized or sworn affidavit attesting to the truth of information furnished and adherence to these standards.

REQUIRED PRACTICES
1. Development and implementation of a conscientious soil building program designed to enhance organic matter and encourage optimum soil health.

2. Rotation of non-perennial crops in accordance with accepted regional organic practices.

3. Regular monitoring and assessment of soil nutrient balances at least every three years (and preferably annually) in each field to be certified.

4. Use of careful management, resistant varieties, intercropping, and maintenance of soil health as the first line of defense against weeds, pests, and diseases.

5. Generation of an audit trail which will permit tracing the sources and amount of all off-farm inputs, date and place of harvest, and all steps between harvest and sale to the wholesaler, retailer, or final consumer.

6. Maintenance of machinery and equipment in good enough condition to avoid contamination of soil or crops with hydraulic fluid, fuel, oil, etc.

7. Use of pre- and post-harvest handling procedures and packaging materials which ensure maximum product quality (appearance, hygiene, freshness, and nutrition) using techniques and materials that are consistent with these standards. Irradiation of certified foods is prohibited.

Organic farming definitely involves more than planting a seed and watching it grow!

PRODUCE BUYING TIPS

•Seasonal fruits and vegetables are always the best buy. Out of season produce costs more and is not as flavorful. Price, appearance, abundance, and flavor are the best clues as to what is in season.

•Imported fruits and vegetables generally are highly sprayed and fumigated. Often they are used to substitute for produce during the "out of season" periods for a particular fruit or vegetable in the United States. This is one place where the phrase "buy American" has some validity.

•Fruits and vegetables are occasionally waxed to retain moisture content. Apples have a naturally occurring wax on their skins but even these are often coated with either vegetable or petroleum based waxes. Some waxes are not harmful, while others are questionable. If there is a choice, buy unwaxed produce. If not, peel before using unless the wax is known to be harmless.

LESS COMMON VEGETABLES

Sometimes the thought of eating another carrot or apple seems so unimaginative. Take advantage of these feelings to experiment with a less common fruit or vegetable.

Arugala has dark green jagged leaves and a pungent hot flavor. Use raw or cook briefly.

Burdock root is a long slender root vegetable with an earthy flavor. Scrub but do not peel. It is somewhat tough and often is boiled 10 minutes before adding other vegetables. Plan on twice as much cooking time as carrots. To keep firm during long storage, wrap the burdock in a damp cloth before refrigerating.

Celery root or celeriac is a tough, knobby root that comes from a different variety of celery than the one raised for its stalks. Since it is difficult to clean due to its tough skin, it is often peeled before use. Celery root has a subtle celery flavor. It can be cooked like carrots or turnips or used in its raw state. It is especially good when grated and combined with a mustard salad dressing. To soften the root when used raw, it is advisable to add 1-1/2 teaspoons of salt per 1 pound of celery root with 1-1/2 teaspoons lemon juice or vinegar. Refrigerate for 30 minutes, rinse thoroughly, and use a towel or paper towel to squeeze out moisture. Then add a salad dressing and marinate for 2 hours.

Chayote is a squash with a soft, pale green rind that has a flavor somewhat similar to zucchini but with the fibrous texture similar to a winter squash. It can be baked, steamed or sautéed.

Daikon is a white radish that is similar to an icicle radish but much larger in size. It has a hot taste that is good raw in salads. When cooked in soups, stews, or alone as the feature vegetable, daikon becomes surprisingly sweet.

Belgian endive looks like a cigar made from pale yellow leaves. Its bitter flavor is a good contrast to milder flavored lettuce in a salad. Braise in vegetable or chicken broth for 5-10 minutes for a delicious hot vegetable.

Endive (also called chicory) has curly, frilly, coarse leaves with dark green edges and pale yellow stems. Use raw in salads for a bitter accent or cook briefly for a more mild flavor.

Escarole has broad, coarse, flat leaves that are slightly bitter. Use raw in salads or cook briefly to mellow the bitter flavor.

Fennel/Anise—Anise is a compact, greenish white bulb with a licorice flavor that can be used raw or cooked in casserole salads, soups, stews, stuffings, or by itself. Fennel is the feathery tops which can be used as an herb for seasoning. Truly a unique, delicious flavor!

Jerusalem artichokes have no resemblance to an artichoke. They are a brown skinned root which can be cooked like potatoes - either sautéed, boiled, baked, simmered in soups, eaten raw in salads, or used as a substitute for water chestnuts.

Jicama (pronounced: hé cah mah) is a light brown colored root grown in Mexico that can be sautéed, boiled, or used raw in salads or for dips. Peel the tough skin before use. When raw, it has a texture similar to an apple with a somewhat sweet, refreshing flavor. It stays crisp when cooked.

Kohlrabi, a member of the cabbage family, has a delicate turnip flavor. The green tops can be used in salads or steamed. The bulbs can be simmered, steamed, or stir-fried or used raw in salads and relish trays.

Enoki mushrooms are mild flavored, creamy white mushrooms with long slender stems and very small round caps. Their crisp, tender texture makes them a good raw addition to salads or added to stir-fries just before serving.

Shitake mushrooms are large mushrooms whose full flavor and meaty consistency make them a favorite in both oriental and western dishes. Only one or two are needed to impart a delicious flavor to soups, stews, and stir-fries.

Parsnips look like white carrots and are, indeed, related to carrots but are unique in flavor. Their sweet, nutty flavor complements bean dishes, soups, stews, and curries.

Rutabagas are roundish in shape with a yellow-brown skin and yellow flesh. Its nutty, sweet flavor becomes even more sweet the longer it is cooked. Raw grated rutabagas add an interesting flavor and texture to salads.

Winter squash—Mild flavored, fibrous acorn squash is the most familiar winter squash but several varieties ranging from very subtle to very sweet flavors are available. Besides baking squash, add chunks while cooking beans, soups, or stews. Some squashes are so sweet that you may forget about dessert!

Banana squash is a very large, yellow-brown, banana shaped, sweet flavored squash that is often pre-cut into smaller more reasonably sized pieces.
Blue hubbard squash is a sweet flavored, blue grey, thick skinned squash that can also be quite large. It is often stuffed similar to a turkey.
Buttercup squash looks like a dark green globe with a light green crown. Its flavor is very sweet.
Butternut squash is a light yellow, bottle shaped squash with a sweet nutty flavor.

Delicata squash is an elongated yellow vegetable with green stripes with a delicate (!) sweet flavor.

Golden nugget squash is a small round squash with a very thick inedible orange skin. It has a sweet nutty flavor.

Hokkaido squash, with its blue-green skin and pumpkin shape, is the sweetest of all the squashes.

Pumpkins are available in two basic types, the less flavorful jack-o'lantern and the sugar pumpkin which is used for cooking and baking. Pumpkins are not as sweet as other winter squash and often need additional sweetening.

Spaghetti squash, like the name implies, can be a vegetable substitute for spaghetti. Bake or steam this yellow skinned, oblong shaped squash until tender and then use a fork to separate the fibers to produce the mildly sweet flavored "noodles".

Taro root is a vegetable most familiar to people living in Japan, Egypt, Syria, New Zealand, Hawaii, and other islands in the Pacific Ocean. It looks like a hairy potato and can, indeed, be cooked like a potato—baked, steamed, boiled, or used in soup. Remove skins after cooking.

Recipes

CELERY ROOT SALAD   *serves 4-6*
Mustard and celery root make a perfect combination. Use this as an elegant side dish or delicious sandwich condiment.

1 lb. celery root
1 1/2 teaspoon salt
1 1/2 teaspoon lemon juice or apple cider vinegar

2 TB. prepared mustard
1/4 cup boiling water
3 TB. olive oil
2 TB. vinegar
salt (opt.)
parsley

1. Cut off or peel coarse outside layer of the celery root.
2. Grate root and combine with salt and lemon juice.
3. Set aside for 30 minutes.
4. Rinse in cold water, drain, and dry grated root with towel to remove excess moisture.
5. Whisk or blend remaining ingredients.
6. Add to grated celery and marinate in the refrigerator 2-12 hours.
7. Garnish with parsley.

DAIKON PICKLE
Borrowed from classic macrobiotic cuisine, this quick pickle adds a zesty bite and helps digest an oily meal.

1 small or 1/2 medium daikon radish
2 TB. tamari shoyu (naturally aged soy sauce)
1 lime, juiced
2 TB. water

1. Slice radish on the diagonal as thin as possible.
2. Combine sliced radish with rest of ingredients in a bowl or Japanese pickle press.
3. If using a bowl, cover radishes with a plate or small bowl that fits INSIDE the bowl. Place a heavy object on the plate and let radishes marinate for 2-24 hours. If using a pickle press, screw down lid and let marinate same length of time.
4. Drain the marinade and serve a few pickles on each plate.

Recipes

TAMARI BAKED SQUASH

If you haven't experimented much with winter squash, delay no more. This recipe is so good you won't be sure whether to serve it as a main course, a vegetable side dish, or as a snack!

1 winter squash, cut into any sized serving pieces
safflower or corn oil
tamari shoyu (naturally aged soy sauce) or salt (opt.)

1. Preheat oven to 425°.
2. Rub winter squash pieces with oil and shoyu. (If using salt, sprinkle a small amount over the individual pieces.)
3. Place on oiled cookie sheet.
4. Place sheet in oven and bake, uncovered, for 1 hour.
5. Squash is done when the pieces have a crisp crust and soft, creamy flesh.

VEGETABLE CURRY- AMERICAN STYLE   *serves 4-6*

Although not a traditional Indian recipe, curry powder is delicious with this combination of vegetables. Here is an opportunity to try the relatively unknown parsnip at its best.

water
1 teaspoon curry powder
1 onion, thinly sliced
2 medium rutabagas, cut in 1" chunks
2 parsnips, cut in 1/2" diagonals
1/2 small head red cabbage, thinly sliced
1 cup peas, fresh or frozen
salt or shoyu to taste
roasted cashews

1. Fill a large cooking pot with 2" depth of water and bring to a boil.
2. Add curry powder and onion.
3. Lower heat and cook, uncovered, until onion is translucent.
4. Add rutabagas and parsnips, cover and simmer 15 minutes.
5. Add cabbage, peas, and seasonings.
6. Cook 10 minutes longer.
7. Garnish with roasted cashews and serve.

_____ Recipes

HIDDEN VEGETABLE SAUCE   *makes 2 1/2 cups*
This sauce will make a "vegetable lover" out of the most adamant "vegetable
hater". They won't even realize what they are eating!

3 cups vegetables cut into 1" chunks (Choose 1 or a variety: carrots, cauliflower,
winter squash, parsnip, rutabaga, or daikon radish)
2 TB. sesame tahini
pinch of salt or 1 TB. miso (aged soy-based seasoning paste)

1. Place cut vegetables in a saucepan with water covering half the vegetables.
2. Bring to a boil, cover, and reduce heat.
3. Simmer until very soft, about 30 minutes.
4. Combine carrots, tahini, and miso in a blender or food processor.
5. Add enough water from cooking vegetables to make a sauce consistency.
6. Serve hot over grain, noodles, beans, or other vegetables. When cold, it also makes
    a good spread for bread, crackers, pancakes, or tortillas.

_____

CHUNKY CHICKEN SOUP   *serves 4*
Soups are an easy way to eat a variety of vegetables. This recipe combines both
familiar and unusual vegetables into a quick delicious soup that could even be
appropriate as a main course.

6 cups poultry or vegetable stock
1 small onion, diced
1 clove garlic, minced
3 ribs celery, diced
2 cups winter squash, cut in 1" chunks
1 turnip, diced
1/2 teaspoon dried (or 1 teaspoon fresh) thyme
1/2 teaspoon dried (or 1 teaspoon fresh) oregano or sage
salt to taste
1/2 cup lima beans (opt.)
1 cup broccoli florets
1 1/2 cups diced, cooked chicken

1. Combine water, onion, garlic, celery, squash, turnip, and seasonings in a large
    pot.
2. Bring to a boil, cover, and simmer 30 minutes.
3. Add lima beans, broccoli, and chicken and cook another 20 minutes.
4. Serve with crackers, crusty bread, or cooked whole grain.

Recipes_____

VEGETABLE STOCK

There is no real recipe for making a vegetable stock. It could simply be the leftover liquid from cooking vegetables. It also could be made from the scraps of vegetables leftover from meal preparation.

Avoid strong flavored cooking liquids and large amounts of the cabbage family: broccoli, brussels sprouts, cabbage, turnips, etc.

Carrots, onions, leeks, and celery are especially good.

Cover vegetables with cold water, bring to a boil, and simmer 30-60 minutes. Strain. The vegetables, whose flavor is now mainly in the stock, can be pureed to thicken the soup, added to your pet's dinner, eaten by you, or composted.

SPROUTS

Sprouts are often the freshest vegetable available. Some stores grow their own while others are supplied by local vendors on a frequent basis to insure flavor and optimum nutrition.

Sprouts also are very easy to grow yourself. No special equipment is needed, no large growing area is needed, and no large amounts of money need be invested.

Almost any seed, bean, or grain will sprout. Basic equipment includes a wide mouthed quart sized jar, a rubber band, and cheesecloth or clean nylon stockings. Special equipment can be bought ranging from sprouting jars with lids of plastic or stainless steel grids to 3 tiered or dome shaped mini sprouting greenhouses. The amount of seed needed depends on the size of the seed. Seeds as small as alfalfa seeds require 1 TB. to fill a quart jar while seeds as large as beans or grains require 4 TB.

Place the seeds in the jar, add water to cover the seeds plus 1" depth, cut a piece of cheesecloth or nylon stocking 2" larger than the diameter of the mouth of the jar, and fasten it tightly with the rubber band. Let the seeds soak overnight or 8 hours. Then invert the jar to drain the soaking water. (Instead of pouring it down the drain, use it to water your plants. The nutrients in the water will make your plants thrive.)

Fill half the jar with water through the cheesecloth covered opening, shake it to moisten the seeds, and drain again. Water should remain in the jar only the first night. Place the jar on its side or in a dish drainer upside down with the mouth pointed toward the sink. Cover with a towel to provide a dark environment. Most seeds require this rinsing technique twice per day. Some of the beans, such as garbanzo beans and soybeans need 5-6 rinsings per day to prevent spoilage.

Sprouts are ready within 2-5 days depending on the seed, bean, or grain used. In general, seeds need 3-5 days to grow 1-2 inches, beans need 3-5 days to grow 1 inch, and grains need 2-3 days to grow the original length of the grain used.

Store in the sprouting jar or a plastic container and use quickly. Sprouting increases the vitamin A, B, C, and E levels and the amino acid content but the benefits will be negated if the sprouts get old. Use delicate sprouts like alfalfa or red clover raw. Bean and grain sprouts can be used raw or cooked. Soybeans are the exception; they must always be cooked.

Sprouts are good in soups, salads, stir-fries, and omelettes. You can make your own natural sweetener, malt powder, from grain sprouts by drying wheat or barley sprouts in an oven at a low temperature for about 2 hours. When dry, grind in a seed mill or blender. Use on or in cereals, breads, and cookies. Refer to recipe books for more creative uses of sprouts. One warning is needed: potato sprouts are toxic. Never eat them!

Recipes

SCRAMBLED SPROUTS   *serves 4*
Sprouts give an interesting flavor and texture to an old standby....

6 eggs or 1 lb. tofu
1/3 cup milk (for eggs)
4 green onions, thinly sliced on diagonal
1/2 cup mung bean or alfalfa sprouts, coarsely chopped
1 TB. sesame oil
2 teaspoons tamari shoyu (naturally aged soy sauce) or 1/4 teaspoon salt
1/4 teaspoon turmeric (for tofu)

1. Whisk together eggs and milk or mash tofu with a fork.
2. Combine either the eggs or the tofu with the green onions and sprouts.
3. Heat oil in a skillet over medium heat.
4. Add egg or tofu mixture and seasoning.
5. Cook, stirring often until eggs are fluffy or tofu is thoroughly warmed (about 10 minutes).
6. Serve with toast, bagels, or tortillas.

SPROUTS SALAD WITH TAHINI DRESSING   *serves 2*
Simple, yet energizing!

1/4 cup sunflower sprouts
1/2 cup alfalfa sprouts
1/2 cup mung bean or bean sprout combination (lentil, aduki, mung)
2 carrots, grated
2 scallions, chopped
2 radishes, thinly sliced

Dressing:
2 TB. sesame tahini
1 TB. vinegar or lemon juice
water to thin
dried shiso leaf condiment or other salty seasoning such as tamari shoyu, salt, gomasio, kelp, or prepared herb seasonings to taste
(see CONDIMENTS for description of unusual seasonings)

1. Mix salad.
2. Blend dressing in blender, food processor, or Japanese suribachi.
3. Pour dressing over salad and serve.

FRUITS

Apples are suitable for pies, sauce, baking, or raw in salads or out of hand. Red delicious is the most popular variety but familiarity with the other types will provide interesting contrasts in flavor and texture.

CHARACTERISTICS OF APPLES

VARIETY	FLAVOR	TEXTURE	COMMENTS
cortland	tart	semi-firm tender, juicy	flesh slow to darken when cut; all purpose
golden delicious	very sweet	crisp, juicy	flesh slow to darken when cut; all purpose
red delicious	very sweet	crisp, juicy	best raw; avoid cooking or baking
gravenstein	tart	crisp, juicy tender	late summer apple, good raw and in sauce
granny smith	very tart	crisp, crunchy	all purpose
jonathan	tart	crisp	avoid baking
lodi	very tart	soft, tender juicy	summer apple, best for cooking
McIntosh	slightly tart	firm, crisp, very juicy	all purpose
pippin	tart	crisp, firm	all purpose
rome	slightly tart	firm somewhat crisp	all purpose but best cooked or baked
stayman	tart	firm, crisp	all purpose but best raw
winesap	somewhat tart wine-like flavor	somewhat crisp	all purpose excellent raw

LESS COMMON FRUITS

Cherimoya is a beautifully textured green fruit with a flavor that resembles a combination of pear, pineapple, strawberry, and banana with a hint of lemon-lime! When ripe, it will yield to gentle pressure. Although quite expensive, its custard-like consistency and incredible flavor will convince you it is well worth the price.

Kiwi fruit has a fuzzy brown skin with a bright green interior dotted with tiny black edible seeds. Peel before using. It is delicious raw and because of it beautiful color, it is often used as a garnish. Use only cooked kiwi in gelatin dishes since raw kiwi has an enzyme which inhibits jelling.

Passion fruit is a dark purple plum-sized fruit with a sweet/sour flavor. To eat, cut the fruit in half and scoop out the yellow gelatinous meat. The seeds may be eaten.

Persimmon is a deep orange red tomato-shaped fruit which is ready to eat when the fruit is very soft, like "jelly in a bag". It is very sweet and is eaten raw or pureed for use in pies, cakes, and custards.

Quince is related to the apple family. It has an acidic taste and is never eaten fresh. Usually it is used in marmalades or jellies or baked in the same manner as apples.

Tamarinds are fuzzy brown colored pods from an evergreen tree grown in the tropics. They can be cooked with rice or eaten raw for the pulp which has an apricot-date flavor.

Recipes

APPLESAUCE

Remember the delicious flavor of Mom's homemade applesauce but don't have the foggiest how to make it? It's easier than you thought!

1-2 lb. golden delicious, McIntosh, gravenstein, or granny smith apples
1 cup water
1/2 teaspoon cinnamon

1. Cut apples into chunks. Discard seeds.
2. Place apples in pot with water and cinnamon.
3. Cover, bring to a boil, and simmer 15 minutes or until apples are very soft.
4. Leave chunky or mash to desired consistency.
5. Serve or cool and refrigerate.

BAKED STUFFED FRUIT

This recipe can conform to the season. The same basic filling can be used to stuff apples, peaches, nectarines, or pears.

6 pieces of favorite fruit (apples, peaches, nectarines, or pears)
1/2 cup raisins
1/2 cup walnuts or pecans
1/2 teaspoon vanilla
dash of cinnamon (opt.)
apple juice

1. Preheat oven to 375°.
2. Prepare the fruit:
   Apples: Core and peel a 1" strip around the center of the apple.
   Peaches, nectarines: Cut in half and remove pit.
   Pears: Cut in half lengthwise and remove seeds.
3. Place fruit in a baking dish.
4. Combine raisins, nuts, vanilla, and cinnamon in a blender or food processor with just enough apple juice to facilitate blending to a coarse texture.
5. Stuff mixture in center of the apple or in pit/seed area of the other fruit.
6. Pour apple juice into the baking dish to a depth of 1/2".
7. Cover with foil.
8. Bake at 375° for 30 minutes or until just tender.
9. Serve plain or with a dollop of yogurt or other favorite topping.

8

CONDIMENTS, HERBS, & SPICES

VINEGAR

What is a salad dressing without vinegar? Vinegar has been used since 5000 B.C. as a flavor enhancer and preservative. Often traditionally served at a high protein meal, a good quality vinegar may also help digestion if it has not been distilled or over-filtered. Unlike distilled or over-filtered vinegars, the most nutritious vinegar will be slightly cloudy or contain the "mother", a living mixture of beneficial bacteria and enzymes that resembles a strand-like substance floating in the bottle.

 Various vinegars are available. The acidity and flavor depends on the source of the vinegar.

Distilled vinegar is from an alcohol source and is the least nutritious and flavorful of all the vinegars. Its strong acidic flavor is too sharp for salad dressings. Its most common use is in pickling when the use of other vinegars would discolor light vegetables and fruits.

Apple cider vinegar is a good all-purpose vinegar for salad dressing, pickles, and for adding some tartness to a dish.

Brown rice vinegar has about half the sharpness of cider vinegar with a touch of sweetness. It is good in salads, and on fish, grains, vegetables, and rice dishes.

Fruit vinegar, most notably raspberry and blueberry vinegars, have a light fresh flavor that is delicious over both vegetable and fruit salads. Adventurous cooks don't stop there.

Malt vinegar is from barley or other cereal grains. The flavor may be too strong in salad for some people. It adds a distinctive flavor to hot and cold vegetable dishes, sauteed potatoes, and of course, fish and chips.

Wine vinegars differ as to the source of wine. Red wine vinegars are robust and go well with pungent greens, meats, and cheese salads. White wine vinegar is more delicate and excellent with tender lettuce.

Ume plum vinegar is the liquid drawn off from pickled umeboshi plums and shiso leaves and not a true vinegar. Its flavor makes it good for salad dressings and the pickling of vegetables. Substitute for salt and lemon in chickpea-based hommus for a new tasty spread. 1 1/2 teaspoon ume plum vinegar = 1 umeboshi plum.

Herb vinegars are cider, red wine, or white wine vinegars steeped with herbs. The particular flavor depends upon the herb added. Delicious with salads.

Balsamic vinegar is an aromatic, syrupy, dense, dark, slightly sweet and sour type of vinegar that is at least 3 years old, but at its best when older than 10 years. The complex process involves transferring the vinegar each year into a smaller barrel made of high quality wood. The evaporation of the vinegar in the various exotic woods gives the vinegar its noted bouquet and flavor. Add to salad dressings, vinaigrettes, and marinades.

PREPARED CONDIMENTS

Good prepared **salad dressings** range from simple, basic oil and vinegar combinations to thick blends of oil, vinegar, honey, herbs, and vegetable gums. Many use inexpensive refined soy oil as the base to subdue the oil's flavor but oils made with olive, sesame, or safflower oil are a better choice. Oil-free dressings are thickened with vegetable gums to provide the body an oil usually provides. A dash of lemon juice or vinegar with some herbs and tamari shoyu might be all you need on a salad if you want to avoid the oil. Tofu based dressings provide a creamy alternative that contain only 40 calories per tablespoon!

Mustard varieties range from the runny, yellow mustards found on hot dogs at the baseball park to the thick grainy mustards from England. The flavors vary according to the type of mustard seed used, the way the seed is ground, whether vinegar or wine is used, and the other herbs and spices that are added. Yellow mustard seeds are mild, brown are pungent, and oriental seeds are sharp in flavor. Most mustards are made from a combination of many types of seeds rather than one isolated variety of mustard seed.

When cooking with mustard, most people prefer a smooth mustard like Dijon. Dijon mustard is made from a mixture of seeds that is strong but not overly aromatic so it works well with other flavors. Grainy mustards are also good in cooking and excellent in salad dressings. Recognizing the increased interest in quality foods, many excellent mustards are available without artificial flavors, colors, or preservatives.

Ketchup is notorious for its high level of refined sugar— about 6 tablespoons per cup! Many delicious products are made with honey replacing the corn syrup and sucrose but remain almost or just as sweet. Try an unsweetened ketchup. It will make you wonder why any type of sweetener was needed at all! Certain seasonings and a particular variety of tomato make all the difference.

Mayonnaise is available honey sweetened, sugar sweetened, with or without eggs, with or without salt, or made with particular types of oil. A unique tofu based mayonnaise provides a creamy, no-cholesterol (no eggs) alternative that tastes remarkably similar to traditional mayonnaise but contains only half the calories.

Both **pickles and sauerkraut** are now available in lower sodium varieties for those who need to restrict their intake.

Every culture has its specialties. The following **Japanese condiments** add another dimension even to your traditional American meals. Experiment!

Goma muso is a crumbly powder made from lightly cooked barley miso and sesame butter. Sprinkle on grain or vegetable dishes.

Gomasio or sesame salt is a combination of ground roasted sesame seeds and sea salt used as a low sodium alternative to salt and as an additional source of protein and calcium. The proportions of sesame seeds to sea salt in prepared, moderately salty gomasio ranges from 8:1 to 14:1 depending on the brand. A gomasio with 20:1 proportion can easily be made at home if a less salty condiment is preferred. Sprinkle on grains and vegetables as you would salt.

Mirin, a sweet cooking wine made from sweet rice is an essential in Japanese cuisine. Its 14% alcohol content dissipates when heated. Use in marinades, salad dressings, sauces, noodle dishes, and vegetables or to balance overly pungent or salty dishes. Many brands of commercial mirin are made from cornstarch, ethyl alcohol, sugar, and chemical fermenting agents. Quality authentic mirin is made from sweet rice, rice koji, and water.

Nori condiment is a combination of nori seaweed, tamari, rice malt, and mirin. Spread on sandwiches as a seasoning or mix with grains or vegetables.

Pickled daikon radish is a crisp textured and sharp, tangy flavored condiment that is traditionally used as an accompaniment to a meal to promote digestion. Use only extremely small amounts as it is very salty.

Pickled ginger is made from young, tender, thinly sliced ginger roots that are briefly salt pressed and pickled in rice vinegar and shiso leaves. Buy only pickled ginger that is free of preservatives, sugar, and food colorings. A frequently used condiment in sushi bars, pickled ginger cleanses the palate, increases the appetite, and settles the stomach.

Ponzu sauce is a blend of brown rice vinegar, tamari shoyu, and mirin for a delicious vinaigrette that brings out the best in vegetables and salads. It can also be used in cooking.

Sesame Sprinkle combines toasted sesame seeds, green nori flakes, and dried pickled shiso leaves for a delicious, nutty, slightly salty condiment that is also high in protein, calcium, and iron. Use to season any food.

Shiso leaf powder is made from the dried purple leaves of the beefsteak plant which are pickled with Japanese plums (ume). The shiso leaves impart the familiar red color to the pickled plums as well as contribute to its tangy flavor. Use instead of salt for a mineral rich, salty, zesty flavor on vegetables, salads, or grains. Really worth trying!

Tekka is a combination of miso, carrots, burdock, lotus root, ginger root, and sesame oil cooked for 7 hours until it is crumbly and dry in texture. Use a *small* spoonful on grain dishes.

Umeboshi plums are made from sour green Japanese plums (actually a type of apricot) pickled with sea salt and shiso, the purple leaves from the beefsteak plant. Used for centuries for their alkaline, bacteria killing medicinal properties, umeboshi plums have a salty, sour flavor. In cooking they may be substituted for salt, tamari shoyu, or miso. One plum is equal to a 1/4 teaspoon of sea salt, 1 1/2 teaspoons of tamari shoyu, or 2 tablespoons of miso. Blend with oil and vinegar for a salad dressing, spread thinly on corn on the cob instead of butter and salt, or use in making rice balls or nori maki or sushi rolls. **Umeboshi paste**, the smooth pitted puree of umeboshi plums, is available for convenience. 1 1/2 teaspoons of umeboshi paste is equal to 1 umeboshi plum.

Wasabi is Japanese powdered horseradish that is less sharp and more aromatic than regular horseradish. Natural wasabi will have a dull greenish color. Avoid artificially colored wasabi which contains little or no wasabi powder. Mix equal amounts of water with the wasabi to form a paste. Cover and let sit for 10 minutes to mingle flavors. Warning: wasabi is very hot! Only small amounts are needed.

MISO AND SOY SAUCE

Miso is a fermented soybean paste made by mixing cooked soybeans with koji (grain inoculated with aspergillus mold), salt, and water and fermenting the mixture from 2 months to 3 years depending on the type of miso. It is a good source of protein, enzymes, and may contain traces of B^{12}. Miso has also been reported to neutralize the effects of smoking and environmental pollution and to alkalize the blood.

Use in soups or sauces instead of bouillon for a rich flavor or as a base for stews, gravies, salad dressings, dips or spreads. Season beans or grains with miso instead of salt or tamari shoyu for variety.

Flavors vary according to the type of miso. Basically, misos can be divided into 2 types— short term misos and long term misos. Each miso has its own unique ratio of ingredients and proper fermentation time.

A **short term miso**, aged for about 2 months, is achieved by the use of more koji and less salt during fermentation. Because its color can be white, yellow, or beige, short term miso is sold by names such as mellow miso, sweet miso, or sweet white miso. It is appropriate for summer cooking, dips, sauces, and salad dressings. Its high carbohydrate content yields a sweet flavor. Short term miso also contains twice the niacin (B^3) and 10 times the beneficial lactic acid bacteria of dark salty miso.

Long term miso is aged 6 months to 3 years with more salt, more soybeans, and less koji to yield a dark red or brown miso that is higher in protein, essential fatty acids, and salt. It is the preferred miso for soups, stews, and colder weather cooking but it is considered an all purpose miso for year around use. Varieties of long term misos include— mugi or barley miso; red, rice, kome, genmai, or brown rice miso all made from rice; soba or buckwheat miso; and hatcho or 100% soybean miso.

Natto miso is a chunky condiment made from soybeans, barley, barley malt, kombu (a sea vegetable), ginger, and sea salt. Use as a relish or chutney on grains, beans, vegetables, or in sandwich spreads. Try seasoning a squash or sweet potato soup with natto miso or add to your favorite barbeque sauce for sweet, salty, pungent zip!

Since miso is a concentrated food, use no more than 1/2 to 1 teaspoon of dark miso or 1-2 teaspoons of light miso per person. 1 tablespoon of light miso or a heaping 1 1/2 teaspoon of dark miso equals 1/4 teaspoon of sea salt.   Dissolve miso in a small amount of liquid before adding to soups, sauces, or other dishes to activate the beneficial enzymes in miso.   Steep 3-5 minutes in the hot liquid at the end of cooking but do not boil. Miso used in spreads, dips, and salad dressings is primarily used for flavor, so the heat activation step is generally eliminated. However, many of the health benefits will still be present.

Unpasteurized miso is preferred since it leaves the beneficial lactobacillus bacteria and other enzymes intact, thus insuring the medicinal benefits and full flavors of miso. Previously, unpasteurized miso was available only in bulk, since, due to on-going fermentation, naturally occurring carbon dioxide expanded and burst packages of miso. Small refrigerated tubs of unpasteurized miso seem to have no problem. Some brands of packaged miso have been heated at temperatures lower than pasteuriziation levels to delay overzealous fermentation. Therefore, technically, they can be called unpasteurized.

Previously, most miso was made in Japan. Now much is being made in the United States using traditional methods and often organically grown soybeans and grains.

Soy sauce quality and purity varies tremendously.

Standard soy sauce is made from defatted soy meal that is treated with hydrochloric acid, heated, then treated with sodium carbonate to neutralize the acid. It is unfermented and contains additives such as caramel color, corn syrup, and preservatives.

Traditional Japanese soy sauce is naturally fermented in wooden kegs for many months and then pressed. What we call "tamari", the product made from soybeans, wheat, water, and sea salt, is technically **shoyu**. Traditional **tamari** is wheat free, originally the liquid which rose to the surface or settled on the bottom of miso kegs.

The confusion in names stems from a lecture George Ohsawa (the person responsible for introducing macrobiotic princples to the West) gave in Hamburg, Germany. A man in attendance was so enthralled with the shoyu that he sampled there, that he registered the word "shoyu" as his own trademark and brand name, thereby giving himself exclusive rights to the name in Germany. Because of the problem, the Ohsawas renamed shoyu with the term "tamari" and "tamari" became a generic term for both shoyu and traditional tamari.

Attempts are now being made to return to the original names. Soy sauce containing soy, wheat, water, and sea salt is labeled as **tamari shoyu** or **shoyu** while the name **tamari** indicates the real wheat free product.

Tamari is not as readily available or as popular as its counterpart, shoyu. Genuine traditionally made tamari made from soybean miso is in small supply since extracting too much of the tamari adversely affects the quality of the miso. Now most companies utilize a process developed specifically for making tamari. Because tamari has a stronger, sharper flavor which is retained in longer cooking, tamari is extensively used in commercial food processing. Likewise, home cooking which benefits from a salty seasoning added early in cooking is best seasoned with tamari. Wheat sensitive individuals use tamari since, unlike shoyu, it is made with no wheat. Tamari also contains 36% more glutamic acid (a natural flavor enhancer) than tamari shoyu.

In contrast, tamari shoyu has a mellow rich flavor that is suitable for both cooking and condiment uses. Add only during the last few minutes of cooking since with longer cooking its delicate flavors are lost as the alcohol (which results from the fermentation of the wheat) evaporates.

Tamari shoyu contains 1055 mg. of sodium per tablespoon. Tamari has 743 mg. per tablespoon. If on a salt restricted diet for medical or personal reasons, consider a low sodium shoyu which contains 133-560 mg. per tablespoon in comparison, depending upon the brand.

Good quality **low sodium shoyu** is made from a double fermentation process. After the normal 2 years incubation of regular shoyu, extra wheat and soybeans are added to the fermentation mash but without the salt, thus lowering the salt concentration. It is then fermented for an additional 1 1/2 to 2 years to yield a 9% salt content instead of the normal 16% of regular shoyu. The double fermentation process insures a full bodied flavor similar to regular shoyu without tasting like some watered down low sodium soy sauces.

Another technique used by some companies is to heat the soy sauce at lowered atmospheric pressure. The moisture content is reduced until the salt forms as a precipitate. The salt is then removed by a centrifuge.

Lower quality low sodium shoyu uses an ion exchange process which removes much of the salt from regular shoyu. The shoyu passes through a tank containing two electrically charged plates. The salt precipitates out onto the plates resulting in a shoyu that is of questionable chemical and nutritional quality.

High grade shoyus form a thick head of foam when shaken that may take as long as 15 minutes to dissipate, while an inferior brand will form a weaker foam that dissolves quickly.

Another quality control test involves placing a drop of shoyu in a glass of water. Good quality, natural shoyu will sink to the bottom of the glass before dispersing, while an inferior shoyu disperses almost immediately near the surface.

High grade, naturally aged shoyu enhances the flavor while aiding digestion of countless foods. Use in marinades, vegetable dishes, soups, stews, beans, salad dressings, and grain dishes instead of salt or miso for variety. To preserve the flavor and chemical structure of shoyu, store away from sunlight and heat, including the stove. Some even suggest refrigeration.

SALT

Salt has the most notoriety of any of the condiments since much is written about the pros and cons of its use. Too much can lead to increased cardiovascular disease, sleeping difficulties, hypertension, and kidney stones, while too little can cause weakness, depression, digestive and elimination problems and even death in extreme cases. Sodium is present in many foods so anyone who eats will get some sodium, but tolerated amounts will vary for individuals depending upon past and present diet, age, activity level, condition and constitution, and the climate in which one lives.

The source of the salt, processing methods, and trace mineral content determine the differences between commercial salts.

Salt can be obtained from land mines or from the sea. Unrefined sea salt generally is higher in trace minerals than unrefined land salt since rain water or other water flowing over the land eventually washes minerals into the ocean. The minerals concentrate as the sun constantly evaporates water.

Good quality salt is either solar evaporated or dried at low temperatures with no additives. The majority of salt processing uses a process of steam heat under pressure to 1200° F. Then it is flash cooled to produce instant crystallization. This is followed by the addition of magnesium carbonate (a naturally occurring mineral) to prevent caking, dextrose (sugar) to stabilize the potassium iodide which is added to provide iodine, and sodium carbonate to prevent the mixture from turning purple.

Sea water contains over 60 elements, most notably sodium, chlorine, magnesium, calcium, sulfur (as sulfate), and potassium. In particular, sea water contains 78% sodium chloride, the compound normally associated with salt.

Most salts, including "sea salts" are processed to conform to federal law requirements that salt be not less than 97.5 % sodium chloride. A typical salt, including some salt labeled as sea salt, is refined to sodium chloride levels ranging from 99.56-99.95%. In contrast, other sea salts, most notably made by Lima and Muramoto, range from 97.5% - 98.49%, containing slightly more trace minerals.

NOTE: all salts should be considered equally as salty. Sea salt, depending on the brand, may retain minute amounts of trace minerals but it is just as harmful as other table salt when used in excessive amounts.

Sea salt should not be considered as a main source of trace minerals and yet some claim the presence of the minerals near the balance that occurs in nature may create a subtle beneficial synergistic effect in the body. On the other hand, a high quantity of certain minerals may cause problems. For example, sea salt which has a dark grey appearance generally contains too much magnesium.

Since sea salt contains no natural iodine, sea vegetables, kelp powder, or ocean seafood should be eaten to maintain proper levels. A deficiency of iodine can lead to goiter, the enlargement of the thyroid gland.

Another salt source is bottled "sea water" derived from the ocean or the Great Salt Lake in Utah, a body of water that is six times more concentrated in minerals (and probably less polluted) than the ocean. The water is purified by filtering. 2 teaspoons of Inland Sea Water is equivalent to 1 teaspoon of granular salt. Some people find it convenient to put a spray nozzle on top of the bottle to lightly spray food with the sea water.

Whether land salt or sea salt is used, moderation is the key. Use only small amounts to enhance the flavor of foods. Remember to include a source of dietary iodine or use an iodized salt.

Recipes

HOMMUS   *yields 3 cups*
This traditional Middle Eastern spread takes on a new dimension when umeboshi plum vinegar is used instead of lemon juice and salt.

2 cups cooked garbanzo beans (chickpeas)
1/2 - 3/4 cup water, vegetable stock, or liquid from cooking garbanzos
3 TB. sesame tahini
3 TB. umeboshi vinegar
3 cloves garlic, minced or 1/4 tsp. garlic granules

1. Combine all ingredients in blender or food processor until smooth and creamy. Add more liquid if necessary.
2. Place in serving bowl and garnish with parsley.

BEAN SALAD WITH MUSTARD MARINADE
This salad is wonderful whether it is stuffed in pita bread or tortillas or served as a main dish salad.   A good entree to make ahead since its flavor improves the longer it marinates.

Dressing:
3 TB. apple cider or rice vinegar
2 TB. tamari shoyu (naturally aged soy sauce)
1 teaspoon prepared mustard
1 TB. sesame tahini
3 TB. water

The salad:
2 1/2 cups cooked beans (pinto, kidney, black, or garbanzo)
1/2 cup green onions, thinly sliced
1/2 cup grated carrot
1/2 bunch parsley, chopped
alfalfa sprouts (opt.)

pita bread or tortillas (opt.)

1. Blend or whisk dressing.
2. Add dressing to beans, green onions, carrots, and parsley.
3. Marinate at least 15 minutes.
4. Stuff pita bread or tortillas with salad or serve on a bed of lettuce.
5. Top with alfalfa sprouts, if desired.

Recipes

MIRIN MARINADE   *yields 1 cup*
Marinades tenderize while adding flavor. Use this recipe for marinating tofu, fish, chicken, or meat.

1/3 cup mirin
1/4 cup tamari shoyu
1/4 cup water
2 cloves garlic, minced
2 TB. lemon juice or vinegar
flour, arrowroot, or kuzu (opt.)

1. Combine all ingredients.
2. Cover food with marinade 30 minutes to 5 hours.
3. Remove food from marinade to broil or sauté.
4. Reserve marinade and thicken if desired with flour, arrowroot, or kuzu just
    before serving for a delicious sauce.
    (**NOTE:** If baking, bake food while immersed in marinade. Check the water level
    periodically as more liquid may be needed during baking.)

MISO SOUP   *serves 4*
This soup tastes great anytime but especially when you crave something basic to balance overindulgence in too many sweets or rich foods.

5 cups water
1 large onion, thinly sliced
8 inch piece wakame (sea vegetable)
1/2 inch piece of ginger root, thinly sliced
1 cup daikon radish, cut in 1/2 inch diagonal slices
1 TB. dark miso
4 scallions, thinly sliced on diagonal

1. Bring 5 cups water to a boil.
2. Add onion. Simmer 5 minutes, uncovered.
3. Quickly rinse wakame under water to remove excess salt.
4. Cut into 1 inch pieces and add to soup along with ginger and the daikon radish.
5. Cover and simmer 20 minutes.
6. Dilute miso with a small amount of the soup and add to rest of soup.
7. Turn heat off from under soup and let soup set for 5 minutes.
8. Ladle soup into bowls and garnish with scallions.

HERBS AND SPICES

Herbs and spices can make the same foods taste remarkably different. For instance, garbanzo beans can be seasoned with oregano and basil for an Italian dinner, with curry for Indian cuisine, with chervil or tarragon for French accent, or mustard, garlic, cayenne pepper, cumin, and cloves for an American barbecue.

Due to the interest in gourmet cooking and the desire to decrease salt intake, seasoning with herbs and spices is becoming even more popular. Technically, **herbs** are from the leaves of a low-growing annual or perennial plants that are usually grown in temperate climates. Popular herbs include basil, oregano, and thyme. **Spices**, most notably cinnamon, ginger, and nutmeg, come from tropical grown barks, roots, fruits, or berries of perennial shrubs. **Seeds** such as dill seed, caraway, and fennel are the seeds of various annual plants. Garlic, onion, and paprika are examples of **dehydrated vegetables** that are used for seasoning. A combination of any of the above constitutes a **seasoning blend**.

Salt has been used for thousands of years mainly as a preservative. Meat and fish were cured in salt to kill harmful bacteria and vegetables were preserved as sauerkraut and pickles. Enhancing the flavors of food with salt is a fairly recent practice. Traditionally, herbs and spices were used as flavor enhancers instead of salt.

Processed foods contain large amounts of sodium. However, because of public awareness of the dangers of excess salt, many manufacturers are returning to using more herbs and spices and offering no-salt or low sodium alternatives.

Cooking "from scratch" enables a person to monitor the amount of salt used. Unsalted foods may seem bland at first since most people are addicted to salt after years of using high amounts. Experimenting with the huge variety of bulk and packaged herbs and spices can make food exciting again. Choose from single herbs and spices and seasoning combinations such as chili powder, curry powder, Italian seasoning, poultry seasoning, and pumpkin pie spice.

Quality varies in flavor, color, and aroma depending on the source and processor of the seasoning. Insist on herbs and spices free of additives which may detract from its flavor, including anti-caking agents. Moisture problems can be remedied by adding a few grains of raw rice to the shaker or container.

Traditional salt substitutes contain potassium chloride, sugar, and artificial ingredients. Potassium chloride tastes bitter, may be harmful in large quantities, and may cause stomach upset in some people. Use salt substitutes only if free of artificial ingredients. However, more people seem to be satisfied with the salt substitutes or herb and spice combinations that are made without the potassium chloride. **NOTE:** some contain small amounts of salt which some people may need or want to avoid. Read the label for specific ingredients.

The secret to effective seasoning is to refrain from using *too much* herbs and spices.

They should remain in the background to merely enhance the food, not to overpower. Use about 1/4 teaspoon ground or powdered seasoning or 1 teaspoon "crumbled" seasoning per 6 servings. The flavor of dried herbs is developed more when soaked in the stock, oil, lemon juice, vinegar, or butter used in a dish. Meat, fish, and poultry should be rubbed with the seasoning instead of merely sprinkled on top. If a stew or soup is to be cooked for a long time, add the seasoning 30 minutes before it is done. Cooking some seasonings for long durations can produce bitter flavors.

Dried herbs and spices should be kept in jars or bottles with tight fitting caps. Store in a cool, dry place away from sunlight *and the stove*. Ground or powdered herbs will keep their flavor up to 6 months while "crumbled" or whole seasonings will keep for 1 year. For best results, buy small quantities and replace frequently.

Don't forget fresh herbs! The subtle flavors of fresh herbs can make a dramatic difference in dishes that normally had been prepared with dried herbs. Use only very fresh herbs, preferably freshly snipped from a plant at home. Figure on approximately 3 times the amount of fresh herb as the same in dried form. Add at the end of the cooking process, avoiding prolonged cooking which destroys the delicate flavors.

No other seasoning gets so many inquiries as **saffron**, especially about its price. Saffron is so expensive simply because it takes 75,000 flowers to produce 1 lb. of saffron! Each flower has 3 reddish orange stigmas which are hand picked and dried for 1 month. Besides imparting a beautiful yellow color to the food, it contributes a distinctive warm, pungent flavor. Dry roast the "threads" for 3 minutes in a 350° oven or steep them untoasted in liquid for 10 minutes to amplify the color and flavor.

Flour is the most commonly used thickening agent but, at times, the flavor and opaque appearance it gives to soups, gravies, or sauces is not desired. Cornstarch has generally been the next choice when transparent, shiny sauces are needed. However, because cornstarch is treated with chemicals to improve its stability as a thickening agent and is sometimes difficult to digest, arrowroot and kuzu have become more popular.

Arrowroot is the dried and powdered cassava plant which native American Indians used to draw out poisons from arrow wounds—hence, the name. It is very digestible, contains trace minerals, thickens at low temperatures, and produces a shiny, translucent sauce. Use 1/2 the amount required for flour. Dissolve in cold water and then add at the end of cooking. Be careful not to overcook or the thick consistency may break down.

Kuzu is the powdered root of the kuzu plant. It is used both for its thickening and medicinal properties. Traditionally in the Orient, it is used to alkalize an acidic condition such as colds, nausea, indigestion, and to help treat diarrhea. Like arrowroot, kuzu must be dissolved in cold water before adding to hot liquids. Use 1/2 the amount required for arrowroot and 1/4 the amount required for flour to thicken. Because kuzu is so expensive, arrowroot is often substituted, however, the superior gelling, translucence and sparkle are unique to kuzu.

FLAVORS AND EXTRACTS

The most popular flavor is vanilla. Puddings, ice cream, cakes, cookies, and other baked goods just would not be the same without it. Real vanilla is expensive but preferred.

Artificial vanilla, called **vanillin**, is derived from the waste products of the wood pulp industry. It has a bland taste, medicinal scent, and will ruin the flavor of any product after freezing.

Mexican vanilla is prized by many, but the basis for its delicious flavor and aroma is coumarin or tonka bean extract instead of the more expensive vanilla beans. A derivative of coumarin, dicumarol, is used in anti-coagulant drugs. It also is an effective ingredient in rat poisons; when rats eat enough of it, they bleed to death. Although there is no indication that coumarin itself produces the anti-coagulant effect in humans, the FDA banned it as a food or food additive since 1954 because of potential poisonous and harmful effects, including liver damage. U.S. tourists may bring it into the country, but it is illegal to import and sell in the U.S.

Despite the name, many **"pure" vanilla extracts** contain ethyl alcohol, glycerine, propylene glycol, sugar, and corn syrup along with the vanilla. All pure vanilla extracts are extracted with alcohol. Besides extracting the flavor, the alcohol keeps the vanilla in suspension, otherwise the vanilla particles would sink to the bottom. The alcohol does not add any flavor of its own to the extract.

When vanilla is extracted, a certain proportion of alcohol is added to the vanilla beans. Most use what is called a double fold proportion—26.7 oz. of vanilla bean to one gallon of alcohol. A double fold extract containing 35% alcohol could be used except that all recipes are based on single fold concentrated vanilla. A single fold concentration is obtained by diluting the double fold concentration in half with water. At this point the vanilla contains 19% alcohol. Since the legal definition of an extract stipulates 35% alcohol, most companies add extra alcohol to reach 35%. Some companies make a vanilla with no added alcohol but, because it contains only 19% alcohol, it must be labeled as pure vanilla *flavor* instead of pure vanilla **extract**. Less alcohol yields a more concentrated vanilla flavor. Read the label to get the desired concentration of alcohol. The best quality vanilla extracts are free of sugar, caramel coloring, and other additives.

Homemade vanilla extract can also be made with or without alcohol. Soak sliced vanilla beans in brandy or vodka, shaking the bottle once per day for 2 weeks. To make without alcohol, cut a vanilla bean into small pieces, pour 1/4 cup boiling water over the pieces, cover, and let steep overnight. Put the mixture in the blender and blend at medium speed until the pieces are pulverized. Strain through cheesecloth. Return the liquid to the blender and add 1 tablespoon each of honey, sunflower or soy oil, and liquid lecithin. Blend and put the mixture into a tightly capped bottle. Store in the refrigerator.

Another substitute for vanilla extract is to scrape the seeds from 1/4 of a vanilla bean to equal 1 teaspoon vanilla extract. Whole beans can also be added to simmering sauces and puddings, removed, wiped off, and stored for future use. They can be used over and over, as long as the flavor is retained.

Some companies manufacture a non-alcoholic, vegetable oil based solvent to extract flavors such as almond, vanilla, lemon, and peppermint.

Flavor oils are steam distilled except when citrus fruit is used. Steam distilling is done by placing the botanical on a tray and passing it through a pressure steam operation, bursting the cell of the plant. The oil is then separated off. Different plants yield different amounts of oil. Some herbs get a 3-8% yield of oil while barks and woody plants yield only about 1/10 of 1%. Therefore, pure cinnamon bark oil is much more expensive than oil of thyme.

Citrus oils are easily extracted using an expeller press since there is so much oil in the rind. Lime flower oils, unlike orange and lemon, taste better if steam distilled.

Recipes

BOUQUET GARNI

This traditional combination of herbs enhances the flavors of soups, stews, and sauces. Tie fresh sprigs together or add dried herbs to a teaball or reusable cloth teabag in order to easily remove the herbs before serving.

1 bay leaf
2 sprigs fresh or 1 1/2 teaspoon dried parsley
1 sprig fresh or 1 teaspoon dried thyme

HERBED RICE PILAF   *serves 3-4*

Ever wonder how some restaurants make such wonderfully tasting rice? The secret is in the seasoning...

1 cup brown rice
(maybe try rose colored "wehani" rice for something special)
2 cups water
pinch of salt (opt.)
1 TB. sesame oil
1 clove garlic, minced
1/4 teaspoon each: oregano, basil, dill

1. Rinse rice and place in a saucepan with water and salt.
2. Bring to a boil, cover, and reduce heat.
3. Simmer 40 minutes, remove from heat, and let sit, covered for 10 minutes.
4. Add herbs and let sit 15 minutes before serving.

Recipes

DILL-ICIOUS POTATO SALAD   *serves 8*

Dill, parsley, and chives were made for each other. Enjoy them in this special low-fat potato salad which is certain to make a hit.

14 small or 5 large red potatoes
1/2 cup peas, fresh or frozen
4 hard boiled eggs (optional)
1 TB. chopped fresh or 1 teaspoon dried dillweed
1 TB. chopped fresh or 1 teaspoon dried parsley
1 TB. chopped fresh or 1 teaspoon dried chives
4 green onions, thinly sliced
1/2 cucumber, chopped
1/3 cup plain yogurt
2 TB. lemon juice
1/2 teaspoon salt

1. Cut unpeeled potatoes in 1" chunks and steam until just tender.
2. Lightly steam fresh peas or thaw frozen peas.
3. Combine with rest of ingredients and let chill for at least 2 hours before serving to let flavors mingle.

ANNEMARIE'S APPLEJUICE PUDDING   *serves 3-4*

Some men pride themselves on their ability to make pancakes. My husband, Terry, is our resident "pudding chef." Inspired by Annemarie Colbin, natural gourmet cook and author of two excellent books: *The Book of Whole Meals* and *Food and Healing*, this recipe is quick and easy enough to make during a "midnight food raid." Good hot or cold.

3 cups apple juice
1 cup water
2 TB. sesame tahini (hulled sesame butter)
1/3-1/2 cup kuzu (Japanese arrowroot)
2 teaspoons vanilla extract

1. Dissolve kuzu in 1 cup of water.
2. Mix with juice and vanilla and cook over medium heat, stirring constantly.
3. When mixture becomes thick and creamy, slowly add tahini and stir 1 minute more.
4. Remove from heat. Serve hot or cold.

9

SWEET THINGS

SWEETENERS

Often the first step people use as a transition towards a better diet is to replace white sugar as a sweetener with honey. Since many believe honey is so good for them, they use it liberally in and on *everything*. Honey, however, is a concentrated sweetener which, like all sweeteners, can affect blood sugar levels adversely.

The preference for sweet flavors seems to be innate. Many foods besides sweeteners, namely, root vegetables, fruits, fruit juices, cashews, and grains can provide sweet flavors as well as nutrients. But, let's face it, the thought of steamed carrots bedecked with birthday candles instead of a cake loses something in the translation. The biggest problem with sweeteners is not so much the sweeteners themselves, but their out-of-proportional use in some people's diets. This imbalance crowds out the nutrients available in foods that could have been eaten instead. Chronic behavior problems, "addictions" to sweets, depression, reduced attention span, etc. are now seen to be connected with simple, sometimes even marginal, malnutrition. Sweets should be used as occasional treats eaten in moderation rather than as a regularly occuring reward for eating a nutritious meal, surviving yet another day, suffering a letdown, or as a means to help alleviate boredom. Experimenting with new foods, finding nutritious foods that can be eaten "on the run", and finding other psychological outlets besides food can help bring nutrients back into balance.

The fact remains, however, that some people may indeed be more sensitive to certain sweeteners than others and that some blood sugar abnormalities do exist. Medical advice needs to be followed for certain conditions such as diabetes. In non-threatening conditions, the personal experience of how the person *himself* reacts to certain sweeteners can lead one to prefer one type over another.

Reviewing the different types of sweeteners will show that a few are slightly better than others but moderation is needed no matter which is used. Although all are processed to some degree and none can be considered to be a rich source of nutrients, preferred sweeteners still contain some "whole food" aspect.

"Sugars" occur naturally in many foods: fruit contains both fructose and sucrose molecules, milk contains lactose, maltose is present in sprouted grains. When sugars are isolated and concentrated from the accompanying food components which slow down absorption or help with digestion, the body can experience a sweetener overload. How fast and how high the blood glucose rises with a particular kind of sweetener and how quickly the body responds by bringing it back to normal is another very important indicator. The ultimate goal is flavor with the least amount of negative impact on the body.

White table sugar is a highly refined product made from sugar cane or sugar beets. In their original state, both sources are nutritious foods and contain 16-20% sucrose. During processing into sugar, however, fiber, vitamins, minerals, amino acids, and trace elements are stripped leaving a substance that is 99% pure crystalline sucrose. Since refined sugar is lacking in fiber, it gets absorbed too quickly causing the pancreas and adrenal glands to overreact to the excess sugar in the blood by lowering the blood sugar too much. This is the "let down", fatigue, and irritability people experience after eating or drinking something too sweet, resulting in what is often called "reactive hypoglycemia". The next urge is to eat something sweet in order to raise the blood sugar level, thus starting the cycle over again. Refined sugar contains no nutrients other than carbohydrate, but requires some vitamins and minerals to be metabolized. Therefore, it takes nutrients away from the body's other needs such as cell growth, protein synthesis, etc.

The sale of **raw sugar** has been banned by the FDA for quite some time because of contaminants such as fibers, yeast, soil, molds, lints, and waxes. Containing about 96% sucrose, it is the raw product that comes from the sugar mill just before refining.

Turbinado sugar is not much better than white table sugar with its 95-97% sucrose level. It has gone through the same refining just short of the final extraction of the molasses.

Brown sugar is white sugar with more molasses added back to it than was originally taken out. It is 93.8% sucrose.

Molasses is a by product of sugar refining. Toward the end of the sugar refining process, a final extraction is made resulting in blackstrap molasses. Unlike other types of sweeteners, it is significantly high in minerals. One tablespoon contains 137 mg. of calcium, 4.42 mg. of iron, and 585 mg. of potassium. Do not use this as a reason to eat it by the tablespoonful as a supplement, however. Its sticky adherence to teeth make it a dentist's nightmare. Use it only in baking and cooking. Molasses has a strong, distinct flavor and has half the sweetening power of white sugar with a 55-65% sucrose level.
Despite its nutrient value, molasses results from the final extraction of sugar refining and therefore can contain all of the residues from chemicals used in growing and refining the sugar.

Barbados molasses or **unsulphured molasses** is not a by-product, but is manufactured for the molasses itself. Sugar cane stalks are crushed in roller mills to extract the juice. The juice is then filtered and slowly boiled down to a syrup. Barbados molasses has a mellow, light flavor with fewer nutrients than blackstrap, but on the positive side, less chemical residue. One tablespoon of medium molasses contains 49 mg. of calcium, 1 mg. of iron, and 213 mg. of potassium. (Again, use it in baking and cooking and not straight off the spoon.) Look for unsulphured molasses to avoid sulphur dioxide which can cause severe reactions in sensitive individuals, ranging from nausea to difficulty in breathing.

Sorghum molasses or syrup is from the boiled down juice of the sweet sorghum plant, a cereal grain. It tastes similar to molasses but has a lighter, tart, more fruity flavor. Sorghum is 65% sucrose and contains 35 mg. of calcium and 2.6 mg. of iron per tablespoon.

Cane sugar syrup is made from sugar cane processed similar to barbados and sorghum molasses. Its nutrient content is also similar to them.

Fructose is a highly refined product which is not made from fruit, despite what many people assume. Granular fructose is made by chemically splitting sucrose into its simple sugars— glucose and fructose, and then isolating and purifying the fructose. Liquid fructose (high fructose corn syrup) is made by treating corn syrup with enzymes to convert some of its starch to fructose. Fructose has no nutrient value but is popular because it is absorbed more slowly than sucrose and does not require insulin from the pancreas for its assimilation in the body, thus being easier to metabolize.

The only problem is that there are different concentrations of fructose— pure fructose, 90% fructose, and 55% fructose-high fructose corn syrup (which can contain a high percentage of glucose and thus need insulin to be metabolized), and yet all are labeled as "fructose". This could be a serious problem for those with diabetes or hypoglycemia who are depending upon a product that does not involve insulin.

Fructose is about *60% sweeter than* white table sugar, so only half the amount is needed to achieve the same sweetening power as sugar. Its sweetening power is greatly reduced when used in cooking, so best results occur with recipes specifically formulated with fructose in mind rather than substituting it in a family favorite recipe.

Fructose tends to be converted into fat rather than glycogen (stored form of glucose in liver and muscle cells) which, in turn, contributes to high levels of fat in the blood. Therefore, the use of too much fructose may lead to elevated triglyceride levels in the bloodstream and increase the risk of arteriosclerosis or hardening of the arteries.

Corn syrup is commercial glucose from chemically purified cornstarch with everything removed except the starch. An acid enzyme treatment yields a crystal clear flavorless syrup. Most corn syrup sold also contains added sugar syrup since pure glucose is only half as sweet as sugar. Corn syrup is a highly refined cheap sweetener is absorbed into the bloodstream very quickly, often causing too quick and high an elevation of blood sugar.

Maple syrup sap straight from the tree consists of 2-3% sucrose, but by the time it is fully processed, maple syrup contains 65% sucrose. Forty gallons of sap are boiled down to make 1 gallon of syrup. Some producers may use formaldehyde pellets to prevent the tap holes in the tree from healing and use polyvinylchloride tubing to a main collector or use vacuum pumps to suck the sap from the trees. (Vermont has banned the use of pellets by its state's producers.) Chemical antifoamers and mold inhibitors can also be added. Fortunately, good brands combining traditional and modern techniques are more the norm.

The previous quality standard classifications of Grades A, B, and C have been changed into 2 categories: Grade C has been retained and Grades A and B have been combined into the Grade A classification. Grades A & B have a delicate flavor and light amber color while stronger flavored Grade C is thick and dark and contains more minerals. Maple syrup is about 60% as sweet as white table sugar.

Products labeled simply as "pancake syrup" contain no more than 2-3% real maple syrup (if any!) with corn syrup or sugar syrup and artificial flavoring and coloring making up the balance.

Maple sugar is crystallized maple syrup concentrated to 93% solids.

Honey is refined by bees instead of man. Bees collect nectar which is primarily sucrose and transform it with enzymes in their stomach into glucose and fructose. All we need to do is extract it from the comb. Good quality honey is strained and heated only to remove beeswax and parts of the bees. Some honey producers overheat the honey to facilitate packing and prevent crystallization and then proceed to overfilter it in order to produce a crystal clear product. Overprocessing ruins the flavor and removes the bee pollen from the honey. When buying honey, look for somewhat cloudy honey that is uncooked. Raw honey has a tendency to crystalize. If this happens, simply place it in a pan of lukewarm water to restore it to a liquid state.

Honey ranges from *20-60% sweeter than* white sugar, so a little should go a long way, although most recipes call for quite a large amount. In fact, many honey sweetened products send the blood sugar reeling much more than those sweetened with white table sugar! The type of sugar in honey depends on the bees' source of pollen and the particular batch of honey. In general, honey is approximately 38% fructose, 31% glucose, 18% water, and 2% sucrose. The flavors also vary according to the flower source, i.e., buckwheat honey is strong while orange blossom and clover are known for their mild flavor.

NOTE: Honey can transmit infant botulism, so it should *not* be given to a child under 1 year of age.

Barley malt syrup is available in two varieties: 100% barley malt syrup and 60% barley/40% corn malt syrup. The barley is soaked and sprouted which changes the starch into primarily maltose and some glucose. The sprouts are dried, mixed with water, and cooked slowly until a syrup is produced. Since barley malt is only 40% as sweet as white sugar and still contains some complex carbohydrates, the "sugar punch" has a more reduced impact than any of the sweeteners. However, when corn syrup is combined with barley malt, the percentage jumps back up to 70% as sweet as white sugar. Barley malt has a strong, although pleasant flavor that is delicious in baked beans, cookies, and other baked goods. In general, use as you would molasses. The majority of manufacturers of "natural" breakfast cereals are using barley malt to impart a mild, sweetening free of the cloying aftertaste and intense sweetness of honey.

Rice syrup contains 45% maltose, 3% glucose, and 50% complex carbohydrates. **Rice malt syrup** is made from traditional methods by adding dried sprouted barley (malt) to cooked rice. The rice is cultured until the enzymes from the malt have transformed the starches of the rice into maltose and easily digested complex carbohydrates. It is then strained and cooked to yield a delicious sweetener with a slight barley flavor. Consistencies vary. Some rice malts are extremely thick while others have been developed to pour like honey. Many rice malt syrups are imported and somewhat more expensive, but are definitely a unique product different in manufacture and flavor than enzyme-treated rice syrups.

Enzyme-treated rice syrups are made by using enzymes *extracted* from sprouted barley rather than adding the sprouted barley directly to the cooked rice. With the ability to now control the amount and type of enzymes, the manufacturer can create different types of rice syrups according to the specifications of the various companies who contract his work. Even though rice malt syrup involves more of a whole food process, the lower price of domestically produced rice syrups make them quite attractive. Rice syrup is generally sweeter than rice malt syrup because of its higher glucose content. No residues of barley malt enzymes remain in the product so rice syrup has a mild, almost butterscotch-like flavor.

Both rice malt syrup and rice syrup are similar in sweetening power as barley malt and, therefore, are much less sweet than white table sugar and honey. Nonetheless, try substituting rice syrup in equal amounts required for other sweeteners. Many people prefer its sweet, subtle nature.

Date sugar is made from ground, dehydrated dates and can be used like brown sugar. It will contain virtually the same nutrient values as dried dates. Even so, date sugar must be used in moderation since it is almost as sweet as white sugar. To use in baking, enough hot water should be added to date sugar to make a syrup in order to prevent burning. If date sugar is to be sprinkled on coffee cakes or baked dessert toppings similar to brown sugar, it should be added after baking to avoid burning. Use to sweeten fruit salads, cereals, quick breads, muffins, and cakes.

Amasake is a whole grain sweetener made by adding koji (cultured brown rice) to a cooked rice. After an incubation period, the koji reacts with the grain's starch, transforming it into primarily maltose and glucose, making it sweet and easy to digest. The thick "pudding" is blended for a smooth consistency and used as a sweetener, as a leavener in breads and muffins, the base for creamy puddings or pies, or diluted with water for a delicious beverage similar to a malt or shake. Diluted amasake can also be used instead of milk on cereals. Amasake can be made at home or purchased in small quantities ready to use straight or diluted, depending upon its use. Amasake "malteds" also available fresh or frozen in plain, carob, and almond flavors for an incredible creamy, dairy-free, soy-free malt-like treat.

Fruit juices, purees, and dried fruits are very sweet and can easily function as a sweetener in baking. **Fruit juice concentrates**, fruit juices with the water removed, are being used commercially as sweeteners in cookies, breakfast cereals, and syrups. Most commonly used are concentrates from pineapple, pear, peach, and apple. Fresh, undiluted fruit juice is very sweet; fruit juice concentrate is *extremely* sweet. To find out how sweet, just taste a spoonful of frozen juice concentrate at home before adding the water. Fruit juice concentrate contains mainly sucrose with some fructose. Although less processed than some sweeteners and probably containing some of the original nutrients from the fruit that survived the processing, fruit juice concentrates can be up to 2/3 as sweet as white table sugar. Apple juice concentrate is less sweet than most of the other fruit juice concentrates.

Aspartame (Nutrasweet, Equal) is a sugar substitute made by combining 2 amino acids; phenylalanine and aspartic acid. It is 200 times sweeter than sugar, non-caloric, and free of the bitter aftertaste of saccharin, an artificial sweetener shown to be carcinogenic that is scheduled to be banned in 1987. Aspartame breaks down into its original amino acids when it is baked or cooked in products. However, aspartame can be added shortly before foods are finished cooking. Aspartame was approved for use in dry food in 1981 and for soft drinks since 1983 despite claims that the testings done on aspartame were sloppy and unscientific. People with the genetic disorder, phenylketanuria (PKU), can experience seizures and mental retardation when given foods high in phenylalanine (hence the PKU warning labels on aspartame sweetened products). Some scientists believe that the isolation of the amino acids, especially phenylalanine in high doses can affect the balance of anyone's two major neurotransmitters in the brain, serotonin and the catechol-amines, chemical messengers that control moods, thinking, and behavior. Headaches, depression, seizures, mood swings, high blood pressure, insomnia, and behavior and appetite problems could be the result. "Nutrasweet" is used in so many products such as cereals, candy, snacks, yogurt, and soft drinks, that it is fairly easy to use too much. The two highest risk groups are unborn fetuses and children under 6. In response to several consumers' groups demanding that the FDA hold public hearings on the use of aspartame in soft drinks due to inadequate testing, the U. S. Circuit Court of Appeals for the District of Columbia affirmed the FDA's approval in September, 1985. Many still question long term effects of increasingly common high doses of aspartame. Use sparingly if at all.

Mannitol is derived from corn glucose and is 65% as sweet as sugar. It is not fully absorbed in the intestines and therefore can cause diarrhea in some people, especially children.

Sorbitol is also from corn glucose and is 60% as sweet as sugar. Because of its slow absorption rate and because it needs little, if any, insulin, it is a common sweetening agent in diabetic foods. Sorbitol also does not promote tooth decay. Like mannitol, it is not fully absorbed in the intestines and can cause diarrhea.

Xylitol is a Finnish import derived from birchwood chips. It has been shown to reduce cavities by neutralizing the acids in the mouth that demineralize tooth enamel. It is as sweet as fructose and is used mainly in sugarless chewing gums. An English study in 1977 brought up the possibility of Xylitol causing bladder tumors. However, subsequent tests have revealed that the problem was inherent in the rats themselves and the product appears safe for humans.

Sucanat is a natural sweetener made from dried granulated cane juice. In fact, its name is derived from the words "sugar cane natural." A traditional sweetener used for hundreds of years in areas where sugar cane is grown, the manufacture of Sucanat was perfected about 20 years ago by a Swiss pediatrician, Dr. Max Henri-Beguin, to provide a natural "whole food" alternative to white sugar for his patients. Nothing is added; only water is removed. The natural complex sugars and all the molasses are still retained and, unlike refined sugars, Sucanat contains up to 3% vitamins and minerals. Since any pesticides and herbicides used on sugar cane are concentrated during the processing of sugar, Sucanat is made only from organically grown sugar cane that is certiifed to be free of chemical residues.

Use equal amounts of Sucanat as required in recipes using white sugar.

The following chart shows how to convert a recipe from white sugar to an alternate sweetener. The amounts are equivalent in sweetening power to one cup of sugar. Remember that these can *easily* be reduced.

SWEETENERS EQUIVALENT TO 1 CUP WHITE SUGAR

SWEETENER	AMOUNT	LIQUID REDUCTION NEEDED
honey	1/2 cup	1/4 cup
maple syrup	1/2-2/3 cup	1/4 cup
molasses	1/2 cup	1/4 cup
malt syrup	1-1 1/4 cup	1/4 cup
crystalline fructose	1/3-2/3 cup	——
date sugar	2/3 cup	——
(dissolve in hot water for syrup)		
Sucanat	1 cup	——

Recipes

APPLE CINNAMON COUS-COUS CAKE   *yields 8X8 inch cake*
No flour, no oil, no sugar! Everyone will love it!

1 1/4 cup cous-cous
2 cups apple juice
1 cup water
pinch of salt
1 tsp. ground cinnamon
1/2 cup chopped roasted walnuts
1/2 tsp. vanilla

1. Bring juice, water, and salt to a boil.
2. Add cous-cous and cinnamon.
3. Stir and adjust heat to low.
4. Simmer 10 minutes.
5. Remove pan from heat.
6. Add walnuts and vanilla and let sit another 10 minutes.
7. Rinse an 8X8 inch baking dish or mold with water. Do not dry.
8. Add cous-cous mixture and pack down.
9. Let cool before cutting into squares or inverting onto a serving platter.

NOTE: Refrigerate leftovers (if there are any!)

OATMEAL COOKIES   *yields 2 dozen cookies*
Rice syrup gives a delicious, subtle sweet flavor to an old family favorite, but feel free to
substitute 1/2 cup maple syrup or honey instead.

3 cups rolled oats
1 1/2 cup whole wheat pastry flour
pinch of salt
1 cup roasted walnuts
1/4 cup raisins
1/2 cup safflower oil
1/2-3/4 cup rice syrup, honey, or maple syrup
1 tsp. vanilla
1/3 cup water

1. Preheat oven to 350°.
2. Mix dry ingredients together in a large mixing bowl.
3. Mix liquid ingredients separately and then add to dry ingredients in the mixing bowl.
   Mixture will be stiff.
4. Wet hands. Make walnut size balls and flatten into 2 1/2 inch diameters.
5. Place on an oiled cookie sheet and bake 15 minutes.
6. Turn over cookies and bake another 10 minutes until lightly browned.

Recipes

PUMPKIN CREME PIE WITH PECAN TOPPING

This recipe, created by Eden Foods to highlight their amasake and barley malt, combines the best of two famous holiday pies.

1 prepared pie crust
1 cup soymilk or whole milk
1 TB. agar flakes
2 cups cooked pumpkin puree
8 oz. thick amasake (1 package) or make homemade
1/2 teaspoon vanilla extract
1/8 teaspoon salt
1/4 teaspoon ground nutmeg
1/8 teaspoon cinnamon

Pecan Topping:
2 cups pecan halves
1/3 cup barley malt
2 TB. corn oil
1/4 teaspoon salt
1 TB. orange rind

1. Preheat oven to 350°.
2. Bake pie crust for 8 minutes and then remove from oven.
3. Increase oven temperature to 425° in preparation for baking the pie.
4. Combine agar flakes with soymilk or milk in a saucepan and simmer for 5-8 minutes until dissolved. Stir frequently.
5. In a food processor or blender, blend pumpkin, amasake, vanilla, salt, spices and soymilk mixture.
6. Pour into prebaked crust.
7. Combine pecan topping ingredients together and spoon carefully over the top of the pie.
8. Bake pie at 425° for 20 minutes.
9. Turn heat down to 350° and bake for another 20 minutes.
10. Cool for 4 hours before serving. If desired, reheat 15 minutes before serving.

SNACK FOODS

We're a nation of snackers. Parties, clubs, TV, movies...all seem to involve some type of snack. Busy lifestyles are often fueled almost exclusively by a quick "this or that" eaten on the run. In fact, the average teenager consumes 1/4 of his/her total kilocalorie intake from snacks. Since snacks are an important part of our lives, it is important to choose the best quality and, for the majority of our snacks, the ones most dense in nutrients. "Fun" foods that are lower on the nutrition scale are best eaten only occasionally. Quality standards vary even for the "fun" foods. Look for those that are at least chemical-free.

Snack items such as **chips** are often labeled as "natural" if they are free of preservatives. It is common knowledge that eating a plain potato is more nutritious than eating potato chips. The biggest difference involves the amount of fat that is added during processing. While 1 large baked potato has only .2 grams of fat, after being fried in oil, 10 potato chips end up with 8 grams of fat, constituting 62% of its calories!

Some manufacturers have tried various methods to produce a more healthy chip from the use of retaining the potato skins to making the chips in small, limited run batches. Consumers can also choose to avoid chips that are fried in highly saturated coconut or palm oil as well as those fried in hydrogenated oils. High amounts of sodium can be avoided by buying unsalted chips. Even though large bags of chips are often the best buy for the money, 1 oz. bags are the best buy for health. Not many people have the will power to eat just a couple chips from a large bag. An 8 oz. bag of chips has between 50-80 grams of fat compared to 10 grams of fat in a 1 oz. bag. The smaller bags are not only satisfying but are helpful guides to moderation.

Ice cream...what would birthday parties or summer days be without it? There is an enormous quality difference in the ice creams that are sold in the world. A federal law passed in 1979 indicates that ice cream manufacturers have a choice whether to list specific artificial colors and flavors on the label. There are chemicals to thicken, chemicals to stabilize, chemicals to replace cream, and chemicals to preserve it. Some brands are 50% air. A half gallon of high quality ice cream with 33% air will weigh 3 pounds. A brand with 50% air will weigh 2-1/4 pounds. Therefore, the more an ice cream weighs, the less air and more substance it will contain.

Natural and gourmet brands, pride themselves in using only the traditional basic ingredients: cream, milk, whole eggs, honey or sugar, and natural flavorings with no additives. Some varieties are even made without eggs. Nonetheless, ice cream is best used in moderation. Besides the high amount of sweeteners, a 4 oz. serving of ice cream contains between 10-20 grams of saturated fat, contributing to 50-65% of its calories.

Frozen yogurt has a consistency similar to "soft-serve" ice cream, but unlike most of the commercial "soft-serves" which contain mainly gums and stabilizers and little, if any, milk, frozen yogurt is a good, low fat source of calcium. Depending upon the brand, frozen yogurt can also be quite high in sugar and chemical additives and stabilizers. Read labels to choose one of the better alternatives. Most frozen yogurt does not contain live yogurt cultures and therefore should not replace regular yogurt with live cultures that can help replace the "friendly bacteria" in the colon.

Allergic to milk? **Soy ice cream** production increased 600% from 1983-1985. Nationwide marketing was originated by a vegetarian community, The Farm, after they devised a way to transform their honey sweetened soymilk into a frozen dessert called "Ice Bean". Since then many other brands have become available. Its popularity stems from being a non-dairy, non-egg frozen dessert that contains less calories. Soy ice cream contains the same amount of fat as ice cream; however, only 15% of the fat is saturated as compared with the 50-65% saturated fat in many milk based ice creams. Since it contains no animal based fat, soy ice cream is free of cholesterol and lactose. Sweeteners used vary among honey, fructose, or sugar.

"Tofu" soy ice creams also contain the same (or even more in some varieties) amount of fat and calories as regular ice cream but the fat is primarily unsaturated and cholesterol-free. These frozen desserts are highly processed with fairly complex ingredients. Water, high fructose corn sweetener, oil, isolated soy protein, lecithin, vegetable gums, flavorings, salt, and *very little tofu* are used to obtain a creamy consistency and sweet flavor.

Another non-dairy, but also soy-free frozen dessert is **Rice Dream**, a sweet creamy dessert made from a modified type of amasake, a sweet, rich, non-dairy milk made from brown rice. Because the much of the starch is converted into primarily maltose and glucose during the culturing of the rice, Rice Dream contains no extra sweeteners. Unrefined safflower oil, vegetable based stabilizers, and natural flavors make up the rest of the ingredient listing. With flavors ranging from traditional vanilla to the exotic, a 4 oz. serving of Rice Dream has only 5 grams of fat and no cholesterol.

Amasake "malteds" are creamy, dairy-free, soy-free thick beverages made from diluting thick amasake, the cultured rice drink (see Rice Dream). Amasake "malteds" are also available fresh or frozen in plain, carob, and almond flavors. An 8 oz. serving contains 150 kilocalories for the plain amasake and up to 250 kilocalories for the almond variety.

Sorbet is fat free and relatively low in calories. Although often a concoction of sugar, water, and flavoring, a healthy alternative that offers much more nutrition is one that is based on fruit and fruit juices, water, and fruit pectin.

Frozen fruit juice bars are a nutritious alternative to popsicles. Some varieties also contain some sugar and vegetable gums for a creamy consistency.

CANDY AND COOKIES

One of the easiest ways to introduce a healthier mode of eating can be, oddly enough, through desserts and snacks. Almost all children and adults enjoy something sweet at least occasionally. A favorite cake or cookie recipe can be transformed into a more wholesome dessert by substituting bleached refined flour and sugar with whole grain flour and a less refined sweetener. As you and/or your family becomes accustomed to the texture and flavor differences of desserts, you can then gradually transform your main course family favorites. Make it a painless, enjoyable transition!

Commercial ready made treats fill the gaps for those unable to prepare their own home made snacks. Although most homemade recipes use basic ingredients such as flour, water, milk, salt, spices, and sweetener, many commercial products contain artificial colors, preservatives, flavors, and additives to "improve" textures. The words "natural," "old fashioned," or "homestyle" are as enticing as the beautiful packaging which connotates simpler lifestyles and ingredients. However, a close look at the ingredients label will often reveal that the "purity" implied is quite the opposite in reality.

Look for candy and cookies that contain no artificial colors, flavors, additives, or preservatives. Even these should be eaten in moderation since most of them are equal to traditional candies in regard to calories, fat, and, especially, sugar, despite the kind of "sugar" used.

Don't always look for the word "sugar" on a label to determine the total sugar content of a product. Although food labels must list the ingredients in order from highest proportion to the least used, sugar content is generally split into its individual components. Thus, a label may list 4 or 5 different types of sugar in one product. Even if a product consists of primarily sugar when analyzed as a whole, it may not seem so obvious when a sugar is not listed as the most prominent ingredient.

Coconut oil and palm kernel oil are frequently seen on labels. Coconut oil and palm kernel oil resist rancidity, are solid at room temperature, and contribute richness and texture to many "natural" and traditional candies. Their presence can make the difference between a carob coating remaining on the candy and one that melts on one's hand. Unlike most vegetable oils which are high in polyunsaturated fat, both coconut oil and palm kernel oil contain as much saturated fat as lard. "Fractionated" palm kernel oil is even more highly saturated. When manufacturers fractionate the oil, they separate the less saturated fat from the more saturated "fractions". Better sources of fats include nuts, nut butters, and unrefined vegetable oils— all in small amounts.

Say "chocolate" and many people automatically think "carob". **Carob**, a delicious alternative to chocolate, is made from the dried, roasted, and pulverized pod of the honey locust tree that grows primarily in Mediterranean countries. Some people believe that the Bible story about the "honey and locusts" that John the Baptist ate during his time in the desert were actually carob pods; hence the origin of the carob tree's nickname: St. John's Bread tree.

Carob contains all the positive aspects of chocolate and few of the negatives. Chocolate contains small amounts of caffeine and a similar stimulant called theobromine. Additionally, chocolate is a common allergen, highly sweetened to counteract its naturally bitter flavor, and high in fat.

In contrast, powdered carob is free of caffeine and has only 3 mg. of theobromine in 100 grams of carob instead of the 2320 mg. of theobromine found in 100 grams of chocolate. Carob is easily digested, and high in fiber and pectin. It has its own natural sweetness, and contains only 2.0 grams of fat per cup while the same amount of cocoa powder contains 10.8 grams of fat. An extra bonus is carob's high calcium content: 390 mg. of calcium per 1 cup in contrast to 124 mg. of calcium per 1 cup of cocoa powder.

Carob can be substituted equally for cocoa in recipes, including beverages, cakes, and candies. Because of its high fiber content it can impart a grainy texture unless blended very thoroughly. Use 3 TB. carob plus 1 TB. milk to equal 1 square of baking chocolate in a recipe.

Although carob coatings on candies are delicious unsweetened, some companies sweeten the carob with dates or sugar. Most often palm kernel oil, a highly saturated vegetable fat, is also added for smooth texture and better coating qualities. As a result, the extra sweetener and saturated fat raise the calorie, carbohydrate, and fat levels of the carob coated candies to that of their chocolate counterparts.

Nonetheless, carob still comes out ahead, especially when used in its natural form with little or no added fats or sugars. Carob candies can be a delicious introduction; then try carob powder in your baking and homemade snacks.

The criteria for a high quality **chocolate** includes the source of cocoa bean, the percentage of butterfat from cocoa butter, the roasting method, the time and temperature used during conching (the process of developing the chocolate's flavor and texture), and the addition of flavorings and additives.

The finest, most flavorful cocoa beans from South America are high in cocoa butter content in contrast with lower quality beans from Africa which have vegetable fats or waxes added to raise the fat content. **Cocoa butter** delivers a better "mouth feel" in chocolates because of its melting properties. It melts a few degrees below body temperature, allowing the chocolate to dissolve gradually and the flavor to develop slowly.

Bitter or baking chocolate is unsweetened, hardened chocolate liquor, the solid chocolate obtained from refining the cocoa beans of which 50-58% is cocoa butter.

Bittersweet chocolate contains at least 35% pure chocolate liquor, cocoa butter, and added sugar.

Semi-sweet chocolate contains at least 35% chocolate liquor, 27% cocoa butter, more sugar than bittersweet chocolate, and flavorings such as vanilla or vanillin.

Milk chocolate is made from adding at least 12% milk solids to sweetened chocolate which can include as little as 10% chocolate liquor.

White chocolate contains no chocolate liquor so technically it is not chocolate. It consists of cocoa butter or cheaper fats, sugar, milk solids, and flavoring.

Unsweetened cocoa powder is the portion of chocolate liquor that remains after most of the cocoa butter is removed.

Cocoa (medium fat), the most popular type manufactured, has from 10-22% cocoa butter.

Dutch process cocoa is treated with a mild alkali like baking soda to neutralize the natural acids, modify the flavor, and darken the color.

The best quality chocolates are free of preservatives and artificial flavors.

Recipes

CAROB FROSTING
covers 1 layer cake

Try this frosting to cover that special cake!

1/3 cup carob powder
1 teaspoon agar flakes (sea vegetable thickener)
1/4 teaspoon salt
1/3 cup sesame tahini (hulled sesame butter)
1 teaspoon arrowroot
3 TB. flour
1 cup water
1/3 cup honey or rice syrup
2 teaspoon vanilla

1. Combine all ingredients except the vanilla in a saucepan.
2. Bring to a boil while stirring constantly.
3. Reduce the heat and simmer for 5 minutes. Stir frequently.
4. Remove from heat and add vanilla.
5. Let cool and whip in a blender or food processor until smooth.
6. Refrigerate 1 hour before spreading on cake.

CAROB BROWNIES
makes 8" square pan

Fudgy brownies...yum! Make them now and top with carob frosting.

1/2 cup sesame oil
2/3 cup honey or rice syrup
2 eggs
1 teaspoon vanilla extract
2 teaspoons "grain" coffee substitute.
1/2 cup whole wheat pastry flour
pinch of salt
1/2 cup carob powder
1/2 cup chopped walnuts or pecans

1. Preheat the oven to 350°.
2. Cream together the oil, honey, eggs, vanilla, and coffee substitute.
3. Combine the flour, carob, and salt.
4. Stir in the "wet" ingredients with the "dry".
5. Add nuts.
6. Oil an 8 X 8" pan and spread evenly with the batter.
7. Bake for 30 minutes or until an inserted knife or toothpick comes out clean.
8. Cool 10 minutes before removing from the pan.
9. Top with carob frosting and serve.

Recipes

ALMOND QUICKS
Quick to make! Quick to disappear!

1 cup raisins
1 cup roasted almonds
1 teaspoon vanilla
apple juice
coconut (opt.)
carob powder (opt.)

1. Using a food processor or blender, grind raisins, almonds, and vanilla together moistened with just enough apple juice to facilitate grinding.
2. Form mixture into small balls.
3. Roll in coconut or carob powder if desired.
4. Chill for best results, but go ahead and eat them right away if you can't resist!

FROZEN BANANA POPS   *makes 8*
Frozen bananas are a great substitute for ice cream. Roll them in carob powder and nuts for a frozen treat that more than surpasses any chocolate-covered ice cream bar.

2 TB. hot water
1/3 cup carob powder
2 teaspoons honey or rice syrup
4 bananas, peeled and cut in half horizontally
1/2 cup finely chopped peanuts or walnuts

8 ice cream sticks

1. Stir hot water into carob until a thick, smooth consistency is reached. Add more water or carob as needed for a thick syrup—not too thin and yet not too pasty.
2. Add honey or rice syrup to taste.
3. Insert an ice cream stick into each banana half and dip into syrup to coat completely.
4. Roll in nuts.
5. Place coated bananas on foil and freeze.
6. When hard, wrap completely and return to the freezer until ready to eat.

Recipes

CRISPY RICE TREATS   *makes 8 X 8" square pan*

A more nutritious version of the traditional marshmallow treats many of us devoured as children. Although obviously not the same recipe, these treats are just as rich and even more delicious.

1 TB. sesame oil
1/2 cup honey, maple syrup, or rice syrup
2 TB. peanut butter, almond butter, or sesame tahini
1 teaspoon vanilla extract
1 teaspoon maple syrup
3 cups crispy rice cereal

1. Warm the oil, sweetener, and nut butter over low heat, stirring until blended very well.
2. Remove from heat and stir in the vanilla and maple syrup.
3. Fold in the cereal until completely coated.
4. Spread in a lightly oiled 8" square pan.
5. Cut into squares when almost cooled.

POPPYSEED CAKE   *makes 8 X 8" square pan*

This delicately seasoned cake is one of my favorites. For those who prefer an eggless cake, substitute the tofu for the egg.

1 1/2 cups whole wheat pastry flour
1 cup unbleached white flour
1/4 teaspoon salt
1 TB. baking powder
1/4 cup poppyseeds

1/3 cup sesame oil
1/2 cup rice syrup or honey
1 teaspoon vanilla extract
1/2 cup apple juice
1/2 cup water
1 egg or 4 oz. tofu (1/4 block)

1. Preheat the oven to 350°.
2. Combine the dry ingredients together.
3. Blend "wet" ingredients in a blender or food processor until smooth.
4. Mix the "wet" ingredients with the dry.
5. Pour into an oiled 8 X 8" pan and bake for 45-55 minutes or until an inserted knife or toothpick tests clean.
6. Let cool 10 minutes before removing from the pan.
7. Eat plain or frosted.

JAMS AND JELLIES

What would toast be without jam? How could children develop normally without jelly for their peanut butter sandwiches?!!

All jams and jellies have one common element— the presence of at least some fruit or fruit juice. However, the quality of fruit, sweetener used, and flavor separate the mediocre from the really delicious, more healthy varieties.

Jams and jellies require fruit, acid, pectin, and a sweetener to jell. Pectin is a carbohydrate that is present in most fruits. Fruits high in pectin include tart blackberries, boysenberries, concord grapes, crab apples, cranberries, green gooseberries, logan berries, plums, fresh prunes, quince, red currants, sour guavas, and tart apples. Fruits low in pectin include apricots, blueberries, cherries, figs, peaches, pears, pineapples, raspberries, and strawberries. It is possible to make good jams and jellies from low pectin fruits if they are combined with high pectin fruits or commercial pectin.

In order to jell effectively, jams made with commercial pectin require substantial amount of some type of sugar in addition to the sugar that is already included in the powdered or liquid pectin formulas. The content of most commercial jams and jellies averages 58% sugar and/or inexpensive corn syrup blend. The result is a product that masks the full flavor of the fruit and transforms the jam or jelly merely into a thick sugar product with some fruit flavor. Honey is used to sweeten some jams and jellies. However, its use results in a loosely textured product with a distinctly strong honey flavor. High quality jams and jellies rely upon the fruit itself to carry the flavor.

Two factors determine the amount of natural pectin available from a fruit— the stage of ripening and the processing temperature. Fruit that is almost at its peak of ripeness contains more pectin than underripe or overly ripe fruit. Too much heat destroys the natural pectin.

Perfectly ripe fruit also has the higher acid content that is needed to make a good jam or jelly. Lemon juice or other acids are added if the acid content is too low.

In summary, the best jams and jellies are made from good quality fruit of optimum ripeness for best flavor and pectin. The use of little or no added sweetener allows the full natural fruit flavor to predominate.

Apple sauce and apple butter are the most familiar naturally sweetened spreads, but the list has grown considerably in the past few years. Because the "standard of identity" for jams and jellies specify that sugar be added, naturally sweetened jams and jellies cannot be labeled as a jam or a jelly. The words "spread," "conserve," or "butter" will alert you to products free of sugar, corn syrup or honey. These products are still very sweet, especially the concentrated fruit spreads, so use sparingly (if you can!).

DRIED FRUITS

Dried fruits are a good low-fat alternative snack, concentrated in iron, copper, potassium, fiber, and, in some, beta-carotene, the precursor to vitamin A. Since drying the fruit also concentrates the sugar content to almost 70% by weight, small portions are best. This fact is easier to comprehend considering that it takes 6 pounds of apricots to make 1 pound of dried apricots.

Fruits are dehydrated at about 125° for 24 hours. Even though dried fruits are very sweet, some are sprayed with a honey and water solution to soften, sweeten more, and prevent the dried fruit from turning brown.

Another method to retain moisture and bright colors is to spray the fruit with sulphur dioxide. Since 1959, **sulphites** (sulfur dioxide, sodium sulphate, sodium and potassium bisulphite, and sodium and potassium metabisulphite) have been on the GRAS (Generally Recognized As Safe) list for food, but numerous reports of adverse reactions, including death, have persuaded the FDA to reevaluate. Asthmatics are most sensitive to sulphites, but about 25% of the cases reported occurred in individuals with no known allergies. Symptoms may include nausea, diarrhea, anaphylactic shock, acute asthma attacks, hives, itching, and contact dermatitis.

Sulphites have been banned on fresh fruits and vegetables, but they are still permitted on dried fruits. The FDA requires that dried fruit containing sulphur dioxide be labeled as such on the package, shipping container, and bulk bin. Fortunately, it is possible to avoid sulphites in dried fruits. The unadulterated version may have a leathery texture and dull color but neither affect the excellent flavors. Eat them with or without nuts for a snack or use in cooking.

Dried fruits are especially good when soaked in water for a few hours or overnight. Soaking benefits are two-fold: the fruit is softened and plumped to almost its original size and the soaking water is transformed into a sweet juice. Soaking the fruit also lessens the tendency to overeat the concentrated sugars in the dried fruit. Dried fruit can be a good, satisfying alternative when the selection of fresh fruit is quite low during the winter.

The high concentration of sugars in dried fruit tends to preserve them so although refrigeration is not actually necessary, it still may be a good idea to refrigerate them in hot climates. For best results, store dried fruit in air tight jars or plastic containers to prevent mold and infestation from insects. Occasionally, white crystals will appear on the skin of the fruit, especially on prunes or figs. This is called "sugaring" and is harmless; the natural sugars in the fruit are simply solidifying and crystallizing on the surface.

Some buying tips and suggested uses of dried fruits are listed below.

Apples—when rehydrated may be used in apple pie! Good in trail mixes.

Apricots— Good in trail mixes or fruit compotes. An especially good source of beta-carotene, iron, and fiber.

Banana chips— usually contain a lot of added oil and sugar. Read ingredient labels for ingredients.

Currants— dried currants are usually dried Zantes grapes and are not related to the fresh berries. May be substituted for raisins.

Dates— come in dozens of varieties that differ in moistness. Zahidi, deglet noor, and medjool are popular moist dates. Bread dates are rather dry.

Figs— also vary in moistness. **Black mission figs** are black, very moist, and very sweet. **Calmyrna figs** have a tan color and are drier and less sweet. Figs are an excellent source of fiber and good source of iron.

Papaya— are often dipped in sugar and/or honey. The "unsweetened" variety is soaked in its own juice concentrate to increase sweetness.

Pineapple—are often dipped in sugar and/or honey. The "unsweetened" variety is soaked in its own juice concentrate to increase sweetness. Real, dried, untreated pineapple tends to be sour.

Peaches— somewhat hard to chew when dried. These come to full flavor when soaked. Good sources of fiber and beta-carotene and excellent sources of iron.

Pears— One of the sweetest dried fruits and best source of fiber. Good source of iron.

Prunes— long familiar for their laxative properties are actually a type of dried plum. Good source of beta-carotene and iron.

Raisins— the most popular dried fruit are mainly available in 2 varieties, **Thompson** and **monukka**. Thompsons are seedless while monukkas are a large plump raisin with tiny edible seeds inside. Although Thompson raisins are more common, many prefer the flavor of monukkas. **Golden raisins** are Thompson raisins treated with sulphur dioxide. Raisins are a good source of iron.

NOTE: By law, all imported fruit must be fumigated. Buy domestic, untreated dried fruits, organic when available for best nutrition.

Recipes

DRIED APRICOT PIE   *yields 1   9-inch pie*
An unusual crust and unusual filling make this an exciting, delicious treat.

Crust
2 cups apple juice
1 cup water
pinch of salt
1 1/2 cups cous cous

1. Combine juice, water, and salt in medium saucepan. Bring to a boil.
2. Stir in cous cous.
3. Reduce heat to low and simmer 10 minutes or until cous cous absorbs all the liquid.
4. Remove from heat and let sit 10 minutes.
5. Rinse a 9-inch pie plate with water. Do not dry.
6. Press cous cous mixture into pie plate to form a crust. Let cool.

Filling
2 cups dried apricots
2 cups water
pinch of salt
1/8 tsp. mace or nutmeg
1/8 tsp. coriander
2 TB. arrowroot, dissolved in 1/4 cup water
1/4 cup roasted walnuts, finely chopped

1. Combine apricots, water, and salt. Bring to a boil.
2. Reduce heat, cover, and simmer 20 minutes or until soft.
3. Add mace, coriander, and arrowroot.
4. Bring to a boil and then turn off heat.
5. Let sit, covered 30-60 minutes.
6. Stir in walnuts.
7. Pour into cooled cous cous crust.
8. Chill and serve.

Recipes

RAISIN BARS   *Yields 8X12 inch pan*

Raisins are so sweet that very little additional sweetener is need in this recipe.
Figs could also be used to make your own fig newtons!

1/2 cup safflower or sesame oil
1/4 cup rice syrup or honey
2 1/3 cup oat or whole wheat flour
2 1/2 cup rolled oats
1 cup raisins
water to cover
1 tsp. vanilla
pinch of salt

1. Bring raisins and water to a boil.
2. Lower flame, and simmer 10 minutes.
3. Puree' mixture.
4. Combine oil and syrup and add to flour and oats.
5. Press 2/3 of oat mixture in an oiled 8X12 inch baking dish.
6. Spread puréed raisins on mixture and crumble rest of oat mixture on top.
7. Bake at 350° for 35-45 minutes.
8. Let cool and cut into squares.

10
BEVERAGES

The body requires a daily supply of fluids to lubricate our joints, regulate the body's temperature, serve as shock absorbers inside the eyes, spinal cord, and in the amniotic sac in pregnancy, and to function as the solvent for minerals, vitamins, amino acids, glucose, and other molecules. Cool and refreshing or hot and soothing, fluids come in many forms, some better than others. The best source is good ol' **water**.

WATER

Although a person could live without food for weeks, the average healthy person can survive only 7-10 days without water. Communities have been built around it and wars have been fought over it. A bigger problem facing us now is not so much where to find it, but how to find water fit enough to drink. Studies made by the Environmental Protection Agency in the 1970's revealed the presence of a great deal of chemical contaminants and high levels of heavy metals in municipal water supplies. These findings led to the **Safe Drinking Water Act in 1974** whose standards limit the amount allowed for 10 chemicals, 6 pesticides, bacteria, radioactivity, and turbidity (cloudiness) based on the amount of each substance that an individual could consume in a lifetime without seemingly adverse health effects, taking into account exposure from other sources. Radioactivity found in surface water is from nuclear power plants, nuclear fuel processing plants, and fallout from atomic explosives. Since long term effects of low level radioactivity are inconclusive as to defining a safe threshold and because radiation in water is only a fraction of what is obtained from all natural sources, the present EPA limits for radiation in drinking water are conservative estimations. Turbidity which results from minute particles suspended in the water can interfere with disinfection and with bacteria testing.

Standards for taste, odor, and appearance are also set but are not enforced nationally. All standards are adjusted periodically as new hazards in source water are found, but considering the potential for existing chemicals to form dangerous compounds, the number of new chemicals that are introduced each year, and the careless disposal of thousands of toxic chemicals used in industry, in homes, and on farms, regulation and testing are no small tasks.

Various chemicals are added to our public water systems in order to reach the minimum standards and now even some of these chemicals have been found to have toxic side effects. Chlorine, used as a disinfectant to rid water of harmful bacteria, has been very successful in eliminating waterborne disease from our public water supply, but when chlorine combines with naturally occurring organic matter, it forms triholomethanes—compounds suspected of causing cancer.

Acute sensitivities to toxic chemicals in drinking water vary among people in severity. Effects may not always be immediate, however. Only long term studies can prove the safety and toxicity of low level exposure and sometimes the information comes too late.

Because of the increased concern for safe drinking water, more and more people have been switching to **bottled water**. Bottled water is hardly a recent phenomenon, however. Spas in both Europe and the United States, famous for the therapeutic health benefits attributed to their waters, began bottling and shipping their waters around the world during the late 19th century. Businesses and homes in arid parts of the country have depended upon bottled water since the turn of the century. Tourists have long been advised to drink only bottled water while traveling abroad. Areas affected by natural or manmade disasters have used bottled water until their usual water source was deemed safe. The use of bottled water, once used on a regular basis by only a small percentage of the population, is now becoming the norm for many.

Other factors besides deteriorating water quality account for the increased demand for bottled water. The taste, odor, and appearance of tap water may not appeal to everyone. The source, mineral content, and processing of the water account for the different aesthetics in the various waters. Natural flavors can originate from the surrounding rock that the water filters through on its way to its destination. For example, the metals in quartz impart a bitter flavor while sulphur-bearing rock gives a "rotten egg" flavor and smell to water. Chlorine and other chemicals used in the purifying process of municipal water can also transmit "off flavors".

Health and fitness goals can also lead to bottled water use. Water, free of calories, sugar, preservatives, and artificial colors is a perfect alternative to both alcohol and soft drink consumption. Athletes are rediscovering the importance of plain water, especially mineral waters, as fluid and electrolyte replacement.

Things to consider when choosing bottled water include its mineral content and pH level.

Mineral content is determined by the presence of **"total dissolved solids"** (TDS). "Total dissolved solids" is what remains after all water is boiled off from a water sample. These results are reported in "parts per million" (ppm) and often listed on the bottle. Preferences vary among people depending upon the amount of minerals they deem beneficial. Mineral waters will test high in total dissolved solids.

The **pH level** of the water is the measurement of the degree of acidity or alkalinity. A pH of 7.0 is neutral. A pH greater than 7.0 is more alkaline while a reading lower than 7.0 is more acidic. Depending upon one's condition, a more alkaline water is generally considered more healthy for the average person. An alkaline water can help balance rich, spicy, and sweet foods by normalizing secretion of gastric juices. Some find its results similar to those of bicarbonate of soda.

So what types of bottled water are available? Bottled water can be classified by use— a basic drinking water or a specialty beverage; by its source— spring, well water, geyser, public water supply, and by the presence of carbonation.

FDA truth in labeling requirements state that for any product to be labeled as **spring water**, its source must be a spring and not tap water. A spring rises to the earth's surface from underground aquifers, emerging under its own pressure or through a bored hole without any pumping assistance. Read labels carefully. A company may include the word "spring" in its name without a real "spring" source of water.

An **artesian well** is a deep water source that bubbles up under its own pressure but depends upon a well drilled to tap the artesian aquifer.

Under the guidelines set by the International Bottled Water Association, the word "**natural**" refers to water that is drawn from a spring, well, geyser, or other source whose mineral content is unaltered. It may be filtered or otherwise treated.

The presence of **carbonation** determines whether a water is considered "sparkling" or "still". A labeling claiming "naturally carbonated" or "naturally sparkling" water indicates water that contains naturally occurring carbonation. In order to prevent the carbon dioxide from dissipating once the water reaches the surface, companies capture the gases (mainly carbon dioxide), bottle the water, and re-inject the carbonation. Labels stating "carbonated natural water" or "sparkling natural water" have carbon dioxide added from a source other than its own. Carbonated waters are subject to the standards set for "soda water" instead of those set for "still" drinking water. FDA regulations for purity and safety still pertain but options include the addition of "safe and suitable" ingredients which, if used, must be listed on the label. Chemical analysis of "soda water" is not required to conform to still water standards since it is believed that the amount of carbonated beverages ingested would be well below the average 2 liter daily intake of still waters used in both drinking and cooking. Therefore, the FDA considers miniscule amounts of naturally occurring minerals in carbonated water as harmless.

Distilled or demineralized water is "pure water" containing no minerals. Its total dissolved solids must be less than 10 ppm resulting from distillation (boiling and steam evaporation of water), demineralization, or reverse osmosis filtering.

Processed drinking water is demineralized, treated tap water that has certain minerals added back that are have been found to give water a pleasant flavor. Total dissolved solids must be less than 500 ppm.

Mineral water contains a spectrum of minerals including bicarbonates, calcium, chlorides, flourides, magnesium, sodium, etc. The minerals can occur naturally in the water or be added by the bottler. Except for regulations in California and Florida which specify mineral waters as any water with 500 or more total dissolved solids, there is no national standard definition for a mineral water. As with carbonated waters, mineral water is not under the same bottled "still water" standards. Again, purity and safety standards must be met, but mineral content may vary. The amount of minerals that can significantly contribute to one's diet depends upon the brand used, how much is consumed, and how often. Individuals on a low sodium diet should pay particular attention to labels as the sodium content can vary from very high to almost none detectable.

Club soda is treated tap water that is injected with carbon dioxide and mineral salts.

Seltzer is treated tap water that is carbonated and contains no additional minerals or salts.

Bottled water is required to meet the same quality and purity standards as public drinking water, so **is bottled water really safer than tap water?** Bottled water generally, but not always, has fewer contaminants than tap water because of different purifying methods employed along with filtration and aeration. Ozone is used in bottled water instead of chlorine as a disinfectant. Unlike chlorine, ozone does not combine with organic material to form carcinogenic trihalmethanes. Additionally it is free of a lingering aftertaste or odor that occurs with chlorine. Public systems cannot use ozone since it does not leave a residual for lasting disinfection through the distribution system. Chemicals can be removed with activated carbon filters which serve as a sticky surface to which many chemicals adhere. Even if the source of the bottled water was chlorinated, filtering could be used to remove residual chlorine and other chemicals. Aeration is a method to rid the water of volatile chemicals that dissipate when exposed to air.

The bottled water industry is carefully regulated and must meet all city, state, and federal qualifications of a food processing plant. This includes cleaning the equipment and containers with an approved bactericidal process— usually chlorine at 100 ppm and hot water. Water that is not bottled at the source must be transported in tankers or containers that also have been treated. Many companies filter the water to remove the chemicals included during transport, but traces of chlorine may remain from the actual retail containers. It is a trade-off, of course, since infected bottles and/or processing equipment is, in itself, a health hazard.

Even more stringent self-imposed standards are set by the American Bottled Water Association. This is a voluntary organization which requires potential members to meet and maintain its high standards in processing, producing, and packaging in order to qualify. 90% of all U.S. bottled water manufacturers are members of the American Bottled Water Association.

The label affixed on bottled water must state the type of water source and the name and address of the processor. It may not make medicinal or health-giving claims or refer to the bacterial purity of the water. Although not a federal law, some states also require labels to list the source of the water.

Quality standards for **imported waters** are equally high. FDA guidelines for imported bottled waters require that the water be obtained from sources free of pollution, bottled or otherwise prepared under sanitary conditions, free from microorganisms of the coliform group, and of good sanitary quality when judged by bacteriological or chemical analysis. The FDA routinely checks for radiation levels before allowing any imported water into the country.

Europeans take their bottled water industry as seriously as their wine industry; very strict standards must be met and maintained. France, who leads the world in consumption of bottled water, has different regulations for the three types of water it sells. Its mineral water, both still and sparkling, is initially approved and constantly supervised by the Ministry of Health because of the waters' reputed medicinal benefits. Bottling must be done right at the source under conditions of meticulous sanitation. Both glass and plastic bottles are made at their factories to eliminate risk of contamination. Soft drinks may not be bottled in the same plant for fear of sugar bacteria contaminating the water. To preserve the natural purity of the water, the maximum daily flow of mineral water sources in France is carefully regulated by the Ministry of Mines. Similar standard controls exist in Belgium and Italy.

Plain spring water which makes no medicinal claims is less regulated. Table water may be disinfected or gasified by the bottler. The majority of imported water in the U.S. is the premium mineral water. Europeans consider it a good beverage and an aid to digestion.

The newest trend in the bottled water industry includes flavoring sparkling water with natural fruit essence derived from the pungent oils in its skin to replace sugary soft drinks and appeal to a broader market. But that's not all. Long recognized that coffee tastes better with bottled water, gourmet chefs are cooking with mineral water to enhance soups, vegetable dishes, and sauces. Cosmetologists recommend using mineral water as a facial refresher and moisturizer and cosmetic companies use it in their products. Because a baby's immune system is underdeveloped, bottled water is often recommended for baby foods and formulas to protect against potential chemical residue.

So in the final analysis, **how does one choose** which particular bottled water to buy?
1. Determine how it is going to be used. Sparkling water is not always appropriate for every occasion and use.
2. Read labels carefully.
   a)   Consider the source of the water. Is it from an area relatively free of pollution?
   b)   Is it bottled at the source or shipped to a bottling plant?
   c)   Does it have natural carbonation or is carbonation added?
   d)   What is its level of total dissolved solids?
   e)   If it contains minerals, is it the spectrum that you desire?
   f)   What is its pH?
   g)   Is it within your budget? Waters definitely vary in price.

Not all decisions about which water to buy need to be so technical. There are many to choose from, so just experiment and find one that you really enjoy.

SOFT DRINKS

Soft drink consumption, for the "average" American, has increased from 100 8-oz. servings per person annually to over 600 servings, representing 8 to 12% of the total daily caloric intake. Besides high amounts of sugar, many soft drinks contain phosphoric acid which is used as a buffer to counteract the carbonic acid formed in the carbonation process. High levels of phosphorous may disrupt the body's mineral balance and interfere with calcium absorption and utilization. Possible consequences include bone demineralization, soft tissue calcification, dental problems, and a weakened nervous system. Another common additive in soft drinks, sodium benzoate, destroys vitamin A in the body.

"Natural" sodas usually are quite high in sugar, but they contain no phosphoric acid, artificial colors, artificial flavors, preservatives, or caffeine. They are combinations of fruit concentrates, natural flavors, carbonated water, and a sweetener that is usually fructose and occasionally honey. A better alternative is to combine fruit juice with a carbonated mineral water.

Several manufacturers have capitalized on this idea by offering mineral water based drinks with non-sweetened natural flavors ranging from various fruit flavors to root beer and cola! They are light, refreshing, and delicious without the sugar punch!

SOYMILK

Soymilk is nutritious and versatile...but with all the variety on the market, which one to choose? Soymilks have gone far beyond the watery, beany-flavored liquid that was available until fairly recently. Several companies are producing uniquely flavored soy milks to provide a delicious non-dairy beverage for those looking for an enjoyable drink or for those allergic to or avoiding milk for dietary or philosophical reasons. Because soymilk is vegetable based, it is lactose-free, cholesterol-free and contains mostly unsaturated or polyunsaturated fat. Although it contains only 18% of the calcium found in dairy milk and 50% of the amount in mother's milk, it is still a fairly good source of calcium. Since soymilk is not intended to be a direct substitute for either of these it is important to also get adequate calcium from other sources. Soymilk also contains more protein, fewer calories, and more iron than milk. Studies indicate that soymilk may also help reduce serum cholesterol.

Commercial production goes beyond the simple technique of grinding, cooking, and straining the "milk" from soybeans. Lipoxidase enzymes, which are responsible for producing the beany "off" flavors, and the trypsin inhibitor, a constituent of soybeans which inhibits the body's ability to use the enzyme, trypsin, to digest protein, are modified and deactivated by heat, pressure, and vacuum processing. The complete cycle of production continues with additions of flavors and sweeteners, homogenization, and pasteurization—all done under sterile conditions. The cycle is completed by packaging in "tetra-paks" or retort "flexible" pouches providing a twelve-month shelf life requiring no refrigeration until opened.

The many flavors and textures vary from brand to brand according to the techniques and ingredients used by each manufacturer. For instance, enzyme deactivation is even more complete in some brands producing a product with little or no aftertaste. Sea vegetables such as kombu are used both for flavor and to further deactivate the trypsin inhibitor. Soymilk's sodium content comes from these sea vegetables or added salt. Some manufacturers use pure, demineralized water to minimize "flavor contamination". Sweeteners may include honey, barley malt, rice malt, chicory syrup, maple syrup, or sucanat—a dried, granulated juice of the sugar cane that contains the vitamins and minerals originally found in the sugar cane. Although some brands add oil for extra richness and smoothness, other brands are still rich and smooth without using excess oil. Pearl barley, a unique kind of barley, or brown rice can also be used for both flavor and texture.

As versatile as milk, soymilk can be used in cooking, baking, sauces, or simply as a refreshing beverage. For most recipes, plain or vanilla would be suitable choices. As a beverage, any flavor would be good. Use it to make your own soy yogurt! Pancakes, breads, cakes, and cookies come out more moist and rich. Use it at breakfast on cereal, for smoothies, or to top your favorite fresh fruit. Be creative!

So how does one choose which particular soymilk to buy? Decide what you really want by answering these questions and then reading the labels.

1. How is it going to be used?
2. How sweet do you like it?
3. What type of sweetener do you prefer?
4. What size do you need?
5. Which is the best value?

JUICES

Fruit and vegetable juices are good concentrated sources of vitamins and minerals. The most nutritious juices are freshly pressed and unpasteurized, but these must be kept under constant refrigeration and even then tend to spoil within a week or even less.

To extend shelf life and benefit distribution, most juices are pasteurized by heating to 190° for a few seconds then quickly cooled. Some nutrients are depleted in the process, but pasteurization makes juice affordable, due to lower labor cost and spoilage, both high when unpasteurized juices are retailed.

The best quality juices are made from 100% fruit juice but not all juices on the market fit into this category. Many juices consist of water combined with purees, concentrates, or nectars. Some can only be manufactured this way. For example, prune juice must be a combination of water and prune extract since prunes have no juice in them. Other juices are made into blends in order to lower costs and to provide unusual flavors.

Purees are the least processed. Fruit is reduced to a pulp and strained to remove seeds and skin. It is then frozen or canned for easier shipping and storage for the producer.

Concentrates are made from juice that has most of the water removed.

Nectars are made by thinning purees with water until the desired thickness is attained and then sweetening them. Nectars can be sweetened with sugar, corn syrup, or preferably with white grape juice. Although white grape juice is an extremely sweet source of glucose, unlike sugar or corn syrup, it can contribute at least some nutrients.

Juices can appear cloudy or clear depending on the degree of filtering. All juices are filtered somewhat in order to remove stems and leaves. Lightly filtered juices are labeled as "unfiltered" and still retain the fiber, pectin, and more nutrients than the clear, filtered varieties.

Since juices are concentrations of fruit, pesticide residues from the fruit can concentrate in the juice. Whenever possible, it is advisable to use juices from certified organically grown fruits and vegetables.

High acid fruits and vegetable juices like tomato, orange, grapefruit, and pineapple are best purchased in glass bottles rather than cans since foods high in acid tend to leach metals out of the insides of lead soldered cans.

Juices contain high concentrations of sugar from the fruit or vegetable and should be consumed in moderation. Some people prefer to dilute their juice to minimize blood sugar fluctuations and to save money by extending the juice.

Avoid "juices" labeled as "drink", "fruit drink", "cocktail", or "punch". Many of these contain very little fruit juice but a great deal of sugar and artificial flavors.

NON-ALCOHOLIC BEVERAGES

More people are becoming concerned about the effects of alcohol on their health and safety, and therefore the demand for non-alcoholic beverages is growing. The Bureau of Alcohol, Tobacco, and Firearms of the U.S. Treasury Department has reported that the sales of domestically produced non-alcohol malt beverages have increased from 388,460 barrels (31 gallons each) in 1983 to 536, 540 barrels in 1985. And this does not include the sales of the number of nonalcoholic malts imported from England, Canada, Germany, and Switzerland.

Even though labeled as non-alcoholic, small traces of alcohol may be present, up to .5%. This compares with 4% for regular beer, 3% for light beers, and 12% for most wines. Whether alcoholics can safely use non-alcoholic beverages remains a controversy.

Several alternatives to non-alcoholic beers and wine are available for those wishing to avoid alcohol occasionally or entirely. Sparkling apple juice can substitute for champagne. Wine can be replaced with sparkling mineral water and grape juice or with specific brands using wine grapes for juice. Sometimes they are even bottled in wine bottles to give a more authentic look.

Light and heavy beer alternatives that taste amazingly similar to the alcoholic versions are becoming more popular. Most are made with water, malt, and hops, and some contain yeast for a more similar flavor to traditional beer. Examples include Kingsbury, Texas Select, Moussy, Clausthaler, and Birell.

COFFEE

What makes a good coffee? Like a fine wine, the differences relate to the species of the plant, soil, elevation, weather, harvesting, and the final processing, in this case, the roasting of the bean.

Even though there are many species of coffee plants, the only two grown for commercial use are robusta (ro-boo-sta) and arabica (a-ra-beé-ka). Robusta coffee is grown primarily in Africa at low altitudes on large plots of land. Since the plants have a high yield and mature 2-3 times per year, they are plentiful and inexpensive and yet they lack the flavor and tang of a cup of coffee made from an arabica. Robustas are used in many commercial coffees, especially in instant coffees, either straight or blended with arabicas for improved flavor and aroma. In addition to their lower quality, robusta beans contains twice as much caffeine as arabicas!

Arabica beans are grown at high altitudes, lower temperatures, and mature only every 8 months. Because of the special growing conditions required, arabicas constitute only 10% of the world's coffee crop and, therefore, are higher in price. Unlike the non-descript flavors from less expensive commercial robusta coffees, the unique, superior flavor of coffee made from arabica beans is well worth the extra cost, not to mention the lower amount of caffeine!

Mrs. Olsen was right. The best coffee is mountain grown. Mountain slopes in tropical or subtropical regions offer the best conditions for growing coffee: altitudes above 2000 feet, temperatures between 55-80°, a few hours of sunshine, moderate water, and sustained humidity.

Ideally, harvesting occurs when the coffee cherries, the fruit of the plant, are ripe. Since the fruit ripens at different rates, even on the same branch, hand picking remains the preferred method of harvesting. The fruity pulp is removed either by sun drying the fruit first and then removing the pulp from around the bean (the "unwashed" method) or through the more modern method of soaking the fruit, removing the pulp mechanically, and then drying the bean (the "washed" method). The "washed" method results in more consistent quality of flavor by controlling the amount of fermentation which occurs more readily in the "unwashed" method.

Roasting brings out the flavor and aroma from the dry, green coffee bean. The type of roaster and length of roasting can make a mediocre coffee palatable and a quality coffee exquisite. Most coffee is roasted at approximately 450° for about 5 minutes. The darker the color, the longer it roasts. Liquid flavor extracts or cinnamon sticks are added during roasting to create the variety of flavors present in flavored dessert coffees.

Basic roasts used in most coffees are:

American roast or "regular" roast— medium brown color, dry surface, acid taste yet sweet and rich in flavor

Full city roast— medium dark roast, neutral taste lacking the sharpness of an American roast and the strong flavor (tang) of a darker roast

French roast or continental roast— dark brown roast, oily surface, no sharp acidity but more tang

Espresso roast— very dark roast, very oily surface, very strong flavor, preferred for the fine grind required for espresso machines

Coffees are named by their grade, size of bean, area of growth, type of roast, type, and blend. Different countries use different grading systems which can be misleading or confusing if comparing coffees using similar grading terms. All aspects should be considered when making the final decision as to which coffee to buy.

Terms such as "supremo", "excelso", "AA", and "jumbo" refer to size and uniformity of the beans. Consistent size insures more even roasting and, thus, better flavor.

Coffee is grown across the entire world. The largest quantity of coffee beans is produced in Brazil but the best quality arabica beans come from Colombia whose soil, consistent weather and high elevation create ideal conditions. Even though 75% of Africa's coffee crop are robusta beans, some of the best arabicas come from Africa, especially from Ethiopia, Kenya, and Rwanda who grow only arabica beans.

India is the major producer of coffee in Asia while China exports small quantities of very good coffee from the Yunnan province. A leaf plague destroyed all of southeast Asia's arabica trees in the late 19th century and subsequent 20th century plantings were damaged during World War II, but coffees from Java, Celebes, Timor, and Sumatra have since restored their high quality and superb flavor.

Coffee in Hawaii is grown in pits carved out of volcanic rock. The soil and weather both contribute to the full-bodied and very sweet flavor which distinguish Kona coffee. Limited production makes Kona coffee scarce and expensive.

Central America and the Caribbean take advantage of the mountain ranges and weather. Excellent Mexican coffee called "altura" (high-grown) is grown above 4000 feet. Café Altura, another high quality arabica coffee, is organically grown in Mexico using the Bio-Dynamics agricultural system which restores vitality to the soil and creates an environment that allows the coffee trees to flourish without adding chemical fertilizers, herbicides, fumigants, or insecticides. The beans are available in both a city roast and a darker Viennese roast. After roasting they are ground and vacuum packed in cans or left whole and vacuum packed in 10 lb. bulk bags for retailers.

Guatemala, like Colombia, is also ideally suited for growing coffee, most notably in the region of Antigua which produces a coffee with high acidity and smoky flavor. Costa Rica and the Dominican Republic are also noteworthy. Jamaica is most famous for its delicately flavored Blue Mountain coffee grown at 7,388 feet. Production is very limited and most of that is exported to Japan. Expect to pay a high price when found.

Because caffeine is a stimulant, some people, including heart patients and pregnant women, are advised to avoid caffeine. Decaffeination of coffee originated in Germany using benzene as a solvent. Throughout the years, various solvents have been used directly on the bean. However, the safety of these solvents has been suspect throughout the years and they have eventually proven to be carcinogenic.

Methylene chloride is another solvent that had been commonly used until recently. This same solvent has been used in hairsprays as a propellant, flame retardant, and to help dry and set the resin in the spray that holds the hair in place. The FDA has proposed banning its use in hairsprays since experiments have shown that it causes cancer in laboratory animals and may be a health hazard to humans when inhaled. However, at this time, it continues to be allowed in decaffeinating coffee claiming that the residue that is, indeed, present is too miniscule to cause harm. Nonetheless, many companies are switching to other solvents such as ethyl acetate, an FDA approved derivative of coffee beans and other fruits believed to be safe.

Besides applying solvent directly to the bean, two other methods of decaffeinating coffee exist: the indirect contact method and the Swiss Water Process. In the indirect contact method the beans are soaked in hot water to draw out the oils in the coffee and the caffeine. The solution is poured into another chamber and treated with a solvent, preferably ethyl acetate. The solvent absorbs the caffeine and is removed from the water by a steaming process. The water containing the flavor oils is added back to the beans to reabsorb the original oils.

The preferred method overall is the Swiss Water Process which involves soaking the beans in plain water for several hours until 97% of the caffeine is removed. This solution is filtered through activated charcoal or carbon filters to remove the caffeine. No solvent is used at any stage of the process. Like the indirect contact method, the filtered solution is added back to the beans to allow them to absorb the natural flavor oils.

Even though labeled as decaffeinated, all decaffeinated coffees still contain a small amount of caffeine. A 5 oz. cup of decaffeinated coffee contains about 4 mg. of caffeine in contrast to the average of 65-115 mg. present in a cup of regular brewed coffee.

Once coffee beans are roasted, oxidation begins which can eventually lead to an old, stale flavor if the beans are not used quickly or stored properly. Whole beans keep fresh up to 6-8 weeks when refrigerated or stored in an airtight container in the freezer. Buy small amounts at one time, grinding only enough to last 1 week. For best results, grind immediately before brewing. Small electric coffee mills are quite inexpensive and can also be used for grinding spices, herbs, nuts, and small amounts of grains.

What are the secrets to a good cup of coffee? A quality arabica coffee, freshly roasted and ground is an essential. Add 1 rounded tablespoon or 2 level tablespoons of coffee for each 6 oz. cup desired to good tasting hot, not boiling, water. (Some people insist on using a bottled spring water or distilled water instead of water straight from the tap.) Don't overbrew and serve as soon as it is ready. Reheating coffee cooks away delicate flavors and aromas to produce a bitter taste. Unlike most percolators which essentially "cook" the coffee, drip coffee makers such as Melitta and Chemex use the simple, effective method of pouring hot water over a paper filter filled with the ground coffee and allowing the coffee, free of sediment, to drip into a carafe below. The hot water passes through the ground coffee only once, releasing the natural flavor oils without bringing out the bitter tannic acid in the bean.

Experiment with a new coffee or coffee blend each week. Or create your own "house" blend by combining three coffees you especially like that have different characteristics.

Coffee substitutes are generally based on chicory, a plant whose root has a coffee-like flavor when roasted and ground. Roasted barley, dandelion root, molasses, and figs are other common ingredients for beverages similar to coffee but without the kick!

Absorption of iron vs. consumption of coffee and tea

Both coffee and tea, whether decaffeinated or not, contain certain compounds which interfere with the absorption of non-heme iron, the type of iron contained in legumes, vegetables, and grains. Some herbal teas, such as peppermint, also contain these naturally occuring polyphenol compounds. Tannins are one example of polyphenols.

In order to avoid impairing iron absorption, drink coffee or tea at least one hour before or after eating instead of with the meal. Adding milk to tea to inactivate the tannins as well as eating Vitamin C-rich foods will help increase absorption of non-heme iron. Absorption of heme-iron, the kind found in meat, does not seem to be affected.

TEAS

Black and green teas, as with coffee, are best grown in the cooler, higher altitudes. All tea is grown from the same type of plant but differences in flavor depend upon where it is grown, when and how the leaves are harvested, and what is done to it after it is harvested. Tea picked too soon or too late will yield an inferior tea.

Leaves used for **black tea** are allowed to ferment before they are dried. Black tea has a hearty flavor with a rich, full amber color. Green tea leaves are dried immediately after they are picked, before they have a chance to ferment.

Green tea has a distinctive flavor and a pale, greenish-yellow color.

Oolong tea leaves are partially fermented, then dried. Oolong has a subtle flavor and bouquet with a light brownish-yellow color.

The words pekoe or orange pekoe refer only to the size or cut of the leaf, not the point of origin or degree of fermentation which are the two most important indications of flavor.

Black teas appeal to most people, especially English Breakfast, Irish Breakfast, and Darjeeling, a more aromatic black tea. Earl Grey, Russian Caravan, and Lapsang Souchang have unique, unusual flavors.

Kukicha and **bancha** teas are often mistaken for one another. Bancha leaves contain caffeine while kukicha consists of roasted twigs and stems from tea bushes that are at least 3 years old. Kukicha is a mellow, soothing tea with a rich nut-like flavor and contains virtually no caffeine due to four roasting and cooling processes. It is reported to have an alkalizing effect on the blood stream and is traditionally used to relieve nausea and other digestive upsets.

The caffeine content in tea is less than coffee, around 48 mg per cup. Decaffeinated teas are available but so far no non-chemical method can be used on teas. Methylene chloride is used as it is in the European Process of decaffeinating coffees.

To brew tea, use 1 teaspoon or 1 tea bag for each 5-1/2 oz cup. Bring freshly drawn cold water to a boil, steep the tea for 3-5 minutes, remove the leaves and serve.

You can thank a sweltering summer for the refreshing concept of drinking tea iced. During the St. Louis World's Fair in 1904 sales in Richard Blechynder's hot tea concession booth were anything but hot. His solution, of course... put the tea on ice!

HERB TEAS

Iced black tea is more commonly served when iced tea is requested, however, in many homes and restaurants cold glasses of **herb tea** are now being offered. Iced herb teas are refreshing, tasty, and the most economical of all warm weather drinks. One box of 24 tea bags or approximately 1 1/4 cups of loose tea makes 6 quarts of tea. Additionally, herb teas are sugar-free, primarily caffeine-free, preservative-free, and less than 6 calories per serving—a perfect alternative to soda pop!

The flavors of herb tea range from minty, fruity, flowery, to bitter. Peppermint and chamomile are the most popular single herb teas although most people take advantage of the many blends available which create unique and delicious flavors. Some teas could easily pass for spicy fruit punch, lemonade, or even a wholesome version of 'Kool-Aid' as evidenced by the names of some of the blends available— Cinnamon Rose, Lemon Iced Delight, Mandarin Orange Spice, Pirate's Punch, Lime Lite, Wild Forest Blackberry.

Iced herb tea is so easy to make that there is no reason not to have some in the refrigerator all the time. There are a number of ways to make iced tea.

1) **The Tea Concentrate**: Bring water to a boil. Use 2 tea bags or 2 teaspoons loose tea per cup of water. Steep 5-10 minutes and pour over ice cubes in a glass.

2) **Normal Brewing**: Bring water to a boil. Use 1 tea bag or 1 teaspoon loose tea per cup of water. Steep 5-10 minutes. Remove tea bag or strain tea. Chill before serving.

3) **Sun Tea**: Place 8-10 tea bags or 6-8 TB. loose tea in a gallon jar. Fill 2/3 full with water. Place in direct sun outdoors or at a sunny window. Steep about 5 hours or until tea looks twice as dark as you would normally brew it. Fill jar with ice cubes and refrigerate or serve immediately.

4) **Brewed Quantity Method**: Bring a pot of water to a boil. Add 1 cup loose herb tea (2/3 cup if using peppermint). Steep for 10 minutes. Strain the tea and add water to make one gallon.

More hearty roots and barks need more time for the flavors to be extracted. Boil 1 ounce in 3 cups of fresh water for 30 minutes, uncovered, and then strain. Add ice cubes to dilute to the desired strength.

In addition to their use as a flavorful beverage, some herbs are also used for their medicinal effects. Therefore, it is important to be very familiar with the herb you are drinking as a tea. Not all teas should be used on a regular basis. Be cautious and consult a qualified herbalist and/or an herb book if contemplating the use of a less common herb or when drinking large amounts of one type of tea. Moderate amounts of the more popular single teas or blends are generally quite safe.

However, some herbs may also cause allergic reactions in sensitive people. For example, chamomile, the tea made famous by Peter Rabbit's mother, is an excellent tea but should be avoided if one is allergic to ragweed. It should also be avoided during pregnancy, along with buchu, shepherd's purse, uva ursi, dong quai, mugwort, pennyroyal, blue cohosh, ginseng, false unicorn, cascara sagrada, senna, barberry, chapparal, ma huang, guarana, or yerba santa. As far as refreshing beverages go, the aforementioned herbs, excluding chamomile, generally are not considered flavorful and usually would only be used medicinally.

A new, less familiar ingredient in some tea blends is **stevia leaf** or "sweet herb". This herb from Paraguay, which is 300 times sweeter than sugar, has been used for years in South America and Japan as a sweetening agent.

Sample the many varieties of teas to find your personal favorites. Your favorite herb tea blend originated as the result of someone experimenting with the flavors from teas.

Celebrations, small parties, intimate conversations, relaxation, a good meal...all seem to be enhanced when accompanied with a cup of coffee or tea, a non-alcoholic drink, or a glass of beer or wine. Beneath the pleasure is the art of production methods passed on through centuries of craftsmanship. That quality difference can turn a mere beverage into an experience.

BEER

Naturally brewed beer is experiencing a renaissance. Small, regional microbreweries who brew beer with traditional methods are making a comeback and imported European beers are experiencing a great deal of popularity despite their higher price. The major difference between these and lesser quality beers lies in the pure, fresh, additive-free ingredients that contribute to the quality flavor of naturally brewed beer.

Naturally brewed beer has unique, distinctive flavors that tend to be heavier and more full bodied than the beers sold by the domestic large scale breweries. Two basic types of beer are produced: **lighter lagers and wheat beer** (wheat plus barley for a different flavor) which use bottom fermenting yeast, and **heavier ales and stouts**, which use top fermenting yeast. Lagers and wheat beers are fermented and slowly aged at cool temperatures resulting in the yeast settling to the bottom of the brew. Top fermented ales and stouts are fermented at warm temperatures for very short periods of time. For best results, serve lager and wheat beers cool or cold, ales cool, and stouts and the heaviest of beers at room temperature.

All brands of Bavarian (the main beer producing area of Germany) beer are governed by a law called the "Reinheitsgebot" (the law of purity) which makes it a crime to brew beer with ingredients other than hops, malt, and water.

Since there is no full disclosure law for alcoholic beverages, beer can have fifty-two other ingredients besides the traditional ingredients of natural beer - water, malted barley, hops, and yeast. For example, sulphites (see dried fruits for explanation) are used as antioxidants to prevent loss of flavor and color, EDTA (ethylenediamine tetraacetic acid) prevents gushing when the container is open, gum arabic and propylene glycol alginate stabilize foamy heads, heptyl paraben and hydroxybenzoate act as preservatives, plus dozens of other additives are added to provide artificial color and flavor! Is nothing sacred?

"Light" beers were devised in response to calorie-conscious consumers, but the term itself can be misleading. Although "light" beers contain less kilocalories, they are only slightly lower in alcoholic content. A beer's full-bodied flavor will more than likely be affected since some ingredients are taken out or manipulated to reduce the caloric content.

Recognizing the trend in consumer demands, more of the domestic major breweries are eliminating the preservatives once so prevalent in their beers. Many, however, still cut costs (and quality!) by using a malt extract or other carbohydrate sources such as corn or rice instead of pure malted barley or hop pellets instead of fresh hops.

A sample, but by no means all, of a few breweries throughout the world dedicated to the most pure, fresh ingredients without preservatives or coloring agents includes:

Anchor Steam Beer— San Francisco, California

Belhaven— Scotland

Chimay Ales— Belgium

Collin County Beers— Plano, Texas

Panlaner Products— Munich, Germany

WINE

The entire ceremony connected with **wine**—choosing the proper wine for the occasion, the appropriate glass, serving temperature, pouring technique, and actual method of consumption—pays tribute to one of the most ancient and highly respected arts of creating a high quality wine.

It all starts in the vineyard. The type of grape, the soil, moisture, temperature, level of ripeness, time of harvest, all make an impact on the flavor, body, and bouquet of the finished product. A deficiency in one aspect cannot be made up by the others. These along with the actual production methods, separate the exquisite from the mediocre.

Although additives can be used in wine, several wineries exist which utilize traditional methods. Quality wineries are very serious about the highest standards possible; their name depends upon it. Therefore, rely upon reputable wineries for the purest ingredients. Since alcohol is a natural preservative, no additional preservatives are needed.

Choosing a wine depends upon the type of occasion and the amount of money you wish to spend. High quality wines are not always high in price. Many reasonably priced, excellent wines are available, both domestic and imported.

Some wines are made by companies who buy grapes or juice and blend them for best flavor before bottling. These wines are usually inexpensive and good values, perfect for simple dinners. Table wine blends labeled "red" or "white" can also be good.

In general, you can be assured of a higher quality wine from designated regions such as Bordeaux, Alsace, Loire Valley, Burgundy in France and Mosel in Germany. However, your better value may be in one of the lesser known areas (or appellations) near those regions: Fronsac (Bordeaux), Saint Veran (Burgundy), and Baden (Germany). New regions such as Australia and Oregon or rediscovered regions such as Rioja (Spain), Cote du Rhone (France), or Central Coast (California) offer good quality wines.

Truly great wines from designated regions are further classified by words such as Grand Cru, Special Cuvee, Reserva, or Premier Cru.

The **vintage** of the wine is also quite important. The vintage indicates the year the grapes were harvested so, technically, every year is a vintage year. But, because peak years vary, it is best to check the quality of the vintage by consulting a vintage chart and your local wine merchant. Depending upon the wine, aging enables the wine to mellow and develop. But, not all wines improve with age. In fact, the majority of all wines made in the world are meant to be consumed within one or two years. However, a standard rule of thumb with good quality wines is to choose the older vintage.

Tannins are a natural compound of wine, present in grape skins, stems, and even oak barrels in which certain wines are aged. Tannins act as a preservative and, without it, certain wines could not be aged. Red wines contain more tannin than white wine. Therefore, those individuals who are sensitive to tannins, may find white wines and lighter reds more enjoyable.

Another concern for some people is the presence of **sulphur dioxide** in many wines. There are two reasons why sulphur dioxide is used in grape juice destined to become wine: 1) it inhibits oxidation and prevents the enzymatic action which causes browning of white grape juice and 2) it kills the natural bacteria and wild yeasts that may spoil the wine or produce "off" flavors. Fermenting yeasts also produce sulphur dioxide from inorganic sulfates which occur naturally in grape juice. The amount produced varies depending upon the yeast strain, nutrient balance of the juice, and fermentation conditions. Even if a wine does not have sulphur dioxide added to the grape juice, because of the naturally occurring sulphites, it is virtually impossible for wine to be *completely free* of sulphur dioxide. (See DRIED FRUIT for discussion on sulphites.) As of January 9, 1988, alcoholic beverages that contain 10 parts per million or more or sulphites must be labeled as they leave the factory or storage declaring the presence of sulphur dioxide. While most people are not adversely affected, those people sensitive to sulphites may need to avoid wines to avoid any possible side effects.

Higher sugar content makes wine **sweet.** In contrast, a wine is **dry** when all the sugar in the grapes is completely fermented into alcohol. The acid content of the wine also determines a sense of dryness. For simplicity's sake, a dry wine tends to be tar, less thick and full and more cleansing to the palate.

Sweet wines have a lingering taste, are richer in body, fruity, and obviously sweeter.

So, go ahead! Enjoy the many types of wines that are available from all over the world. Join a wine tasting group or simply experiment on your own. The chart on the next page can function as a stepping stone for combining certain wines with particular foods.

DINING WITH WINE

The best advice to remember is to make sure whatever wine you choose does not overpower the food and is not overpowered by the food.

WINE	FOOD
pinot noir/red burgundy	lamb, veal, wild game (pheasant) lighter, more delicate meats
red bordeaux cabernet sauvignon	beef, country style paté, pasta with tomato sauce, sharp cheddar, aged gouda with chocolate or coffee at end of a meal
white bordeaux sauvignon blanc (fume' blanc)	poultry, seafood, chicken, brie, soft cheeses, fruit (apples, pears), light pasta dishes or with white cream sauces
chardonnay white burgundy	richer seafoods (shellfish, lobster), brie, soft cheeses, heavier poultry dishes, pasta with cream sauces
champagne	before dinner, hors d'oeuvres, light, delicate seafood or poultry
saké, gewukrztraminer	stir fries, oriental dishes
auslese (sweet German wine) sauterne	dessert
chablis	hors d'oeuvres, fish, lobster, oysters, cream sauces
beaujolais	wild game, monastery cheeses (Chimay, etc.)
chianti	Italian dishes, cheeses

SUGGESTED SERVING TEMPERATURES FOR WINES

major red wines: Burgundies, Bordeaux, Californias, and Riojas	**58-65°**
Chardonnay, Beaujolais, Valpolicella, and Cotes du Rhone	**52-58°**
Champagnes, Sauvignon Blancs, Loire whites, Italian whites	**45-52°**
Sauternes, German Spaetleses, Muscats	**39-45°**

The best chilling method is to use an ice bucket about 9-10 inches in diameter. Place the bottle in the ice bucket and loosely pack in ice. Add cool water up the shoulder of the bottle. The temperature of the bottle will drop 10° from room temperature every 8 minutes of immersion. Once the desired temperature is reached, remove the bottle from the bucket for short periods to maintain temperature.

Recipes

FRUIT "SODA"   *serves 1*
Make your own refreshing natural soda on the spot!

1/2 cup carbonated mineral water
1/2 cup fruit juice
ice cubes (opt.)

1. Pour mineral water in a glass.
2. Add juice, stir, and serve.
   NOTE: If making a large quantity ahead of time, use a tight-fitting lid to retain carbonation.

SMOOTHIES   *serves 1*
Smoothies are the low fat answer to malts and shakes. Include a frozen banana for the ultimate flavor and texture.

1 cup juice, lowfat milk, yogurt, or soymilk
1/2 cup fresh or frozen fruit (frozen makes the drink thicker)
1 TB. nuts or seeds (opt.)

1. Blend all ingredients in a blender until smooth.
2. Serve immediately.

FRUITY TEA   *serves 1*
Endless variations of fruit flavored teas are possible. "Kool-Aid" and sodas may soon be a thing of the past!

1/4 cup apple, apricot or other fruit juice
1 cup brewed herb tea or kukicha tea

1. Brew tea and combine with juice.
2. Serve hot or if preferred cold, refrigerate or add ice cubes before serving.

Recipes

KUKICHA TEA
serves 2

Although generally connected with classic macrobiotic cuisine, the soothing quality and good flavor of this no-caffeine tea have made kukicha a favorite of many.

2 1/2 cups water
2 teaspoons kukicha twigs

1. Combine water and kukicha and bring to a boil.
2. Reduce heat, cover, and simmer 10 minutes.
3. Strain into 2 tea cups.

HERB TEA FRAPPE'
serves 1

Try this new twist to iced herb tea.

1 cup iced herb tea
1 teaspoon honey
cracked ice

1. Process all ingredients in a blender.
2. Pour into a chilled glass and serve while foamy.

11

MEDICINAL HERBS

Herbs have also been used medicinally for thousands of years. Physicians collected herbs from their own herb gardens or from the countryside to treat patients. The modern drug industry has attempted to replace herbs with synthetic concoctions which bring only symptomatic relief. Ironically, many drugs originally were based on herbs. For example, foxglove was the source of digitalis, a powerful heart stimulant, aspirin was derived from white willow bark, and oil of clove was used as a numbing agent. The FDA does not recognize herbs as having any medicinal properties and therefore, it is illegal for a store employee to prescribe or for a product label to make medicinal claims.

FORMS OF HERBS

Nonetheless, there is a surge of interest in herbs. Herbs can be used in various forms. Teas in the form of infusions or decoctions are discussed in detail in the BEVERAGE section of this book. Herbs and roots are available in bulk ground, whole, and cut. Some herbs have a disagreeable taste so encapsulating or making them into a tablet helps eliminate the problem. Other forms include the following:

Tinctures are fluid extracts extracted with alcohol, vinegar, or glycerine. Tinctures require no heat for processing so none of the volatile oils or herbal properties are destroyed. They provide the best and quickest assimilation into the body. One ounce of tincture equals one ounce of the powdered herb so a few drops will equal 1/2 cup of tea. Tinctures can be diluted in a small amount of water or juice or put directly on the back of the tongue. If alcohol must be avoided, put the drops in 1/3 cup hot water to evaporate the alcohol.

Syrups are made by adding about two ounces of herb to a quart of water and boiling down to one pint. It is then strained and combined with one or two ounces of honey and/or glycerine while warm. Syrups generally taste good, are convenient, and suitable for children.

Poultices are warm, moist masses of powdered or macerated herbs applied directly to the skin to relieve inflammation, blood poisoning, insect bites, and skin eruptions.

Linaments are herbal extracts that are rubbed into the skin for strained muscles and ligaments. The properties of the herbs are extracted in vinegar, alcohol, or massage oil.

Salves or **Ointments** are beeswax thickened herbal oils that remain in place due to their thick consistency.

GENERAL USE

Herbs should be used with caution and knowledge. They work best in combinations with other herbs in specific proportions. Many companies provide herbal combinations suggested for specific conditions.

As mentioned in the section concerning herb teas, certain herbs during certain conditions can be harmful. Again, a pregnant woman should avoid pennyroyal, angelica, blue cohosh, goldenseal, rue, dong quai, and false unicorn. Goldenseal can have an adverse effect on a person who has hypoglycemia. People with high blood pressure should avoid goldenseal, ginseng, licorice, and ephedra. Careful study should precede the use of any herb.

Herbs and prescription drugs should not be combined. If both are used, space them at least two hours apart.

Children's dosages vary according to their age. Dosage should be *limited* according to the following chart. Amounts will vary according to the herb. ***Never give a child herbs without knowledge of herbal medicine!***

MAXIMUM SAFE DOSAGES OF HERBS FOR CHILDREN

AGE	DOSAGE
infants 6 months to 1 year	.04 to .08 of a '0' capsule.
ages 2-4	1/8 adult amount
5-9 year olds	1/4 adult amount
10-15 year olds	1/2 adult amount
late teens	full adult dosage

GINSENG

Ginseng is known as a non-specific adaptogen which means that it helps the body adapt to general stress. The adaptation mode includes strengthening energy, increasing resistance to disease, protecting the liver from damage by chemicals, alcohol, and radiation, calming the nerves, and normalizing the cardiovascular system.

Three kinds of ginseng are available: 1) **Panax ginseng**— oriental ginseng from Korea, China, and Japan, 2) **Panax quinquefolium**— American ginseng, and 3) **Eleutherococcus senticosus**— Eleuthero or Siberian ginseng.

Wild ginseng is considered superior in quality and potency to cultivated roots. Wild oriental roots are extremely rare and, therefore, prohibitively expensive. American ginseng is available both wild and cultivated. Much of the American ginseng is shipped to the Orient where it is used in general tonics and patent medicine.

Siberian ginseng is actually a shrub whose leaves and rootlike underground stem are used. It has properties similar to the other two types of ginseng.

The type to use can be determined by experimentation. Each ginseng has its own set of chemical compounds called glycosides which provide pharmacological activity. Some people find that one type may give better results than the others.

Others use the yin/yang balancing theory of harmony in nature and determine what ginseng to use according to the season or according to the person's temperament. American ginseng is considered "yin" as it is moist and cooling and, therefore, is used primarily in the summer or for those with a "yang" temperament. Oriental ginseng is dry and warming ("yang") and is more used in the winter or for those with a "yin" condition.

Whatever ginseng is used, the best quality is the best buy. Quality ginseng is determined by the quality of the soil in which it is grown, the length of time it is grown before harvesting, the handling and processing of the roots after harvest, and the storage of the ginseng product before use.

Oriental roots are generally 4-6 years old. There is little pharmacological activity during the first 3 years. It is difficult to grow Panax ginseng longer than 6 years so few are older than this. After it is picked, the enzymes in the root start to break down the glycosides unless they are preserved. The root is steamed, soaked in date sugar and other herbs, and dried under careful conditions. In addition to breakdown of the starches in the root, the process leaves the roots with a dark red color and a sweet flavor. Steamed roots often have three times the activity of white roots.

Shiu Chu ginseng roots are excellent red cured roots from the Shiu Chu Province in China that are commonly found in retail stores. Although the less expensive **red Kirin ginseng roots** from the Kirin Province are also good roots, they are somewhat lesser in quality. Kirin ginseng is most often used in patent herbal tonics and commercial extracts. In general, Chinese ginseng are said to tonify the "yin" energy.

Although **Korean ginseng** has different qualities than those of Chinese ginseng, it is of utmost quality. Like some Chinese roots, the best Korean roots are steamed and cured. White Korean ginseng is made by drying peeled lesser quality roots in order to prevent them from being illegally steamed. Korean white ginseng roots are used as a light general tonic with less long range effect than the Korean red roots. In general, Korean ginseng is quicker in action than Chinese ginseng and tonifies the "yang" as well as the "yin" energies.

American ginseng can be grown for long periods of time and is most potent when more than 6 years old. The age can be determined by counting the notches in the stem. Wild American ginseng is more potent than cultivated.

Eleuthero ginseng is usually sold in powder or extract form. Production costs are lower than panax or American ginseng, so the retail price is usually lower. Eleuthero ginseng is especially noted for its use to counteract stress.

Besides roots, ginseng is sold in powder, capsules, tablets, pastes, liquid extracts, and instant teas. Buying the root is the only sure way of knowing the quality of the ginseng used. Most instant teas contain high amounts of lactose (milk sugar) or dextrose and less than 15% ginseng. The 4-star rating system pertains only to ginseng in granular form and designates the ratio of ginseng to sugar. A 4-star rating indicates less sugar and more ginseng while a 1-star rating means more sugar and less ginseng. Use spray dried or freeze dried ginseng granules to make an instant tea without sugar.

For best results, ginseng should be combined with a healthy lifestyle and good diet. Only then will its potential have the opportunity to be expressed.

BEE POLLEN AND PROPOLIS

Bee pollen has been used for increasing energy and stamina, and to help treat allergy problems. Pollen is collected by bees from the male seed of flowers, mixed with a secretion from the bee, and held until the bee has enough to form a granule. A pollen collecting device installed by the beekeeper traps the pollen as the bee enters the beehive.

Bee pollen is available in capsule, tablet, extract, and fresh form. Fresh pollen is the most potent and must be refrigerated. Dry pollen is also good providing it has not been dried at temperatures higher than 130°. Dry pollen is more convenient since it requires no refrigeration.

Bee pollen is a highly concentrated food primarily containing carbohydrate and also small amounts of vitamins, minerals, enzymes, and protein. A little goes a long way. One to three teaspoons per day is generally sufficient eaten by the spoonful, sprinkled on cereal or fruit or mixed into smoothies **unless** you have environmental allergies or are allergic to bees. Even if you think you have no allergies, it is best to start with just a few grains at a time, very gradually increasing to a couple of teaspoons. Taking a lot of bee pollen initially can cause some people to have a severe allergic reaction due to the concentration of the pollen.

To help the body develop immunity to airborne pollens, fresh pollen should be used months ahead of the prime pollen season. It may or may not be effective.

Bee propolis is another product collected by the bee, this time from the resin under the bark of specific trees. Bees apply it to the interior of the hive because of its anti-bacterial and antibiotic qualities. The presence of a bacteria could destroy the entire colony if propolis were not used.

As for its affect on humans, propolis stimulates the thymus gland which boosts immunity and resistance to infections. It also has an antibacterial effect and therefore is used in toothpaste and creams. When fluid propolis is applied to a wound, it forms a thin band-aid-like coating allowing air to penetrate while keeping germs and dirt out.

Most antibiotics become less effective after prolonged or frequent use because bacteria develops a resistance to them. However, bacteria do not become resistant to propolis, so it maintains its effectiveness even if used frequently. It can even increase the effectiveness of penicillin and other antibiotics so the dosage of the antibiotic may need to be regulated by the doctor. Besides toothpaste and creams, propolis is sold in its dry form as a tablet or capsule, in lozenges, cough syrup, and in a liquid form combine with herbs. Propolis should not be used instead of an antibiotic prescribed for a specific serious condition without discussing the matter with one's doctor.

12

NUTRITIONAL SUPPLEMENTS

Remember all the predictions that claimed we would be using perfectly balanced concentrated food tablets by the year 1990 instead of eating real food? Although food is far from being totally replaced, food supplements do play a major role in many people's lives. Ideally, a person should be able to rely on food to supply all the nutrients needed to remain in excellent health. However, where and how food is grown, the processing of the food, how it is stored, and how old it is when eaten can adversely affect the nutritive value of the food. Then too, the uniqueness of the individual must be considered. Age, heredity, environment, activity level, stress, and lifestyle affect how a person assimilates the nutrients and how much of each is needed.

Nonetheless, food is still your best source of nutrients. Our bodies need the proteins, fats, carbohydrates, and fiber from food for the isolated nutrients to be effective. Science is not so sophisticated that is has been able to isolate every factor involved with even basic metabolism. To get the most for your food dollar, shop and prepare to get the most from your food. Choose a variety of fresh, minimally processed foods. Buy only as much produce as you can use in a few days and refrigerate promptly. Minimize cutting and peeling and avoid long soaking in water to retain more nutrients. Stir fry, steam, or pressure cook, cooking quickly using only a small amount of water. Store leftovers in airtight containers and use within a few days.

NATURAL OR SYNTHETIC

So just what **is** a **natural supplement**? A truly natural supplement is one that is a concentrated food source. Vitamins A & D from fish liver oil, alfalfa, rose hips, brewer's yeast, wheat germ oil, lecithin, desiccated liver, vitamin E from soy oil, bone meal, chlorophyll, aloe vera, evening primrose oil, and spirulina fit this definition. However, most supplements are from a **manufactured (synthetic) source**, that is, a laboratory product whose molecular structure is similar to the supplement being copied. Manufactured synthetic supplements are more prevalent due to cost factors, availability of a natural commercial source, size limitations on the pill itself, and the number of pills required for a certain potency.

Vitamins from a natural source can be concentrated only to a certain degree. Most vitamin B and vitamin C supplements are at least partially synthetic to provide quantities that can be used to offset a deficiency; however, high potencies of vitamins A, D, and E can be concentrated from the natural oil source. Since supplements from a natural source may contain synergistic elements (naturally occurring co-enzymes and other vitamins and minerals which facilitate assimilation in the body) many companies add a natural base to their synthetic supplements in order to provide the best results. In contrast, some people prefer pure synthetic supplements to avoid natural substances to which they may have allergies or sensitivities.

The body recognizes natural source and synthetic source supplements as equals. Vitamin E is the only vitamin that is definitely recognized to be more effective in the natural source. Personal preference and the potency required are the determining factors in choosing a natural or synthetic supplement. If you require only minimal amounts to supplement your diet, natural supplements can be suitable. If you need higher potencies to offset a deficiency or if you have food sensitivities, try a synthetic based supplement.

HOW MUCH?

Does everyone need to supplement? With a good foundation of a balanced diet, plenty of exercise, and adequate sleep, many people probably do not need supplements on a regular basis. However, they can be an effective booster if more nutrients are indeed needed. Pregnant and lactating women, heavy drinkers, women on oral contraceptives, persons taking certain medications, and those who are unable to get an adequate diet due to a prolonged illness, digestive disorder, physical or emotional problems, or low-calorie weight reducing diet can find it difficult to get all the nutrients they need from food and may find supplementation beneficial.

Keep in mind that "more is not always better". The U.S. Recommended Daily Allowance **(U.S. RDA) guide** that is listed on food labels is also listed on supplement labels. It is based upon the RDA levels, the recommended daily intakes for normal, healthy people according to age, sex, and the special needs of pregnancy and lactation. The U.S. RDA amounts chosen by the FDA represent the highest level for each nutrient suggested for any of the seventeen different population groups covered by the RDA. The U.S. RDA is de-signed to be used as a standard guide to evaluate and compare supplements as well as foods for all individuals above the age of four through adulthood. Infants have a separate U.S. RDA guide. A 30-50% margin is included to allow for individual variations. Along with a good diet, exercise, and sleep, a low potency supplement that supplies the U.S. RDA will be sufficient for most people as an "insurance" type supplement to fill in the gaps that may occur.

Since no special considerations are given for people with abnormal metabolic disor-ders, severe infections, chronic illnesses, or living under unhealthy life styles or environ-mental conditions, higher potencies may be warranted for some people but the higher potencies should be used with discretion and knowledge, preferably under guidance from a dietician or qualified health practioner. "Hit or miss" evaluation techniques may worsen the situation or cause even more problems. The toxicity symptoms of a nutrient are some-times similar to the deficiency symptoms and large amount of one isolated nutrient may cause an imbalance. Use only the supplements that are necessary and in the proper amounts.

Supplements should be taken with foods for best absorption and to prevent the nausea that can occur when supplements are simply swallowed with water or juice. Note the recommended dosage listed by manufacturer on the bottle. If supplements are taken once per day, generally they should be taken at the largest meal.

Supplements without preservatives will keep 2-3 years if the bottle is unopened and, once opened, up to 1 year. Store in a cool, dry place away from sunlight. Do not store in the refrigerator or medicine cabinet since moisture builds up inside the bottle after con-stant opening and closing. Some companies add a silica gel packet to absorb excess mois-ture. A few grains of rice added to the bottle will give similar results.

FORMS OF SUPPLEMENTS

Supplements are available in many forms to facilitate the particular absorption requirements of the various nutrients and to provide alternatives for individual needs and desires.

Tablets, the most familiar form and easily stored, are made from high pressure compression of the loose materials. They often require the addition of fillers and binders to facilitate formation of the tablet and coatings to protect the tablets from moisture and facilitate swallowing. Some tablets are so compact that some people may have difficulty with absorption and utilization.

Chewable tablets, most often sweetened with sugar, honey, molasses, fructose, or fruit concentrates, are easy to take and generally well absorbed. The sugar content can be *quite high*, so if sugar is to be avoided, use powders, liquids, or capsules.

Powders and liquids are assimilated very well, contain no excipients, and are usually are quite potent. They can be mixed into liquids, foods, or taken by the spoonful. Unpalatable combinations generally are sweetened or flavored.

Capsules rarely contain excipients unless a filler is needed. They are very well assimilated, easier to swallow for most people and usually do not taste of the nutrients contained within. Capsules are not suitable for a strict vegetarian since they are made from gelatin. Vegetarians and those who are allergic to beef can open the capsules, swallow the contents, and discard the capsule.

WHAT DOES IT MEAN?

Excipients are the other ingredients added to a tablet to help in the formation of the tablet itself, to facilitate the absorption and utilization of the nutrient being supplemented, and to make the tablet more palatable. Avoid supplements which use artificial colors, artificial flavors, shellac, propylene glycol, polysorbate-80, and preservatives such as BHA, BHT, and methyl-propylparaben. Excipients are used primarily in tablets and rarely in capsules except when a filler is needed.

EXAMPLES OF EXCIPIENTS USED IN SUPPLEMENTS

CLASS	PURPOSE OR ACTION	EXAMPLES OF COMPOUNDS USED
dilutents or fillers	to increase bulk of the tablet for pressing	di-calcium phosphate, sorbitol, cellulose
binders	substances that hold the tablet together	cellulose, cornstarch, ethyl-cellulose, algin, alginic acid, sodium alginate, lecithin, sorbitol, acacia (gum arabic)
lubricants or glidants	slick substances used to keep the tablet from sticking to the press	silica, calcium stearate, magnesium stearate
disintegrants	used to facilitate disintegration in the intestinal tract	gum arabic, algin or alginate, cellulose, starch, lactose, citric acid, bicarbonate
colors	for appearance only	chlorophyll (green) beet powder (red) riboflavin (B^2) (yellow)
flavors	makes chewable vitamins more palatable	look for natural flavors
sweeteners	makes chewable vitamins more palatable	fructose, sorbitol, honey, malt, sucrose, turbinado sugar
coatings	to protect tablets from moisture; to mask odd flavors or odors; to make tablets easier to swallow	zein (corn protein) brazil wax, sugar, food glaze
drying agents	to prevent tablets from absorbing water during processing	silica

g.-gram. Dosages expressed in terms of weight. 1 gram = 15.4 grains. 1000 grams = 1 kilogram.

gr.-grain. Dosages expressed in terms of weight. 1 grain = 0.085 grams (85 milligrams).

Hypo-allergenic is a term signifying that the product contains none or few of the foods or substances constituting the most common sensitivities experienced by people. In addition to being free of artificial flavors, colors, or preservatives, hypo-allergenic can be free of foods such as wheat, corn, soy, yeast, and milk.

i.u.-international units are the measure of activity used rather than the weight of dosages of vitamins A, D, and E. International units are used with vitamin E instead of milligrams or micrograms to standardize the many forms of vitamin E available while its use with vitamins A and D is simply due to historical application. A more recent method utilized in some charts for expressing vitamin A is in terms of of retinol equivalents (R.E.), the equivalent weight of retinol (vitamin A) actually absorbed and converted.

mcg.-microgram. Dosages expressed in terms of weight. 1000 microgram = 1 milligram.

mg.-milligram. Dosages expressed in terms of weight. 1000 milligrams = 1 gram.

Private label supplements are supplements made exclusively for a store. Even many nationally distributed supplements are formulated and produced by one of the few major supplement manufacturers. Because the marketing and advertising expenses are generally much lower for a store that carries its own private label supplement line, prices are usually much lower than a national brand. Private label supplements are made to the specifications of the store and therein lies the differences in quality among the brands. Quality can be determined by reading the label to be sure that the product is free of starch, artificial flavors, colors, and preservatives.

Sustained release or timed released supplements are designed to provide nutrients over a 6-12 hour period when frequent doses were not taken. Effectiveness varies with the manufacturer and the digestive system of the person taking the supplement.

Vegetarian supplements are supplements free of any animal products or derivatives. They are sold in the form of tablets, powders, or liquids; capsules are usually avoided because of beef gelatin source.

VITAMINS

People usually refer to all supplements as "vitamins" even though minerals, fats, protein, and carbohydrates are also available in supplement form. The actual definition of a vitamin is a substance necessary for proper growth and maintenance of the body which cannot be synthesized by the body but must be obtained from food or supplements. An exception to this is vitamin D which can be obtained from food but more often is produced from the sun activating the precursor to Vitamin D which is present in oil-like substances in the skin. Vitamins act as catalysts or spark plugs in the many chemical reactions within our body. Although often connected with energy, vitamins provide none themselves but speed up the chemical reactions involving the carbohydrates, fats, and proteins that the body *does* use for energy.

Vitamins A, D, E, and K are called **fat soluble vitamins** since they concentrate in fatty tissues and cell membranes, needing fat for proper assimilation. Because they can be stored in these areas and the liver, high doses carry the risk of toxic level buildup.

Water soluble vitamins include vitamins C and the B complex. They are carried by the blood throughout the body and absorbed by the cells where they are needed. They must be replenished everyday from food and, if needed, from supplements since they cannot be stored in the body. Any excess is excreted in the urine although large amounts of an isolated vitamin may create an imbalance if used indiscriminately without adequate knowledge or guidance.

MINERALS

Minerals, one of the most understated classes of nutrients, is finally getting the status it deserves. Although most people recognize the importance of vitamins, the fact remains that without minerals, vitamins cannot be assimilated or utilized by the body.

Minerals are used in our bodies to form bones, teeth, soft tissue, muscles, blood, and nerve cells. Besides functioning as structural components, minerals are also catalysts for many reactions within the body such as transmission of nerve impulses, digestion, and muscle response. In addition, they assist in producing hormones, maintaining the acid/ alkaline balance in the body, and in the manufacturing of antibodies.

We obtain highly assimilated organic minerals from the food we eat: fruits and vegetables from the soil or from the sea or from fish or animals whose mineral content originates from eating land or sea plants. A varied diet containing whole grains, beans, nuts and seeds, leafy greens, fruits, and also dairy products, meat and poultry, fish, and eggs has the potential to provide all the minerals needed for an average person. Avoid refined sugar and carbohydrates since they retain very few minerals originally present in the food.

Calcium, chlorine, phosphorus, potassium, magnesium, sodium, and sulfur are called **macro minerals** since relatively large amounts are needed in the body. Zinc, iron, manganese, copper, chromium, selenium, iodine, and molybdenum are referred to as **trace minerals** since only minute amounts are required. Although like vitamins, most minerals have a general U.S. Recommended Daily Allowance (U.S. RDA) established by the National Academy of Sciences, trace minerals have a significantly narrow margin of safety. It is easy to take too much, develop toxicity, and create a deficiency in another trace mineral by upsetting the delicate balance unless proper levels are maintained and monitored. Some minerals have no official RDAs because of insufficient knowledge about the exact levels needed.

Consider total dietary intake before supplementation. Higher potencies of any of the minerals may be warranted for certain conditions but should always be used with discretion and under guidance. Calcium and iron are the more commonly supplemented minerals since it is difficult for many people to obtain and absorb an adequate amount in their diet. Dosages for minerals are expressed in terms of weight: micrograms (mcg.), milligrams (mg.) or grams (g.).

Chelated minerals-Inorganic minerals from the earth such as dolomite, oyster shell, egg shell, and bone meal must be converted in the body into an organic form that the body can assimilate. Some individuals and manufacturers claim that chelated minerals facilitate the process. A chelated mineral is bound to another substance such as gluconic acid from corn (gluconates), lactic acid from milk, corn, or fermentation process (lactates), fumaric acid from plants (fumerates), sulfuric acid (sulfates), ascorbic acid (ascorbates), citric acid (citrates), amino acids from soy or milk protein (amino acid chelates) or orotic acid from a fermentation process (orotates).

FIBER

Fiber in one's diet or in supplement form gives a sense of fullness and aids digestion. Psyllium seed powders, bran tablets, pectin tablets, and formulas using a multiple of fiber sources have been popular in weight loss programs.

Dietary fiber includes all food substances that our digestive enzymes cannot break down and utilize by the body as an energy source. There are 6 major types of dietary fiber: **cellulose**— the major constituent of plant fiber; **lignin**— the woody compound found not only in wood (!) but also in plant fiber; **hemicellulose**— usually found along with other fibers; **pectin**— the substance found in roots, stems, and fruits of plants, especially apples and in citrus rinds, that is famous for its gelling properties; **gums and mucilages** such as guar gum from legumes used in many prepared food products; and **algal polysaccharides** found in sea vegetables including kelp, kombu, carrageenan and agar which are also gel-forming fibers.

All six types of fiber fit into two basic categories: water insoluble and water soluble. **Insoluble fibers** as found in cellulose, hemicellulose, and lignin, stimulate the intestines, accelerates food transit time, and increase the weight and softness of the stool. Insoluble fiber can be supplied from bran, whole grains, fruits, vegetables, and nuts.

Studies have shown that the **soluble fibers** of pectin, gums, algal polysaccharide and certain hemicelluloses as represented by fruits, oats, barley, legumes, psyllium seeds, flax seeds, and sea vegetables are responsible for most of the beneficial effects of fiber. This class of fiber has been found to lower absorption of cholesterol, regulate blood sugar by slowing the absorption of sugar into the bloodstream, and absorb and remove toxic metals and carcinogens from the body. Although important to all of us, soluble fibers are of special interest to individuals with diabetes. The fiber lowers fasting glucose levels, reduces insulin requirements, and improves glycemic control, while decreasing the high serum cholesterol and triglycerides often found in diabetes. Hypoglycemia is also treated by using the slow sugar absorption properties of soluble fibers. Insoluble fibers have not shown the same results.

How much is suggested?

The average low fiber, refined diet provides only about 10-20 grams of fiber per day. No U.S. RDA exists but suggested optimum amounts range from 30-50 grams per day. Any increase should be done gradually in order to give your digestive system time to adjust to the extra fiber intake. Start by eating a bran muffin instead of a croissant and brown rice instead of white rice. Don't peel your vegetables unless they are waxed or have surface damage. Eat the whole fruit instead of drinking its juice. Conscious counting of grams of fiber generally is not necessary if common sense substitutions for low fiber, refined foods are made.

However, food charts and labels that list the amount of fiber contained in particular foods can function as a comparison guide to insure a diet high in fiber. Previously, fiber was measured in regards to the amount of crude fiber it contained. Crude fiber is the residue left after treating a plant sample first with a weak acid and then with a weak alkali. A new method for analyzing dietary fiber has since been accepted for official use since lab treatment of a food is much harsher than what occurs in the body and generally reported much less fiber than what was actually present. When reading food tables and labels, look for the words "dietary fiber" instead of "crude fiber". To convert crude fiber to approximations of dietary fiber, multiply crude fiber values of whole grains by 6, all high-carbohydrate vegetables, legumes, and fruits by 3, and other vegetables by 2.

Adjusting to increased fiber

Although common reactions to increased fiber in one's diet are flatulence and bloating, both can be minimized (when no other cause is present) if proper precautions are taken. Increasing fiber intake *gradually* will decrease the nuisance of flatulence and bloating. Practically speaking, this means to add just one serving of a high fiber food daily for a week. The next week add another serving per day and so on to make ongoing diet changes that includes proportionally more high fiber foods than refined, low fiber foods. The second important variable is to increase liquid intake considerably, about 8-10 glasses of water per day, to account for the extra liquid that will be absorbed by the fiber. This is the real key for the effectiveness of fiber. Too little liquid can even cause the fiber to be constipating unless enough liquid can create a soft bulk.

Too much fiber has the potential to lead to mineral deficiencies as some fiber compounds, especially phytic acid and oxalic acid, bind with some minerals to block their absorption. Unless the rest of the diet consists of primarily refined foods whose mineral content has been stripped along with the parts of the foods that have been eliminated, under most circumstances a moderately high fiber, complex carbohydrate whole food diet should not present a problem. **NOTE:** much of this mineral-binding phytic acid can be destroyed if grains, nuts, and legumes are sprouted, fermented as in sourdough, or made into a yeast-risen bread.

Individuals with specific medical conditions, especially those being treated for diabetes, hypoglycemia, and elevated cholesterol should discuss an increase in fiber with their doctor, dietician, or qualified health professional. Increased fiber may reduce insulin needs and other medications.

SOURCES OF FIBER

Since all fiber sources except lignin are complex carbohydrates, the best source of fiber is from a whole foods diet high in complex carbohydrates. Overprocessing of foods as in the production of white flour, white sugar, and white rice not only removes a significant amount of fiber but is accompanied by significant losses in nutrients. Canned fruits and vegetables and even fruit juices are much lower in fiber than their fresh, whole counterparts. Overcooking also reduces the amount of available fiber. Include both insoluble and soluble fibers in your diet from a variety of food sources.

Although very effective fiber supplements are available in tablet, powder, and instant mixes, they should be used only as an adjunct, if necessary, and not as a substitute for foods high in fiber. Monitor the amount you take with the amount provided by the diet. Many people find them useful while traveling when, unfortunately, foods high in complex carbohydrates and fiber are harder to obtain.

Wheat bran, one of the least expensive ways to obtain fiber, it is easily added to breads, casseroles, soups, or cereals. Since it is extremely high in insoluble fibers, it accelerates transit time even more than most foods by acting as an irritant to the intestines. Wheat bran must be used with a large amount of water to prevent cramping, flatulence, and constipation.   Unlike soluble fibers, wheat bran increases absorption rate of sugars into the bloodstream which may cause adverse blood sugar fluctuations in hypoglycemic and diabetic conditions. Since it is high in mineral-binding phytic acid, it should be used in moderation.

Oat bran, an excellent soluble fiber noted for its use in lowering cholesterol, it is equally effective in the other benefits of soluble fibers. Like wheat bran, oat bran can be added to breads, casseroles, soups, cereals, and made into a delicious cooked cereal which is ready to eat after cooking only 2 minutes. Its lighter color, texture, and flavor make it even more appealing to many people than wheat bran. Since it contains some natural oils, refrigerate or store in the freezer and use within 2 months.

Flax seeds, similar to psyllium seeds, the outer walls of the seed expand, swell, and absorb water to form a mucilage coating which provides bulk and lubrication. It's most commonly used as a delicious fiber addition to breads and baked goods.

Guar gum is a mucilaginous substance derived from legumes which acts in a similar fashion as pectin.

Pectin, besides its obvious presence in apples, purified pectin, often derived from the inner portion of citrus fruit rinds, is most familiar to people with its use in anti-diarrhea preparations and in making jams and jellies. It does, indeed, form a jelly-like substance and has all the beneficial effects of other soluble fibers when both foods rich in pectin or supplements are used.

Psyllium seeds, derived from the plantago plant, are most used for their fiber-rich husks. The outer walls of the seed expand, swell, and absorb water to form a mucilage coating which provides bulk and lubrication. Since it swells so rapidly, preparations made with psyllium should be used immediately. Psyllium has been used in many commercial laxatives for years. Read labels carefully to avoid added sugar.

HOMEOPATHY

Homeopathy is a scientific system of medicine that uses natural remedies made from animal, vegetable, and mineral substances. The name comes from the Greek words "homoios" and "pathos" which mean "similar suffering." Like glandulars, the underlying premise is "like cures like." In homeopathy, a remedy can cure a disease if it produces in a healthy person symptoms which are similar to the disease. This is called the "Law of Similars". Two other basic laws of homeopathy are the "Law of Proving" and the "Law of Potentization".

The "Law of Proving" is the verification that a certain substance produces a particular medicinal effect. The substance is given to healthy people and the symptoms are recorded in the homeopathic doctor's reference, similar to the PDR, Physicians Desk Reference, that traditional doctors consult to determine what drugs to use.

The "Law of Potentization" concerns the method of preparation for a substance that is used as a remedy. Each remedy is prepared by a controlled process of successive dilutions alternated with shaking or grinding of the substance, which is continued to the point where the resulting medicine contains no molecules of the original substance. This small dose is called a potency. The greater the dilution, the higher the potency. It is this process of potentization which makes it possible to use certain substances such as metals and charcoal as medicine because they are so diluted that they become non-toxic. Each time the substance is diluted and shaken or ground it is designated as 1X potency. A 6X on a label indicates that the substance has gone through the process six times.

A true homeopath is a trained medical doctor who then studies to become a homeopathic physician. Chronic problems should be handled by a licensed homeopath but acute conditions can be cured at home with basic 6X homeopathic remedies.

Homeopathy is recognized by the FDA as a real science so unlike herbs or vitamin preparations, labels can legally state the purpose of a product.

Certain precautions should be followed when using homeopathic remedies. Do not use with caffeine or standard medicines. When improvement is well established, the remedy should be discontinued or the symptoms may develop again.

Nothing else should be in the mouth 15 minutes before or after the remedy is used. The remedies are available in liquid form with an alcohol base and in tablets which are designed to dissolve on or under the tongue with the help of lactose.

Cell Salts are inorganic minerals which exist as part of the cells of healthy organisms. They are not used to cure disease, but to aid the body in healing itself. The twelve tissue salts relate to specific cell functions in the body. They are prepared in a manner similar to homeopathic remedies. They also are available in liquid and tablet form alone and in combinations.

PRENATAL NUTRITION & SUPPLEMENTATION

Although good nutrition is important throughout each person's life, never is it so important as during formation within the womb and early infancy. The unborn baby is entirely dependent for his/her physical and mental development upon the nutrients the mother provides from her daily choices of food and drink.

To supply both her child's and her own nutritional needs, the expectant mother needs extra calories, protein, calcium, iron, and folic acid in her diet. Avoiding caffeine, drugs, and alcohol is also particularly important during this time. Many physicians prescribe prenatal supplements to insure the needs are being met. A **prenatal supplement** is a general multiple vitamin/mineral supplement which includes extra calcium, iron, and double the amount of folic acid.

After birth the breastfed baby continues to depend upon nutrients supplied by the mother and when weaned, upon nutrients supplied by the food and drinks chosen by the mother to feed her child. The best food choices for mother and child are whole foods—minimally processed, low in sugar, and free of artificial color, flavors, and preservatives. This combined with a lot of love will provide the basis for a more problem free pregnancy and the best opportunity for the child to reach his/her full potential happily and healthfully. As mentioned previously in the BABY CEREAL section, iron may be the nutrient most needing attention in infant nutrition.

PROTEIN POWDERS

Protein powders go in and out of vogue periodically. Years ago, excessive amounts of protein were considered important for an athlete and high protein-low carbohydrate diets were considered the best route to weight loss. Anyone who wanted to excel in sports or lose weight usually spent a lot of time at the blender making a protein drink.

In both cases, research has since proven otherwise. Excess protein depletes the body of calcium and overworks the liver and kidneys. The liver can convert protein into glucose for energy when carbohydrate levels are low, but reliance on protein for the major energy source is inefficient. Not only is excess energy needed for protein conversion, dehydration and mineral loss can also occur as the kidneys and liver try to remove excess toxic wastes. Sufficient protein *is* needed for growth, maintenance, repair, and energy, but too much protein and too little carbohydrates can result in sluggishness and impaired performance. Adequate protein is easy to obtain from a balanced diet.

Nonetheless, protein powders are sometimes recommended for certain people in certain conditions. To reflect the latest nutritional research, more manufacturers are changing their formulas. Rather than providing primarily protein, many formulas include a good proportion of carbohydrates in order to provide energy and spare the protein to do its own more essential work. Many formulas also include fiber as well as some vitamins and minerals in the effort to make their protein powders into more of a all-around nutritional supplement drink.

But what about the quality of protein present in a protein powder? Protein is composed of 22 amino acids which need to be in proper proportions in order for the body to utilize them efficiently. The actual protein content of the various protein powders varies according to the source of the protein. The powders which tend to have the optimum balance of amino acids are combinations of protein sources.

The better the balance of amino acids, the higher the Protein Efficiency Ratio (P.E.R.). This is a standard measure of protein quality based upon the growth of laboratory rats fed casein (the milk protein casein used as the government standard for protein quality) as compared with rats fed the particular protein formula in question. The test reveals whether the protein value of the formula is equal to, higher than, or less than the value of casein.

Some protein powders list their P.E.R. level but most do not. To determine the P.E.R. yourself, note the percentage of the U.S. RDA of protein per serving. If the product's percentage is equal to or higher than better than casein, the manufacturer must use 45 grams as the RDA and calculate what percentage of that RDA the recommended daily intake of the product provides. If the protein powder is less than the value of casein, the manufacturer must use 65 grams as the RDA and then calculate the percentage of that RDA number per recommended daily intake. Note also the number of tablespoons needed per serving to obtain the protein listed on the label.

How much protein does one need? The amount of total protein required throughout the day by the "average" adult can be calculated in grams by dividing one's weight by 2.2.

Beyond that, special conditions, illnesses, or stresses on the body may require more protein, especially in an absorbable form. As with any nutrient, each person's needs may vary according to the type of protein ingested, the condition of the body in general, and the condition of the digestive system. Extra protein is needed for pregnant and lactating women, but it can usually be obtained from the extra kilocalorie food intake that is also needed. In general, the average athlete only requires about 10% more protein than the average person. Extra calories and plenty of carbohydrates are more important to the athlete than excess protein.

EVALUATING PROTEIN POWDERS

The most common source of protein in protein powders is **soy protein**. Soy protein is an inexpensive high protein source excellent for vegetarians and those allergic to milk. Although soybeans are low in the amino acid methionine, *for adults*, **soy protein isolate** seems to be comparable to the protein quality of animal protein. Growing children still need some added source of the missing amino acid. Adding protein powders based on soy protein to milk would increase the P.E.R. of the protein powder, but this would not be a solution for strict vegetarians or people allergic to milk. Therefore, some protein powder formulas have added methionine to improve the amino acid balance.

Milk protein is another common protein powder source. Some companies use non-fat dry milk but this provides only about 46% protein. Most use casein which is the chief protein in cow's milk. Some use lactalbumin, the second most abundant protein in cow's milk which has a higher biological value than casein. (It is noteworthy that 60% of the protein in human milk is lactalbumin while casein comprises about 40%.) Products that contain lactalbumin will probably be more expensive than those which are primarily casein. **Whey powder** comes from the watery part of the milk which is separated from the curd. It contains lactalbumin and is high in vitamins and minerals. Because it is high in lactose (milk sugar) it also acts as a natural sweetener.

Egg albumin is the protein found in egg whites. This is included in some protein powders to enhance the protein content since eggs are often referred to as a perfect protein. The egg albumin is used instead of the whole egg or egg yolks to decrease the fat content.

Brewer's yeast can be added to protein powders to provide yet another source of protein and a variance in the proportion of amino acids. It also provides B vitamins and some minerals. Originally, brewer's yeast was a by-product of making beer and had a horrible taste. Now it is grown in laboratories with flavor in mind and is more correctly called **nutritional yeast**. Yeast grown on a molasses medium has a better flavor than torula yeast which is grown on wood pulp. Nutritional yeast is also very high in phosphorous and, therefore, should be balanced with calcium from food or supplement sources.

Spirulina is a new addition to some protein powders. Spirulina is a blue-green micro algae which is dried to provide a source of protein, B-vitamins, and beta carotene (pro vitamin A). In protein powders it enhances both the quality and quantity of the protein. It improves the assimilation and digestibility of the blends and supplies vitamins and other nutrients at the same time. The green color that some people object to indicates its high chlorophyll content and contributes to its vegetable-like flavor.

Lecithin from soy is added to many formulas. While large *pharmacological* doses of a special grade of lecithin have some beneficial affect on several disease conditions that affect memory and muscular coordination, the presence of lecithin in protein powders acts as an emulsifier and, therefore, helps to thicken the drink.

Digestive aids are often included in protein powders to assist the body in breaking down proteins for better utilization. Bromelain from pineapple and papain from papaya are common vegetarian digestive aids. Some companies use animal based pancreatin which contains amylase, protease, and lipase to break down carbohydrates, proteins and fats. Since digestive aids work best if they are enteric coated tablets or specially formulated pellets in capsules (coated to prevent digestion until they reach the small intestine), their presence in protein powders may or may not be effective.

Desiccated liver is added to provide many of the nutrients that are contained in liver. Too much added desiccated liver can affect palatability.

Natural flavoring such as vanilla, carob powder, or natural fruit flavors are used in better quality protein powders.

Carbohydrates, as mentioned before, the presence of some of it allows protein to be used for tissue repair and growth rather than be converted in the body to carbohydrates to be used for energy. Try adding the protein powder to fruit juice or blend in fresh fruit instead of relying upon high amounts of concentrated sweeteners.

One final word regarding the use of protein powders: they are meant to be used as an adjunct to one's diet, not the main source of one's protein or calories. Make sure you get plenty of complex carbohydrates and some fat along with a variety of protein foods for proper nourishment.

SPORTS SUPPLEMENTS

Whether you are a weekend or professional athlete, what you eat will affect your performance, stamina, strength, and endurance. As mentioned before, the massive amounts of protein and salt tablets in vogue years ago have been dismissed in favor of a low fat, moderate protein, high complex carbohydrate diet that provides adequate kilocalories. Sports nutrition is a relatively new and controversial field of research. New claims and new products are introduced continually. However, no supplement can replace a good diet, adequate training, and sufficient rest.

In addition to protein powders, octacosonal, amino acids, glandulars, glucose polymer drinks, electolyte replacements, and anti-oxidants are common supplements advocated by some books, athletes, and supplement companies.

Octacosonal is believed to be responsible for the increase in stamina, strength, and endurance that people experience after using wheat germ oil or isolated octacosonol for 4-6 weeks. Supplemental potencies range from 325 mcg. up to 6000 mcg. Each teaspoon of wheat germ oil yields 325 mcg. of octacosonol. A dry synthetic form of octacosonol is available that is cheaper, wheat free, and helpful for those who have difficulty digesting oils. Most studies have used the concentrated wheat germ oil octacosonol supplements rather than the synthetic forms. Some believe the presence of the essential fatty acids in the oil enhance utilization.

Steroid replacements are becoming more popular as the long term side effects of anabolic steroids are made visible. Disruption in liver structure and function causing cancer and other liver problems, changes in the body's metabolism of carbohydrates and fats leading to arteriosclerosis, heart disease, and high blood pressure, and the possibility of degenerative joint diseases are possible side effects.

Raw glandulars such as adrenal, liver, and orchic or ovarian tissue were the first alternatives suggested. Single or certain combinations of amino acids have been used in the belief that they can replace steriods, help lose weight, increase energy, and build muscle. The use of isolated amino acids is highly controversial and, in high levels, can have some negative side effects. Growing children and adolescents as well as pregnant and lactating women should not supplement with amino acids. Questions are also raised as to whether the amino acids are simply broken down during digestion similar to amino acids found in food proteins. Branch-chained amino acids are now being introduced as a possible alternative. Since no long term studies have been made, caution is advised upon experimentation.

Electrolyte replacements and complex carbohydrate replacement drinks are one way some athletes choose to replenish what is lost through perspiration. Working muscles need water. Athletes who train and compete in hot weather especially understand the value of fluid and electrolyte replacement. The warning symptoms of dehydration: dizziness, nausea, and exhaustion can be avoided by the appropriate means depending upon the intensity and duration of the activity. In many cases, water is enough. By rehydrating with water, we maintain our capacity to dissipate heat produced by exercise and environmental conditions, thus keeping us cool. If the duration of the activity is short, water is the preferred source for rehydrating because nothing leaves the stomach as quickly.

Profuse sweating, especially during long periods of activity in hot weather, could lead to a possible imbalance of electrolytes—the minerals, primarily sodium and potassium that regulate the movement of water in and out of your cells. Electrolytes, along with water, function to ward off possible dehydration.

Adequate sodium is generally not much of an issue since a typical American diet includes plenty of this mineral. In fact, moderate salting of foods is considered fine for athletes. Avoid salt tablets or electolyte drinks high in sodium since they raise the salt concentration in the blood, leading to dehydration and the loss of potassium.

Potassium and magnesium seem to be much more important to replace. Fruits, fruit juices, fresh vegetables, and minimally processed foods are good sources of these minerals. While supplementation is sometimes recommended under extreme circumstances and according to the particular needs of the particular individual, a good, balanced diet may be an adequate source of the electrolytes for the average athlete.

Many electrolyte replacement drinks are available and most of them have high concentrations of simple sugars. Despite its addition for palatabilty and "energy" factors, the presence of sugar can prolong its stay in the stomach and cause cramping, bloating, and posssibly diarrhea. This occurs since the body concentrates on muscle movement and energy production during exercise instead of digestion. The burst of energy from simple sugar based drinks that contain glucose, sucrose, and dextrose, (including de-fizzed soft drinks) is short-lived and, in the long run, impedes performance.

However, carbohydrates do have their purpose. For long athletic events when muscle glycogen is depleted, extra carbohydrate seems to be of benefit. Consider the amount of oranges and bananas that are usually consumed at running and bicycle events. Fruits, fruit juices, and, more recently, glucose polymers, are the preferred sources of replenishing carbohydrates with little gastric upset.

Glucose polymer drinks are one of the more recent formulas used as a concentrated source of energy based on complex carbohydrates. Glucose polymers are hydrolized starches extracted from grain, bean, and/or vegetable, depending upon the brand. In contrast to simple sugar formulas, drinks made with glucose polymers leave the stomach quickly and avoid the problems of dehydration and gastric distress. Individuals with blood sugar disorders such as diabetes or hypoglycemia should use the drinks with caution, especially if used on an empty stomach or if mixed in too high a concentration.

Anti oxidants such as vitamin E, S.O.D., selenium, glutathione, vitamin C, zinc, and beta-carotene are used to counteract the deleterious effects of pollution in the air, the water we drink, and from cigarettes, alcohol, and caffeine. Damage to the cell walls and the actual functioning of the cell occur which, if not checked by our own anti-oxidant guard systems, cause premature aging, cancer, and, of immediate concern for the athlete, narrowing of the blood vessels and impairment of the oxygen transport system. A good diet will supply the anti-oxidant nutrients but some supplementation in reasonable amounts may be beneficial for some people under certain high pollution conditions.

WEIGHT LOSS

Speaking of exercise, it is an important component in an effective weight loss program along with a well balanced, high fiber diet low in fat and sugar. One pound of fat tissue contains 3500 kilocalories. Skipping meals, fasting a couple days, or wearing "sweat suits" can result in quick water weight, but as soon as one drinks again, the "pounds" return quite quickly. Eating much less or nothing at all is not the answer. A caloric intake less than 1200 kilocalories per day for extended periods of time is not only dangerous, but also counterproductive, especially with diets that emphasize protein and very little carbohydrates.

The body requires a steady flow of glucose as fuel. If not enough carbohydrate is provided, the body looks for other sources. Although fat provides energy in a fast, it cannot provide it in the form of glucose, the fuel needed by the brain and nerve. Protein is best used for growth and maintenance and many other factors, but, in the presence of little carbohydrate, the body breaks down lean body protein tissues such as muscles and liver to supply the necessary glucose. As lean body mass is reduced, the body's metabolism slows down. Because of the slower metabolism, the fat loss falls to a bare minimum! In fact, less fat will be used up in a low carbohydrate diet than if a balanced, low calorie diet containing at least 1200 kilocalories were used!

As the carbohydrate-sparing fast continues, in addition to using lean body tissue for fuel, the brain and nerve cells develop the ability to derive about half of their energy needs from a special form of fat known as ketones. These are produced normally in small amounts but larger amounts overtax the kidneys as the body tries to excrete the ketones via the urine and neutralize their acidity. High concentrations of ketones can eventually lead to ketosis, a very serious condition that occurs when the blood concentration of the acidic ketones outstrips normal metabolic capabilities. Death due to a collapse of the circulatory system is a possible outcome. So what is the best way to lose weight?

The best reducing diet should be:
1) adequate in nutrients—carbohydrates, protein, some fat, vitamins, and minerals
2) lower in calories without going below 1200 kilocalories
3) be as near normal a diet as possible while emphasizing nutrient-dense foods.

A good meal can be had for the same amount of kilocalories provided by some weight loss formulas that are based primarily on protein. If a weight loss formula is used, make sure it has a source of carbohydrate, fiber, and is included in a program that emphasizes the importance of eating regular balanced meals.

A major key to weight loss is to establish new eating patterns that will continue to be used. As mentioned before, the other key to weight loss includes some form of exercise.

Exercising is the only way to avoid lean body mass losses while losing fat. The more lean tissue a person has, the higher the rate of metabolism. An added bonus to exercise is that the higher rate of metabolism generated during exercise will continue for hours afterwards.

As one becomes more conditioned, the body burns more fatty acids than glucose as fuel. Therefore, a conditioned body burns more body fat than an unconditioned body. No one needs to become a competitive athlete or become the best in whatever exercise is chosen. Find an aerobic exercise that is most fun and fits into your schedule— but take the time.

It is beyond the scope of this book to provide definitive guidelines concerning each of the nutrients. The science of nutrition is young and dynamic. New research is continually giving us expanded information on the roles of the nutrients, the interactions that take place, and the specific needs for specific conditions, activity levels, and lifestyles.

Many supplement companies are sincere and sell only products that are backed by **solid current research data**. Other products exist that are marketed only to ride the tide of the latest fad or to promote a celebrity and/or book. Take the time to investigate.

13

COOKING FOR
SPECIAL DIETS

COMMON ALLERGIES

Say the word "allergy" and most people think of hay fever, runny noses, watery eyes, or hives. Food sensitivities and food intolerances can manifest in many different ways. Mood swings, inability to concentrate, migraine headaches, diarrhea, constipation, extreme fatigue, hyperactivity, chronic colds, anxiety, depression, and bloating— all may be linked to a sensitivity to a food or chemical.

Clinical ecology is a relatively new area in the field of medical diagnosis and treatment which links illness and chronic "unexplained" health problems to a person's environment— the house and city in which one lives, the food eaten, chemicals in foods and the air, the water one drinks, molds, and pollens. Clinical ecology stresses biochemical individuality. What affects one person adversely may or may not affect another. No food is considered sacred; anything may cause an adverse reaction in someone.

The most common allergens are wheat, corn, milk, yeast, peanuts, soy, eggs, beef, citrus, and potato. These foods are also the most common foods eaten on a regular basis and as ingredients in prepared foods. Often a person will tend to eat the same foods every day. He/she may have the same type of cereal at breakfast with whole wheat toast or a croissant. At lunch the basic menu may be hot sauce and chips, avocado on a wholewheat roll with alfalfa sprouts or a hamburger on a wheat bun. Dinner might be beef again, cheese, or a soy based meal with the same basic vegetables such as green beans and carrots.

Constant or repeated exposure to a food or chemical is a stress on the body. The body can handle a large amount of stress but, similar to one more drop in the bucket causing the bucket to overflow, one more stress can overwhelm the body, leading to various symptoms. A person who has a stressful job, gets little sleep at night, smokes, drinks, or uses drugs to try to relax, and then eats the same foods every day is a candidate for allergies. Some people have higher stress levels than others such as that mythical great aunt everyone seems to have had who smoked like a fiend, drank a six-pack every day, existed on Twinkies and still lived to be 97 years old. The average person is not as tolerant, especially after late teens or early twenties.

Some people eat the same thing every day because they don't feel as good when they don't eat it. Food sensitivities are strange. Early exposure to an "allergen" can make you feel better. Because of the good feeling, a person tends to eat it often or every day. Antibodies to that food or chemical increase until a chronic symptom manifests such as irritability or digestive problems. Many times the source of the problem is unrecognized and the food is continually eaten, exacerbating the problem. This is known as allergy-addiction syndrome, not unlike a drug addiction. When it is finally recognized, the elimination of the food or chemical causes a withdrawal reaction. The symptoms intensify initially but subside after 3-4 days. Some people find the withdrawal too difficult and revert back to the food to diminish the withdrawal symptoms, thus never breaking the cycle. Once it is broken, however, and the offending substance avoided for a while, a rotation diet is often used to prevent future problems with that food or potential problems with other foods.

A rotation diet is a system to limit exposure to all foods by eating or drinking a particular food or beverage only once every 4 days. For example, if you had an apple, applesauce, or apple butter on Monday, you would not eat anything with apples until Friday. This is supposed to increase one's tolerance to foods through less exposure. Some allergists and clinical ecologists have said that if people who had food sensitivities did nothing but rotated their foods, their symptoms probably would diminish by 80%.

A 4 day rotation diet also emphasizes diversity in food selection and can expose people to foods never experienced previously. Diversity in food will provide a wider spectrum of nutrients.

Unless allergies are severe, many people use a modified rotation system which emphasizes diversity and a less strict schedule. A strict schedule can be as stressful as an offending food for some people. Avoiding the use of a particular food every day is a good start in controlling or preventing allergies as well as a way to ensure that a varied diet is maintained in order to obtain the wide spectrum of nutrients.

Discovering that a favorite food is causing some problems can be upsetting. Food selections become habits hard to break. A habit gives some security to people and when it needs to be broken, outrage and self pity are common. These emotions need to be recognized but the focus should be on the alternative food selections available. New flavors and textures may replace old familiar foods. Some substitutions may not be exactly the same, but an open mind and adventurous spirit can turn a negative self-pity situation into a positive exciting experience.

What are some alternatives to the most common allergies? Specific recipes mentioned are included in the RECIPES at the end of this chapter.

WHEAT AND GRAIN ALLERGIES are generally the hardest for individuals to approach. Wheat is included in most breads either as the main ingredient or to provide gluten to other grains which have little rising ability. Thus, a rye bread may be part wheat. Most ready-made cereals are primarily wheat based as are pancakes, desserts, noodles, crackers, gravies, and breaded fish or meats.

A wheat allergy provides the opportunity to experiment with different grains. Anything that is made with wheat flour can be made with other grain flours, but the flavor and texture will be different. Refer to the FLOUR section in this book for the properties of various grain flours.

Many ready-made alternatives are available:

Crackers are made from 100% rye flour and 100% rice flour. Rice cakes can be used as crackers or as a bread alternative. Wheat bread substitutes include 100% rye breads—both sourdough and regular yeast risen, Essene rye bread, mochi (rice), and corn tortillas. Corn pasta and 100% buckwheat soba can replace regular wheat pasta. Ready made cereals include cream of rice, puffed rice, rice flakes, brown rice crispies, cream of rye, rye flakes, corn flakes, corn germ, puffed corn, puffed millet, cream of buckwheat, oat bran, wheat-free granolas, steel cut oats, and oatmeal. Since food manufacturers recognize the prevalence of wheat allergies, an increasing amount of wheat-free products are being made.

Any cooked grain can replace cracked wheat or cous cous used at dinner. Cooked grains can also be used as a breakfast cereal by adding dried fruit before or after cooking barley, millet, buckwheat, etc. Leftover cooked grains can be warmed or served cold with milk.

CORN ALLERGIES are also very common and corn seems to be as widely used as wheat. Cornmeal, dextrose, corn oil, fructose, and corn syrup are included in many products. Even the adhesive used on stamps and envelopes is derived from corn.

For most people the most devastating aspect to corn allergies concerns the inability to eat corn chips and corn tortillas! As always, there is a substitution: wheat tortillas and potato or wheat based chips. They may not yield the same satisfaction for some people but the lack of aggravating symptoms usually makes up for the initial disappointment.

ALL GRAINS in general are allergens for some people. Starchy vegetables such as potatoes, yams, and winter squashes can fill the gap. Cutting the vegetables into 1/4 inch slices and topping with a sandwich spread can be an alternative to an open faced sandwich. Frozen tofu can even replace lasagna noodles. Simply thaw the frozen tofu, squeeze dry, and cut into 1/4 inch thick slices. Follow your lasagna recipe and substitute the slices of thawed tofu for the noodles.

MILK ALLERGIES seem almost beyond comprehension to most people. Milk has been touted as being a good source of calcium for decades, a high quality protein, a healthy beverage, a major cooking ingredient, and the basis from which cheese, yogurt, and ice cream are made.

However, for those who are allergic to milk or lack the ability to digest it, milk is not a good alternative. No matter how nutritious or tasty a milk is for many people, for some it can cause problems.

There are other sources of calcium besides dairy products. Sea vegetables, dark greens such as collard greens, bok choy, mustard greens, kale, and dandelion greens, sesame seeds, almonds, broccoli, and carob provide calcium. A calcium mineral supplement can also be used. Avoid using non-dairy creamers. Although free of milk substances, most are based on coconut oil, an extremely high source of saturated fats.

A sample of non-dairy food sources for calcium listed below. The U.S. RDA for calcium is 1000 mg. per day. To make comparisons with dairy food sources:

cheddar cheese	1 oz.	225 mg.
low fat cottage cheese	1 cup	138 mg.
low fat milk	1 cup	300 mg.
whole milk	1 cup	290 mg.
parmesan cheese	1 TB.	69 mg.
plain low fat yogurt	1 cup	415 mg.

NON-DAIRY CALCIUM SOURCES

almonds	1 oz.	75 mg.
broccoli	1/2 cup cooked	89 mg.
carob flour	1/4 cup	120 mg.
collard greens	1 cup cooked	113 mg.
garbanzo beans	1 cup, cooked	150 mg.
hijiki	1/4 cup cooked	153 mg.
kale	1 cup cooked	94 mg.
kombu	1/4 cup, cooked	76 mg.
mustard greens	1 cup cooked	104 mg.
pinto beans	1 cup, cooked	130 mg.
rutabagas	1 cup cooked	100 mg.
sardines w/ bones	3 oz.	372 mg.
salmon, pink, w/bones	3 oz.	167 mg.
tempeh	3 oz.	129 mg.
tofu (made w/ nigari)	3 oz.	54 mg.
(w/ calcium sulphate)		130 mg.
(w/ both nigari & calcium sulphate)		123 mg.
turnip greens	1 cup, cooked	198 mg.
wakame	1/4 cup, cooked	130 mg.

NON-DAIRY MILK SUBSTITUTES

NOTE: these do not contain all the other nutrients found in milk. Most importantly, they should not be the sole source of nutrition for an infant or child. Consult a dietician or qualified health practioner who can give advise on how to replace the missing nutrients.)

Various soy derivatives can be made into good dairy substitutes. Soy milk can be used as a beverage or cooking ingredient in all recipes using milk. Tofu can replace milk when it is blended with water, but, flavorwise, it is better for cooking than drinking. Blend 1/4 cup of tofu per 1 cup water.

Nut milks are another substitute for milk. Tahini milk is made by adding 1 tablespoon sesame tahini to 8 oz. of water. Mix in a blender adding honey, maple syrup, rice or barley malt syrup, raisins, or dates if desired. Whole sesame seeds, cashews, and almonds also make delicious nut milks.

Coconut milk, the liquid from fresh coconuts, is another alternative. Dried coconut can be made into milk using the same method as nut milks.

Blending 1/2 cup of amasake with 2 cups water makes a good milk. It will keep 5-7 days in the refrigerator.

Finally, plain water or fruit juice can replace milk in a recipe, in making hot cereals, and even to moisten dry cereals. Recipes using water instead of milk yield a dry crunchy crust instead of smooth, more moist texture.

Besides plain milk, other common dairy products have good non-dairy substitutes. Yogurt can be made with soy milk or nut milk. Soy based ice cream as well as the non-dairy, non-soy "Rice Dream" is available. Another ice cream alternative is frozen banana custard. Peel and freeze a banana, cut the frozen banana into chunks, place in a food processer, blender, or Champion Juicer, and process until the banana becomes creamy and whipped with air. Frozen bananas can also be blended with fruit juice to make "smoothies", a non dairy milk shake. Fruit, lecithin, brewer's yeast, protein powder, soy milk, or yogurt are optional ingredients. Thick amasake drinks taste similar to milk shakes.

Tofu is the basic alternative for cream cheese, sour cream, cottage cheese, ricotta cheese, and whipped cream. Digestibility and flavor of the tofu is best when boiled for 10 minutes before use. If the tofu is used as an ingredient in a recipe that will be cooked in some way before eating, the pre-boiling is not needed.

Tofu can also be substituted for soft cheese in sandwiches or on pizza although it will not melt or have the same flavor. In these situations, marinated or seasoned tofu is more satisfying for most people than plain boiled or raw tofu.

Soy based mozzarella "cheese" can provide the gooey, cheesy texture and flavor that is so good in macaroni and cheese, pizza, and lasagna. However, read the label carefully since casein, the principal protein in milk, is an ingredient in many soy cheeses. It acts as a binder in imitation cheeses and although a safe and nutritious food additive, for those allergic to the protein in milk, it may cause some problems.

But, not to worry! Foods that are topped with melted cheese can be topped with mochi, the sweet brown rice "biscuits". When casseroles or vegetables are topped with cubed or grated mochi and then steamed or baked, the mochi "melts" with a texture similar to mozzarella.

Besides using nut milks as the base, non-dairy creamed soups can be made by adding rolled oats or cous-cous to the soup as it is cooking. When the vegetables are tender, purée partially or completely to desired texture.

YEAST and MOLDS are common allergens found in baking yeast, brewer's yeast, beer, wine, and other fermented foods such as tempeh, vinegar, sauerkraut, miso, and pickles. The severity of the sensitivity varies among people. Avoiding yeasted bread may seem initially insurmountable, but many delicious alternatives are available. Rice cakes, mochi, tortillas, chapatis, Essene bread, flat bread, quick bread, pancakes made with baking powder, cooked grains, cookies, and noodles are yeast free.

PEANUTS are inexpensive and therefore are quite common in foods in many forms: whole or ground, peanut butter or peanut oil. People allergic to peanuts can use any tolerated oil and use almond butter, cashew butter, tahini, or sunflower butter as well.

SOY is another inexpensive common ingredient in foods. It also is used quite widely in milk free diets. If a person is allergic to soy but not to dairy products, there will be fewer inconveniences with the situation. If both allergies are present, then other protein sources such as the other beans, fish, meat, and nuts will need to be used. As previously mentioned, nut milk can fill the milk gap.

EGGS are used to leaven, to hold ingredients together, and to eat as a protein source. Different items are substituted depending on the original purpose the egg had in the recipe.

Leavening— Non-egg leavening agents include dry yeast, sourdough, baking powder, and tofu. Recipe books usually include pancakes, muffins, and breads using dry yeast or sourdough instead of eggs. To substitute baking powder for eggs used in a recipe, use two tablespoons baking powder and one teaspoon oil per egg. Another method is to use 1/4 cup mashed tofu to replace two eggs.

Binding— When eggs are used to hold ingredients together or for body, use 3 tablespoons apple or other fruit purée, cooked starchy vegetable purée, flaxseed and water mixture, or nut butters for each egg in the recipe. Agar-agar, arrowroot, gelatin, and kuzu can also be used, especially in puddings, sauces, and gravies.

Eating— Tofu again comes to the rescue when replacing scrambled eggs. Saute' mashed tofu with 1/4 teaspoon tumeric for a yellow color. Onions may be sautéed with the tofu for added flavor.

BEEF is easily replaced with poultry, eggs, cheese, beans, and nuts for protein. Many burger mixes are available made from beans, grains, and nuts. Tempeh is especially good served in a bun with ketchup and mustard. Frozen tofu thawed, squeezed, and crumbled has the texture of ground beef which can be used in chili, tacos, or pizza with good results.

CITRUS is often found in foods primarily in the form of lemon juice. Vinegar can easily be substituted.

POTATOES can be replaced by sweet potatoes, yams, or jerusalem artichokes. All three can be baked, steamed, fried, and used in salads. Since it is not sweet, the jerusalem artichoke is more readily substituted for traditional uses of potatoes. Buckwheat groats are a good substitute for hash browned potatoes.

Substituting for a non tolerated food with another takes some imagination and an open mind. Tastes and textures may vary, but a symptom free existence more than makes up for the loss of foods usually eaten.

Recipes

TOFU CREAM CHEESE   *makes 1/2 cup*
Great on bagels, breads, and as the basis for a dip.

8 oz. tofu
1 TB. sesame tahini or oil
1 teaspoon umeboshi paste or a pinch of salt

1. Boil tofu in water for 10 minutes.
2. Drain and let cool.
3. Combine all ingredients in a blender or food processer and blend until smooth.
   DO NOT ADD WATER.
4. Serve as a spread, dip, or use in recipes to replace cream cheese.

TOFU "RICOTTA"
There is no need to get rid of that favorite lasagna recipe if you are allergic to milk.
Substitute this recipe for the ricotta and use the "mock mochi cheese" for the topping.

8 oz. tofu
1 TB. sesame tahini or oil
1 teaspoon umeboshi paste or a pinch of salt

Instead of blending, mash tofu cream cheese ingredients to ricotta cheese
consistency.

TOFU SOUR CREAM
Great in dips or to top a bowl of borsch!

8 oz. tofu
1 TB. sesame tahini or oil
1 teaspoon umeboshi paste or a pinch of salt

Add 1 TB. lemon juice or vinegar to tofu cream cheese recipe.

TOFU COTTAGE CHEESE
Similar in flavor and texture to cottage cheese.

8 oz. tofu
1 TB. sesame tahini or oil
1 teaspoon umeboshi paste or a pinch of salt
1 TB. lemon juice or vinegar

Instead of blending, mash tofu sour cream ingredients with a fork for a chunky,
cottage cheese-like consistency.

Recipes

TOFU WHIPPED CREAM

You still can be "devilish" with your desserts, even if allergic to regular dairy whipped cream!

8 oz. tofu
1 TB. sesame tahini or almond butter
1 TB. maple syrup
1/2 teaspoon vanilla extract
pinch of salt
water or soy milk (opt.)

1. Boil tofu in water for 10 minutes.
2. Drain and let cool.
3. Combine all ingredients in a blender or food processor and blend until smooth. Add water or soy milk if whipped cream seems too thick, but be careful!

MOCHI MOCK CHEESE

Go ahead, try it! You can't imagine how satisfying it is!

2 squares mochi, plain or sesame-garlic, grated
1/2 cup water
3 TB. sesame tahini
1 teaspoon olive oil

1. Combine all ingredients.
2. Sprinkle over pizza, lasagna, etc. and bake as usual.

NOTE: If your entrée will be cooked or baked covered, the water, tahini, and oil may be eliminated. Experiment to see which method you prefer.

NUT MILK   *makes 1 quart*

A truly delicious beverage, but, admittedly, high in fat (although primarily unsaturated in composition). 1 cup cashews can be substituted for the blanched almonds.

1 cup blanched almonds (Cover with boiling water and allow to cool.
Skins can easily be removed.)
4 cups water
1 teaspoon-1 TB. honey or rice syrup (opt.)
1 TB. sesame oil (opt.)

1. Place all ingredients in blender or food processer and process at medium speed for 3 minutes.
2. Strain through a piece of fine cheesecloth.
3. Chill and serve or use in baking.
4. Will keep 1 week refrigerated.

Recipes

SCRAMBLED TOFU   *serves 4*

If everyone tried scrambled tofu, chickens would be out of work! The addition of tumeric gives the soft textured "eggs" its familiar yellow color.

1 TB. corn or safflower oil
1/4 tsp. tumeric
2 cloves garlic, minced
1 onion, minced
2 ribs celery, finely diced
1 lb. tofu
2 teaspoons tamari shoyu or 1/4 teaspoon sea salt

1. Heat oil in a large skillet and sauté tumeric and garlic for 1 minute.
2. Add onion and sauté 3 more minutes .
3. Add celery and continue to sauté for another 2 minutes.
4. Crumble tofu and add to vegetables.
5. Season with shoyu or sea salt.
6. Cover and cook for 10 minutes, stirring occasionally.
7. Serve with toast, bagels, or tortillas.

CREAM OF VEGETABLE SOUP   *serves 4*

It's non-dairy but still creamy, thanks to the addition of oat flakes.

3 cups of any 1 vegetable or combination, cut in small chunks (Choose from cauliflower, broccoli, carrot, celery, cucumber, etc.)
1 small onion, cut in small chunks
pinch of sea salt or to taste
1 teaspoon of any herb or spice
1/2 cup rolled oats
water to cover

1. Bring ingredients to a boil.
2. Reduce heat and simmer 1/2 hour or until vegetables are soft.
3. Purée soup in blender or food processer to desired texture.
4. Serve hot or cold.

Recipes

HEARTY MEATLESS SPAGHETTI SAUCE   *serves 4*

Frozen tofu comes to the rescue to provide an alternative that fools (or at least appeases) the most vehement meat eater. The cooked, previously frozen tofu has a texture similar to ground beef while the long simmering gives it a remarkable flavor.

2 TB. olive oil
1 onion, diced
4 cloves garlic, minced
1 green pepper, diced
1/2 lb. mushrooms, quartered
1 bay leaf
1 quart tomato sauce
1/2 teaspoon **each** oregano, basil, thyme, and fennel seed
salt to taste
1 lb. frozen tofu (freeze tofu 48 hours without water. Thaw and crumble to texture of ground beef.)
water (opt.)

1. Heat oil over medium heat.
2. Sauté onion and garlic for 5 minutes.
3. Add pepper and mushrooms and sauté 5 more minutes.
4. Add remaining ingredients.
5. Bring to a boil, reduce heat, and simmer 30 - 60 minutes, adding water if necessary.
6. Serve over pasta or spaghetti squash.

14
ET CETERA

CONVENIENCE   FOODS

It would be ideal if everyone had the time or desire to bake their own bread, make soup, and cook full course meals. However, sometimes all it takes is some preplanning and a variety of staples to make a meal in 30 minutes. Always make and freeze extra beans, keep tofu, eggs, and a few types of cheeses in the refrigerator, freeze some fish, stock up on bulgar, mochi, pasta, buckwheat, or cous-cous for a quickly cooked grain, and store some potatoes or yams.

To make things even easier, the natural foods industry has provided an array of convenience foods that are minimally processed and made with good ingredients.

Sauces can transform a plate of pasta, a pot of beans, or chicken into a different meal each night. A variety of dry mixes are available without MSG and artificial ingredients. Tomato and spaghetti sauces are made without the high amounts of sugar, corn syrup, cottonseed oil, animal fats, and starch fillers so commonly found in many commercial sauces. The richest tasting sauces are based on whole tomatoes rather than tomato paste. Other differences include the type of oil used and the addition of salt, vinegar, or other herbs.

In the mood for **beans** for lunch or dinner but you don't have any already cooked? Refried beans can be cooked in 20 minutes with pinto beans that are precooked, dried, and powdered. Just add oil and water, assemble your vegetables and tortillas, and sit down to a delicious quick meal. Cooked beans and soups come in cans and glass jars. Glass jars or enamel lined cans used by some health conscious manufacturers (check the label for claim) are preferrable in order to avoid lead and other metal contamination. Other soups include instant miso soups, ramen, and packaged dry cream soups which rely on whey powder for the creaminess.

The **frozen food** area has nearly as extensive a selection as other traditional grocery stores with the emphasis on quality chemical free ingredients. The use of real cheese, fresh vegetables, natural flavors and spices, whole grains, and choice meats accounts for the prices being somewhat higher than their commercial counterparts.

Don't forget **frozen burgers** made from tempeh, tofu, or grain/seed combinations for non meat/non dairy proteins. Steam, bake, or even put them in a toaster to reheat. All you need is bread, buns, and vegetables for a complete meal. Here is a good way to try preseasoned, precooked tofu and tempeh.

Packaged dinner mixes offer a quick meal at home or while camping or backpacking. Most are grain and bean combinations which cook up into stews, soups, or vegetarian burgers. Quick grain mixes are also available including grain pilafs that cook in 20 minutes and a 10 minute rice which is made from a specially processed brown rice whose nutritional content is almost identical to home cooked brown rice (see RICE for more information).

Dried vegetables such as shredded daikon radish, mushrooms, and tomatoes are easily stored and full of concentrated flavor when rehydrated and cooked with other vegetables, sauces, stews, or casseroles.

Dried mushrooms vary in size and flavor. Soak in warm water for about 20 minutes before cooking and use the soaking water if possible in your recipe.

Cepes have a strong mushroom, nutty flavor.

Delicious but expensive **morels** have a rich woodsy flavor.

Chanterelles have an apricot-like aroma and flavor.

Shitake mushrooms have a strong taste and aroma that is used extensively in Oriental cooking.

Straw mushrooms are small mushrooms that are grown on bundles of soaked rice straw. They are often used in Chinese stir frys.

Oyster mushrooms have a robust flavor and tough texture.

Cloud ear or tree ear mushrooms expand 5-6 times in size after soaking. Although they impart little flavor, these mushrooms add a slippery, crunchy texture to stir fries and soups.

Gluten, the elastic-like fibers that appear after kneading wheat flour, is responsible for making bread rise. This same gluten is a concentrated source of protein which is obtained when a flour and water dough is kneaded under water. Simmering the resulting gluten in naturally aged soy sauce, kombu sea vegetable, and ginger yields **seitan.** Its appearance and texture resemble roast beef and thus it is appropriate in stews, soups, and casseroles. Although it has a delicious flavor of its own, it absorbs the flavors of other vegetables, sauces, or seasonings to create unique dishes every time.

A 3 1/2 ounce serving has 118 calories, 18 grams of protein, and 1 gram of fat. Seitan is sold with the tamari shoyu, ginger, kombu broth which prolongs its freshness up to one week in the refrigerator. Seitan freezes well, too. Complement with beans or animal products for a complete protein.

Fu is a wheat gluten product similar to seitan that is toasted, steamed, and dried into small toast-like doughnut shaped rounds that store well in an airtight container. Soak in hot water for 10 minutes until softened and squeeze out excess water. Fu expands considerably when reconstituted. Add the reconstituted fu to soups or stews, or boil, sauté, steam, bake, or deep fry. Like seitan, it absorbs flavors and adds a meaty texture. 3 1/2 oz. of dried fu contains 28.5 grams of protein and 365 calories. Complement with beans or animal products for a complete protein.

Recipes

FU STEW
serves 4

Funny name, but seriously delicious!

2 leeks
1 medium daikon radish
2 yams
2 parsnips
6 pieces of fu
1 TB. tamari shoyu (naturally aged soy sauce)

1. Cut vegetables in large chunks.
2. Add shoyu and water to cover.
3. Bring to a boil and simmer 45 minutes.
4. Meanwhile, soak fu in water for 10 minutes.
5. Squeeze out and discard excess liquid from soaking fu.
6. Add fu to simmering vegetables for remainder of cooking time.
7. Serve with beans and grain for a hearty, warming meal.

SEITAN STEW
serves 4

Reminiscent of traditional beef stew. Serve with crackers and your favorite spread.

3 potatoes or turnips
6 carrots
1 onion
1/2 cup seitan tamari broth from container
bay leaf
water or tomato sauce
arrowroot or Japanese kuzu

1. Cut vegetables into large chunks.
2. Cube seitan into bite-sized pieces.
3. Combine vegetables, seitan, seitan broth, bay leaf and water or tomato sauce to cover.
4. Bring to a boil, reduce heat, and simmer 30 minutes or until vegetables are tender.
5. Dilute 1 TB. kuzu or 2 TB. arrowroot in cold water. Add to stew, stirring constantly until thickened.

Recipes

SHITAKE MUSHROOM KOMBU BROTH   *yields 5 cups*

One of the best broths for soup or for a sauce base can be made with shitake mushrooms and kombu. Use this broth for cooking stock when making rice or barley for an incredible grain dish!

1/2 cup boiling water
3 shitake mushrooms, dried
4 inch piece kombu
1 onion, thinly sliced
5 cups water
1 TB. tamari shoyu (naturally aged soy sauce)

1. Soak shitake mushrooms in boiling water for 20 minutes.
2. Quickly rinse kombu and place in 5 cups water.
3. Bring to a boil and add onions, soaked mushrooms, and soaking water.
4. Cover, reduce heat to medium and simmer 30 minutes.
5. Remove kombu and mushrooms.
6. Thinly slice kombu on the diagonal.
7. Remove and discard stems from mushrooms. Thinly slice mushroom caps.
8. Return kombu and mushrooms to broth.
9. Add 1 TB. of tamari shoyu and simmer another 10 minutes.
10. Serve hot.

SEA VEGETABLES

Sea vegetable or seaweed? Although commonly thought to be of Japanese origin, many cultures, including our own colonial ancestors in New England, have enjoyed sea vegetables as a delicious food and natural flavor enhancer. Most recently in the United States, the presence of sea vegetables in one's diet has been in the form of stabilizers, thickeners, emusifiers, and suspending agents found in baked goods, ice cream, and cheeses as well as cosmetics and medicines. However, recognition of its superior nutritional content and remarkable textures and flavors has lead to the "rediscovery" of an ancient food source. Nutritionally, it is a rich source of proteins, easily digestible carbohydrates, minerals such as calcium, phosphorus, magnesium, iron, iodine, sodium, and vitamins A, B_1, B_{12}, C, and E.

As with many fruits and land vegetables such as apples, apricots, tomatoes, and mushrooms, the drying of sea vegetables is a method of preservation and concentration of flavors. Most sea vegetables should be quickly rinsed with water to remove any lingering dust, sand, or excess naturally occuring sea salt and then briefly soaked before cooking with other vegetables, grains, beans, or seafood dishes. No soaking is needed when used in long simmered soups and stews. Since rehydrating sea vegetables can expand the volume up to seven times, only a small amount is required in recipes.

Dried sea vegetables will keep indefinitely if stored in a tightly sealed container in a cool, dark place such as a cupboard or pantry away from the stove. Cooked sea vegetables will keep 4-5 days refrigerated.

Adding small amounts of sea vegetables to soups, stews or beans is a good way to experience the unique flavors, textures, and colors. The mild flavors of arame, dulse, and nori make them good sea vegetables to use initially. Use the following guide to acquaint yourself with the extensive variety available.

Agar-agar is a vegetarian source of gelatin and binding agent used to make "jello," aspics, and puddings. Red seaweed is processed into light translucent bars, flakes or powder. Quicker to use, the flakes and powder are also less expensive and yield a harder gel than the more traditional agar bars.   To gel, dissolve agar in warm water, simmer in juice or broth for 10 minutes with optional additions of fresh chopped fruits or vegetables, and refrigerate until firm.

Arame is a brown algae whose large tough leaves are parboiled, shredded, and dried into long black strands. It should be thoroughly rinsed before use and soaked no longer than 10 minutes to retain its rich, yet mild flavor. Use in vegetable sautés, salads, and casseroles.

Dulse is a reddish-purple sea vegetable harvested commercially in eastern Canada. A traditional staple in Ireland, Scotland, Wales, and parts of New England, it can be eaten raw as a salty snack or rinsed and added to soups, stews, salads, or sandwiches.

Hijiki looks like a more chubby version of arame and has a more pronounced although delicious flavor. Soak 15-20 minutes, simmer 30 minutes to one hour, and use in vegetable sautés, salads, and casseroles.

Kelp is most often found in powder and tablet form. Like all sea vegetables, it is a good source of trace minerals, most notably iodine. Use as a salt substitute or condiment.

Kombu is high in natural glutamic acid, making it a good alternative for the flavor enhancing properties of MSG, monosodium glutamate. Kombu resembles stiff, broad flat strands and is used to make soup stocks, broths, and vegetable stews. Beans cook faster and digest and taste better when a small piece of kombu is added.

Nori, the familiar "wrapping" used in making sushi, is a cultivated sea vegetable that is washed, chopped into small pieces, ladled onto bamboo mats, and dried into sheets. Flavor and digestibility are improved when the raw purple nori sheets are toasted. Simply hold a couple inches above a flame or heating element on a stove. Within seconds it will turn green, ready to crumble or cut into strips as a garnish and condiment or to use to make rice balls or sushi.

Wakame, one of the most tender sea vegetables, cooks quickly. Rinse to remove surface dirt, soak 3-5 minutes, and then cook 5-10 minutes. If soaked 15 minutes, it can be cut into small pieces and added to a salad without cooking. Wakame is a common ingredient in miso soup and is a tasty addition to vegetable dishes and salads.

Recipes

AGAR "GELATIN"   *serves 4*
Gelatin-type desserts are light and refreshing, but so often they are overly sweet
and artificially flavored. Try this fruit juice sweetened version thickened with agar.
It is just as easy to make as the traditional gelatin-based packaged varieties.

3 cups juice
1 cup water
1/3 cup agar flakes or 2 bars agar
pinch of salt
1 cup sliced fresh fruit (opt.)
1 TB. kuzu (Japanese thickening agent- opt.)

1. Add agar flakes to juice, water, and salt, bring to a boil.
   NOTE: If using agar bars, first break bars into small pieces and soak in juice,
   water, and salt for 15 minutes before bringing to a boil.)
2. If a creamier texture is desired, dilute the kuzu in a small amount of water and
   add to the boiling mixture.
3. Reduce heat and simmer 10 minutes.
4. Add fresh fruit and simmer an additional 3 minutes.
5. Pour into heat-proof mold or glass dish and let cool to room temperature.
5. Refrigerate 2 hours or until firm.

VEGETABLE STIR FRY WITH ARAME   *serves 2-3*
This recipe is a hit with everyone, despite any preconceptions about eating
something made with sea vegetables!

1 TB. sesame oil
1 large onion, thinly sliced
1/4 cup dry arame
1/2 lb. tofu, cubed
water
3 carrots, cut in 1/2" diagonal slices
1 TB. tamari shoyu (naturally aged soy sauce)
1 TB. sesame tahini (hulled sesame butter-optional)

1. Rinse the arame under cold water and soak 10 minutes.
2. Meanwhile, heat the oil in a skillet and sauté onion until translucent.
3. Drain arame. Add arame and tofu to onions.
4. Stir fry 3 minutes and add 1" depth of water.
5. Cover and simmer 20 minutes.
6. Then add carrots and tamari shoyu and simmer about 10 more minutes until the
   carrots are tender. Add more water if necessary.
7. Dissolve the sesame tahini in a small amount of the cooking water and return to
   the vegetables in the skillet.
8. Stir to coat the vegetables and let cook 3 more minutes over low heat.
9. Serve with noodles, rice or other grains.

Recipes

DULSE AND RED ONION SALAD   *serves 4*

Use this delicious salad to accompany a meal or as a condiment in a sandwich.

1 cup dry dulse
2 red onions, thinly sliced
pot of boiling water
1 TB. apple cider vinegar or rice vinegar
pinch of salt

1. Rinse dulse and soak 5 minutes.
2. Place red onions in a strainer and dip quickly into boiling water to mellow the onion's pungent taste.
3. Allow onions to thoroughly drain and cool and then place in bowl.
4. Drain dulse and squeeze out excess liquid and chop into small pieces.
5. Add dulse, vinegar, and salt to onions and mix well.
6. Marinate 2 hours and serve.

ENHANCED VEGGIES   *serves 3-4*

Monosodium glutamate (MSG) is used frequently in Chinese foods to enhance flavors. Similar but non-toxic effects can be accomplished with kombu.

2 inch piece of kombu
1 onion, 1/4 inch slices
4 carrots, cut in 1/2 inch diagonals
1/4 head cabbage, shredded
4 ribs celery, cut in 1/2 inch diagonals
1 tsp. tamari shoyu (naturally aged soy sauce)
water

1. Rinse kombu quickly in water and place in bottom of cooking pot.
2. Add 1 inch of water and layer onions, carrots, celery, and cabbage—in that order.
3. Bring to a boil, cover, reduce heat, and simmer 15 minutes.
4. Stir shoyu into vegetables and simmer another 5 minutes and serve.
   NOTE: Kombu may be eaten along with the vegetables or saved to flavor another dish.

Recipes

SPLIT PEA WAKAME SOUP   *serves 4*
A delicious broth can be flavored with a ham bone, but wakame is a wonderful substitution. Besides flavor, it gives a body to the soup without having to resort to conventional thickening agents.

1 cup split peas
4 cups water
2 ribs celery, cut in 1 inch diagonals
3 carrots, cut in 1 inch chunks
wakame, 4 inch piece
1 onion, chopped
1 bay leaf
salt, tamari shoyu, or miso to taste

1. Rinse split peas to remove any dirt.
2. Rinse wakame quickly in water to remove excess salt and cut into 1 inch pieces.
3. Add split peas and wakame to rest of ingredients.
4. Bring to a boil, lower flame and simmer 2 hours or until done.
5. Add salt, tamari shoyu, or diluted miso 15 minutes before serving.
6. Garnish with croutons, chopped parsley or scallions.

PET PRODUCTS

EVALUATING PET FOODS

Friends, companions, always eager to see you no matter what mistakes you made that day...the unconditional love from pets knows no bounds. Good friends deserve the best and that includes providing them with the best food possible.

A good, well balanced diet must supply sufficient energy to meet the pet's needs, be nutritionally adequate, provide balanced nutrients in proportion to calories, consist of usable nutrients, and, of course, be acceptable to the pet. Nutrient needs vary according to the specific type of animal, its age, weight, activity level, environment, temperament, and health status.

How to read a pet food label is an art in itself. Commercial pet foods became available about 70 years ago in the United States, partially as a way to use products generally considered unsavory for human consumption. Early dog foods based on horse meat were sold straight from a town's local rendering plant. Since then, minimum standards of nutritional requirements for pets have been set by the government's National Research Council (NRC). Foods labeled "nutritionally complete and balanced" indicate that the NRC's minimum requirements have been met or exceeded. Of even more significance is the product's claim to have passed the voluntary feeding tests approved by the Association of American Feed Control Officials (AAFCO). These tests insure that beyond supplying certain percentages of nutrients, the food is nutritionally adequate and *usable* to match the amounts listed for each nutrient.

By law, each ingredient must be listed on the product label in descending order by weight to provide a general indication of the product's contents and quality. Other listings which may appear on the label include: "guaranteed analysis" which indicates the minimum/maximum tolerances established for those nutrients, "average analysis" which lists the actual percentage of each key nutrient, and "metabolized energy" (ME) which measures the percentage of food content that can be utilized by the pet. Ingredients used within the products are added according to a "lease formula" or "line formula". "Lease formulas" are made according to specifications demanded from the company under whose label the pet food will be sold. A "line formula" pet food is made from a variety of sources chosen by the manufacturer just as long as the finished product maintains label requirements.

Homemade pet foods based on high quality, easily digestible foods, are ideal for pets. However, although it is superior, it is also very time consuming and involves a great deal of knowledge and adherence to a nutritionally sound guide designed specifically for pets. A diet of more than 10% mere table scraps (i.e., leftovers from your plate) is not recommended since, even though it may sustain you (hopefully), it most likely lacks the nutritional balance needed by your pet. However, dedicated owners who even occasionally want to take the time can find specific recipes for the particular age and situation of a pet in many books such as *Dr. Pitcairn's Complete Guide to Natural Health for Dogs & Cats* by Richard H. Pitcairn, D.V.M., Ph.D., and Susan Hubble Pitcairn and *The Natural Cat* by Anitra Frazier with Norma Eckroate. Rich gravies, sweet desserts and candy, soda pop, alcohol, and spicy foods must be avoided as they are very harmful to an animal's digestive system. Even milk may cause diarrhea in both cats and dogs. Do not let your pets chew on small bones since they may break and splinter possibly resulting in choking or internal injury. Avoid using too much liver. Although an excellent food, too much can lead to vitamin A toxicity. Cats are wild about tuna, primarily because of its aroma. While some manufacturers add tuna to their cat foods to entice the cat to prefer their brand, too much tuna can cause a vitamin E deficiency.

Without a doubt, **protein** is necessary but not the most important aspect in a pet's diet. Even in the wild, the grains within the stomach, bones, hair, and fat would be eaten with as much gusto as the muscle tissue of its prey. Fats and carbohydrates are needed to supply sufficient energy. Proteins, in absence of fats and carbohydrates, can be converted into an energy source but only at great expense both to the digestive system of the pet and pocketbook of the animal's owner.

What is important is that the supplied protein be of utmost quality and usability. The higher the biological value, the less amount of protein is actually needed. As in human nutrition, biological value is measured by the amount and proportion of essential amino acids, the building blocks of protein that must be supplied by food. In addition to the 8 or 9 essential amino acids required by humans, current thought is that arginine (needed only in puppy stages) and taurine (needed by cats to prevent degeneration of the retina) are considered essential in pet nutrition.

Both digestibility and biological value are important when evaluating a source of protein. The "crude protein" listed in the guaranteed analysis states the amount of total amount of protein but not necessarily how much is utilized or of what value. Feathers and hair, which have 0% digestibility, are not allowed to be used. "Meat by-products" is a common inexpensive protein source based on bonemeal and leftover meat products that are not sold for human consumption. It has between 50-100% digestibility and varies in its nutrient proportions and bioavailability due to its composition. "Poultry meal" or "poultry by-product meal" refers to whole (including feet and beaks but no feathers), processed chickens that are dried and ground. There is nothing inherently wrong in using these types of sources since an animal would normally eat almost all the parts of its prey. In all states except California and Florida, 4D animals (dead, dying, disabled, or diseased) are allowed to be used in pet foods. Certain standards of safety must be met before its use. Diseased animals are used only if inspection shows the disease or damage is isolated in certain areas which are then, consequently, removed. The rest of the disease-free material is rendered and cooked at extremely high temperatures to make it virtually sterile, free of harmful bacteria and organisms. Since some animals receive drugs such as antibiotics during various stages of their life, drug testing is done to detect the amount still present in the meat.

Carbohydrate quality and usability are also important. Sugar is often used as a preservative and for palatability. Although sugar, corn syrup, and other simple carbohydrates can supply calories, they are "empty calories" devoid of any nutrient value that can result in hyperactive pets as the sugar is quickly metabolized. Devitalized, partial grain sources such as brewer's rice and wheat middlings provide starch but little vitamins and

minerals. In contrast, complex carbohydrates as found in cooked whole grains and vegetables provide sustained energy, fiber, B vitamins, and trace minerals.

Fats, another energy source, needs to come from quality, usable, rancid-free fats.
Essential fatty acids are important for healthy skin, shiny coat, and for proper maintenance
of the nervous system. Both saturated and unsaturated fats are important. Chicken fat is
higher in essential fatty acids than fats from beef or lamb. Unsaturated fats from corn oil
and safflower oil are more suited for dogs while cats, who don't metabolize unsaturated fats
as well, do better with olive oil. Old, rancid fats create unstable chemical reactions in cell
membranes and alter cell duplication resulting in decreased immunity and premature
aging. Fats oxidize quickly and need to be stabilized somehow but, all too frequently, pet
foods will include preservatives such as BHA, a chemical shown to cause cancer and behavioral changes in rats. Natural, effective alternatives to chemical preservatives include
vitamin C (ascorbic acid), vitamin E (d-alpha tocoperol), and the herb, rosemary.

Other additives seen on some pet food labels include sodium nitrite, artificial flavorings, and artificial colors. Sodium nitrite is used to preserve color and inhibit the growth of
bacteria that might otherwise cause spoilage. Nitrites can react with other chemicals in
foods to form nitrosamines which, even in extremely small amounts, have caused cancer in
laboratory animals. The addition of vitamin C to a product containing sodium nitrite
appears to help prevent the formation of nitrosamines. But, since pet foods can be made
without sodium nitrite, it is easy to avoid products containing it.

Like sugar, artificial flavors are added to "hook" the animal to the product's palatability. Many artificial flavorings have not been tested for their long term effects which may
include cancer, birth defects, and mutations. A product will have no need for artificial
flavors if it actually includes the food that the additive is trying to match. "Poultry digest",
"liver digest", and similar terms are natural flavoring powders that are made by drying the
liquid residue from cooking the source material.

Lack of research is also the reason to avoid artificial colors. The presence of artificial
colors is simply for owner appeal; dogs and cats are color-blind.

Dry or canned food can be used equally as well. Pets will prefer the type of texture
they are most conditioned to receive. In fact, after a steady diet of soft canned food, most
animals will refuse dry kibble.

Canned food contains between 75-78% water. Because it is more easily digestible than
the dry, it is good for small puppies. Since it is the most expensive source of pet food, many
people use canned food as an occasional treat or to act as a carrier for a supplement or
medicine that may be unpalatable on its own. Canned food can also be extended by thinning it with more water to form a gravy to pour over dry kibble that is being ignored.

Dry kibble is the least expensive and the most convenient. Unlike canned food which
will spoil if left in a food bowl during the day, dry kibble can safely be left out for your pets.
Dry food is made in two basic ways— expanded (extruded), or baked. The expanded process is a more modern, improved version of the hard pellets that were originally used in dry
pet foods. The protein and grain sources are mixed with a vitamin/mineral premix,
ground, and then sent to the extruder. Within the extruder, steam is added to cook the
ingredients and to make them moist enough so that the resulting dough can be pushed
against a die to form the particular shape desired. Cats are especially fond of star shapes
while dogs, who are not as particular, like virtually any shape. At this point, the kibble is
dried and screened to remove excess crumbs from the whole material. Animal fat and,
quite often, flavorings are then sprayed on the dried kibble and sent on to the bagging unit.

Baked kibble is made by mixing the ingredients into a dough and spreading it on long sheets. After baking, the "biscuits" are broken up into bite sized pieces. Because baked kibble has a lower moisture content than expanded kibble, it is best soaked with a small amount of hot water for a few minutes before serving your pet. Supplementing with oil is particularly important with baked kibble since it generally is quite low in fat. Soaked baked kibble retains its firm texture without changing to a mushy consistency.

Feline facts— A diet too high in mineral content ("ash"), especially if it contains high levels of magnesium in the presence of alkaline urine, is one of the contributing factors of a serious group of disorders called feline bladder disease or F.U.S (Feline Urologic Syndrome). F.U.S. is a serious disorder in which the excess minerals crystalize and irritate the lining of the urinary tract causing an inflammatory condition called cystitis. In turn, the inflamed bladder produces mucus that binds the crystals into extremely hard material which can plug the uretha. If the uretha is not unblocked, the cat will die of a toxic condition called uremia. Good quality cat food will address this potential problem by keeping the ash and magnesium content to a minimum and by providing a more acid internal environment. The amount of minerals needed and tolerated by dogs is different than cats, so this is one reason why in households which contain both cats and dogs, cats should be discouraged from eating food left out for the dog.

Unlike most animals, cats depend on protein as their primary energy source, and, consequently, need a great deal more protein than dogs and less carbohydrates. Cats have different dietary needs during different stages in their lives. Kittens need more of some nutrients and more calories pound per pound than adult cats. Pregnant and nursing cats require more protein and 2-3 times the calories needed by adult cats.

Poochie particulars— Similarly, dog dietary needs vary according to age and activity. A puppy needs twice the nutrients and calories of an adult dog. Pregnant and nursing females need more protein, vitamins, and certain minerals while old dogs need more digestable foods, less vitamins, minerals, and protein and lower sodium levels. Most dog food companies offer specific formulas for puppies, adult foods for maturity to age 7, and senior formulas for older dogs.

Is it possible to feed a vegetarian diet to pets? Dogs and cats are carnivores by nature and require concentrated sources of protein. Too much food may be required for an animal to obtain all their protein from plant sources. Cats, especially, will have a problem with a total vegetarian diet since they are unable to convert beta-carotene from vegetables into usuable vitamin A. Their requirement for taurine is much higher than can be supplied in plant protein. However, it is possible to eliminate the meat from a pet's diet if eggs and/ or dairy products are included. Soybeans also are useful for their high protein content. Although considered at one time to contribute to bloat or gastric dilation in large dog breeds, the theory has since been disproved. The whole cooked soybean meal has more protein, fats, and carbohydrates in contrast to soy flour or fractionated soybean products.

Supplementation needs— If a complete and balanced commercially prepared food is used 90% of the time, extra supplementation is unnecessary and could create imbalances. However, certain conditions may require more nutrients added with adequate knowledge and/or guidance. When homemade pet food is prepared, it may be necessary to add extra vitamins and minerals if specified in the advice given in the recipe or guide.

A tablespoon of corn oil or safflower oil can be added to both commercial and homemade dog foods daily to help alleviate dry skin and produce a shiny coat. A daily teaspoon of olive oil will achieve the same purpose in cats. Small amounts of grated or finely chopped fresh vegetables can "wake up" both dried and canned foods nutritionally and flavor-wise. Take a hint from your dogs and cats who love to graze upon your household plants or garden. Sprouts, grated carrots, cooked root vegetables— especially sweet pota- toes— are welcome additions. Instead of tossing leftovers that seem too miniscule to bother storing for another meal, purée and add them to your pet's next dinner. Figure on about 1 tablespoon of vegetables for cats and up to 1/4 cup for dogs.

Brewer's yeast, a good source of B vitamins and protein and garlic, is a famous combi- nation reported to help deter fleas and other parasites by both boosting the immune system and creating a smell that vermin hate. Brewer's yeast and garlic can easily be added to your pet's food, especially because they really love the flavor! If preferred, the combination is available in a pre-mixed powder and in tablets which serve as an delicious treat that helps deter fleas at the same time.

Feed your pet nutritious, delicious foods free of sugar, artificial flavors, colors, and preservatives that are based on high quality proteins and whole grains. Read your labels. Pet foods that are too much of a bargain are suspect. Support companies that are sincere enough about quality control to check their sources to insure only the best quality, disease free meat and meat by-products. Along with plenty of love, exercise, water, fresh air, and sunshine, a good diet is what your good friends deserve.

KEEPING PETS PEST-FREE

Let's face it. Anyone who has a pet is going to experience fleas and ticks. An all and out war of "Them vs. Us" has been waged all over the world for centuries. Not only are these external parasites annoying, they also increase potential sores and infection from constant scratching and transmit internal parasites and diseases.

Numerous products have been developed to curtail them. Unfortunately, many are also potentially toxic to the animal being treated, its owner, and the rest of the environ- ment. Piperonyl butoxide, an insecticide synergist, can suppress enzymatic detoxification in human and pet livers and may increase susceptibility to a wide range of environmental toxins. Carbamates (including carbaryl and sevin) and organophosphates (malathion, ronnel, vapona, diazinon, dichlorvas, and parathion) are the two groups responsible for most pet deaths by insecticide poisoning.

Consider the warnings on room foggers to vacate the premises for hours after detona- tion and the cautions on bottles of chemical dips about avoiding contact with clothing and skin. What else do these do to your pet beyond controlling their fleas and ticks?

Chemical insecticides are specially formulated to resist natural decomposition proc- esses. Although this makes them effective over a more long term basis, highly toxic levels can accumulate and be stored in the fat tissues of humans, animals, and plants or other animals that both our pets and ourselves eat as food.

It is impossible to completely eradicate fleas and ticks whether chemical or natural means are adopted. Using preventative pest control based on the Integrated Pest Manage- ment (IPM) method is not only an effective pest control means but also the most ecologically responsible. The IPM method is a biological approach to pest control. It first considers the natural life cycle of the flea or tick and applies effort directly on their developing stages. It then chooses the treatment that is least likely to disturb the total environment. The treatment is applied strategicallly where the pests hide or breed, not just where they are seen.

FLEAS

The life cycle of the flea is very dependent on high temperatures and high humidity. At cool 55° temperatures, larvae mature in 140 days, but in 95° heat, maturation occurs in only 14 days! The whole process starts with the eggs that are laid by the female flea while on the animal's body. These eggs fall to the ground, floor, or bedding and, under optimum conditions, hatch in 2-3 days. After feeding for 4-8 days on dust, pet dandruff, and dry drops of partially digested blood produced by adult fleas feeding on the host, the larvae spins a cocoon from debris found in its environment. When the temperature and humidity are perfect, the adult flea emerges. This can take from 5 days to as long as 5 months. Until that occurs, the cocoon provides a physical barrier against insecticides.

TICKS

A tick's life cycle is much more complicated. One female tick can lay between 1000-3000 eggs. Within 30 days, these eggs hatch into six legged larvae or "seed ticks". Immediately, each larvae looks for a host from which to feed. A tick attaches itself to an animal either by dropping from a bush or blade of grass or by crawling onto a prone animal. The larvae's fishhook-shaped mouth hangs on tenaciously as it digs in and gorges itself for 3-6 days. At that point, it falls to the ground, molts for 1-2 weeks, and changes into an eight legged nymph. Still with an insatiable appetite, it binges for a week and falls to the ground for yet another molting process, this time to change into an adult. After mating, the adult female lays eggs and the cycle starts once again.

Effective control of both fleas and ticks requires termination of the cycle of presently emerging adults and prevention of future emergence by killing the larvae. These parasites thrive in hot, humid, untidy conditions. It's difficult to change the weather unless one moves to another state, but a clean environment is possible to change and maintain. This includes daily grooming of the animal and consistent, thorough cleaning of its bedding, and special attention to the house and yard, as well. Both ticks and fleas are sometimes hard to detect. Adult ticks are much easier to find then the "youngsters". Brown in color with long, oval bodies and six or eight legs, depending upon how old they are, ticks are encased in a gray "bubble" which continually increases in size as they gorge themselves with blood. Direct special attention to the pet's head, inner ears, and neck for ticks. If any are found, use a tweezers to remove, taking care to pull off the head along with the rest of the body. A head buried in the animal's skin may cause an infection or cyst.

Constant scratching may indicate fleas. Look for "flea dirt" in the pet's coat, dark, gritty particles that are actually the flea's feces. To determine if it is "flea dirt" or regular dirt, put a few specks on a paper towel and add water. If the specks turn red, your pet has fleas.

NON-TOXIC ALTERNATIVES

Shampoos are common ways to fight fleas and ticks. Insecticides and harsh detergents in some pet shampoos destroy the hair's natural oils and cause irritation. Better options include mild, non-toxic pet shampoos that includes herbal essential oil repellents. The soapy solution drowns the fleas which then float away with the rinse water.

The presence of essential oils interferes with the insects' ability to sense moisture, heat, and the breath of a prospective victim. Even ticks begin to voluntarily pull themselves out.   Useful essential oil repellents include citronella, cedarwood, eucalyptus, rosemary, and bay leaf. To make a non-chemical "dip", add 1/4 tsp. essential oil repellent to 1 tsp. shampoo and 1 cup of water. Mix thoroughly and pour over your pet making sure to avoid the eyes and mouth. Let the "dip" dry on your pet's coat. Some pets may be extra sensitive to the oils. If so, decrease the amount applied. Irritations are only temporary; rinse thoroughly with plenty of water to dilute the degree of sensitivity. Never rub undiluted essential oils directly on your pet's coat.

Apply a **non-toxic flea powder** when your pet is dry and between baths. Herbal flea powders are ground aromatic herbs such as sage, wormwood, eucalyptus, and bay leaf which have similar repellent effects as the essential oils.

Pyrethrins are often mixed with toxic insecticides in many commercial flea powders. This powerful product is related to a particular species of chrysanthemums. Even though considered to be the least toxic of all insecticides, pyrethrins work by causing convulsions and paralysis of the insect's nervous system.

The paralyzing effect is immediate when dusted on insects living on the pet and its bedding. Many insects die, but frequent applications are needed since some insects recover within a few hours.

Diatemaceous earth (pronounced die-ah-toe-may'-shus) is a finely ground fossilized diatom, a one-celled algae with shells. Diatemaceous earth can be found in vast deposits originating from ancient oceans over much of the world. Much of what is sold in this country is mined in the southwestern United States. When this material is finely ground, the microscopically sharp edges of the particles pierce the protective coating of insects so that they dry out in a few hours and die. In addition to its use on eradicating fleas and ticks, it is used by gardeners as a non-toxic dust to control insects on plants, as a natural means of fumigating grains and seeds for long term storage, and as a method to aid intestinal tone and prevent worms in animals when added to a pet's food on a daily basis. The U.S.D.A. has approved up to 2% by weight of ration as animal feed supplement to control internal parasites, including worms transmitted by fleas. The diatemaceous earth passes harmlessly through the digestive system. Use 1 tsp. daily for cats, small dogs, and puppies and 1 TB. for dogs over 55 pounds.

The effectiveness of using diatemaceous earth for external parasites is related to the thoroughness of application. One cup will deflea a dog. Put it in a salt shaker or similar container and shake it on the animal, and comb it through to get it down to the skin. Be particularly thorough around the ears, between the legs, and around the tail. Repeat this process in 7 days and then another 7 days after that. Since the diatemaceous earth particles can irritate the eyes and the respiratory system, keep the dust out of the animal's eyes, nostrils, and mouth. These precautions are equally important for you. A dust mask may be advisable when using in an enclosed area or when working with a large quantity. Refrain from applying diatemaceous earth on windy days.

Never use filter type diatemaceous commonly used in swimming pool maintenance. This type is treated unti it no longer resembles the state in which it left the mine. After being air dried, it is treated with soda ash and placed in a kiln. At heats of 2000°, some of the residue is burned off and the primary ingredient, amorphous silica, changes physically and chemically into needles of glass with a tough, ceramic-like coating.

Herbal flea collars help prevent fleas from hopping on for a ride. Unlike dimethyl dichlorovinyl phosphate (DDVP), a spinoff from nerve gas warfare research that is found in chemical flea collars, herbal flea collars take advantage of the benefits of essential oils. Two types are available, a plastic collar impregnated with herbal oils and a rechargeable cotton variety. Herbal flea collars work best in areas of low infestation.

The house and yard— Once the pet is brushed, shampooed, dusted, the house and yard need attention. Fleas spend only 10% of their time on the animal so treating the immediate environment is essential. Clean up any debris which may harbor food and lodging for fleas and ticks. Wash bedding regularly in hot water. Vacuum carpets and crevices regularly. Remove cushions and vacuum the bottom of sofas and chairs. After vacuuming, dispose of the vacuum cleaner bag at once so flea eggs won't have a chance to hatch and reinfest the house. Another effective idea is to put a piece of herbal flea collar inside the bag to deter hatching. Then dust the carpet lightly and refrain from vacuuming for a week. After 7 days, vacuum the carpets and dust lightly with more diatemaceous earth. Repeat the application once again in 7 days. Dust the yard on the same schedule. Moisture will not hurt the diatemaceous earth, but it could wash it away.

Final attention needs to be geared toward **nutrition**. Parasites love sick, old, and rundown animals. Add something fresh and raw to your pet's diet. As mentioned in the previous discussion about pet foods, many people depend on supplementing their pet's food with yeast and garlic or using yeast and garlic wafers for treats. Results vary but the scent of the pet's skin seems to be altered by the combination. Yeast and garlic can aid but do not substitute for an intensive flea eradication program.

Controlling fleas and ticks naturally reduces problems to a minimum and eliminates the use of chemical insecticides in your home and on your pet. Don't create potential problems. Maintain the beauty of the environment while you maintain the health of your pet as well as your own.

BODY CARE

The term "natural cosmetics" suggests products which are pure and fresh with no preservatives. Besides products such as henna and clay, however, most body care products are processed, have some additives, and also include preservatives. Why bother buying natural body care products? The following information will highlight the differences between them and those of lesser quality.

Natural body care products contain fewer artificial colors, artificial fragrances, and potentially harmful preservatives, such as formaldehyde, than conventional cosmetics. Here lie the basic differences. Many conventional cosmetics have joined the trend of adding aloe vera, jojoba, keratin, etc. to their products in small amounts while retaining the cheaper, more harmful additives. But, in order to be of highest quality, natural body care products must also pass the following criteria:

1. the action of a product must be harmless to the user
2. it must be effective in what it does
3. free from harsh chemicals
4. free of ingredients not needed for its purpose
5. formulated to prevent the growth of potentially dangerous bacteria, fungi, or other micro organisms.

The **colors** found in "natural cosmetics" are generally based on herb and vegetable colorings. Most lotions, shampoos, and conditioners are either white, orange, or green with very few bright colors. Lipsticks, on the other hand, are at least partially FD&C colors in order to get the wide range of colors and the staying power that people demand. Some companies also use colors classified as Lake D&C colors which are mixtures of soluble color dyes (no stains) and earth minerals such as iron oxides. Lake D&C added to regular D&C colors dilutes the negative aspects of using 100% D&C colors.

Earth minerals by themselves are sometimes used. The effects are not as long lasting as a lip color and the range of colors is limited but no toxicity is involved. *Indian Earth* and *Aubrey Organics*, to name a few, have 100% earth mineral products which are used for eye shadow, blush, contouring, and can be used on the lips and fingernails. Those who desire a completely natural product will be satisfied with these. The color varies according to individual skin chemistry.

Fragrance can be a problem since many people are sensitive to both natural and synthetic scents. In recognition of this, more companies are formulating a wide variety of both unscented products and those with natural fragrance derived from materials such as herbs that are used in the manufacturer of the product, such as herbs.

Traditionally, the word "fragrance" on any cosmetic item is a catch-all term to describe up to 250 ingredient combinations; many are synthetic. Trade secrets and the enormously long listing of what constitutes a particular fragrance necessitates the plain listing of "fragrance". Some companies list the actual plant or flower oil used. Products that smell highly perfumed often are highly synthetic.

Preservatives are necessary in all bodycare products. Some preserve with chemical preservatives, while others pasteurize the product or by using a preservative derived from a natural source.

Water based products are particularly susceptible to contamination by staphlococcus and streptococcus bacteria. While many conventional cosmetic companies use formaldehyde, better quality products use methyl or propyl paraben when a synthetic preservative is used. Some advantages of using the methyl and propyl paraben are that very little is needed to be used as a preservative (1/10 of 1%) and it does not alter the characteristics of the product itself.

Products preserved with natural preservatives should be bought frequently in small quantities. When appropriate (i.e., oils), refrigerate for extended life.

Ingredients labels are sometimes difficult to understand. In addition to the preservatives listed on ingredient labels, many other "unpronounceable" chemical names appear that seem more ominous than they are in reality. Most of these fall into a few basic categories:

1) Soap or Detergents act as cleansers
2) Emollients help prevent drying of the skin
3) Humectants help other ingredients retain moisture
4) Sudsing agents make everything foam up nicely
5) Surfactants boost a product's wetting, cleansing, and dispersing properties

Generally, people expect a shampoo to produce a large amount of suds, a lotion to remain emulsified and not separate, and a product to retain moisture and not dry up. Various ingredients are needed to retain these properties. Nonetheless, a few less expensive basic products are available that minimize the "extras".

Some extras that do have a pronouncable name and add value to the product include jojoba, aloe vera, and clay.

Jojoba oil is often added to shampoos, conditioners, and moisturizers. It lubricates the skin and hairshaft with no greasy feeling and helps prevent split ends. Its chemical structure and lubricating properties are similar to sperm whale oil and therefore can be a suitable replacement. To judge the quality of jojoba products, check the ingredient listing. If the jojoba oil is listed before the other emulsifiers, the amount may be significant enough to do some good.

Aloe vera has about the same pH factor as human skin. Combined with emollients and moisturizers it can help skin tone and soften the skin. Its antiseptic action treats infections, stimulates circulation, and promotes healing. In shampoos, it adds luster and manageability to the hair. Aloe vera also helps heal all types of burns including sunburns.

Clay is a natural blend of earth minerals that is activated when moistened to act as a deep cleanser and to stimulate circulation. When used dry, it absorbs moisture and odors. Clay is used in soaps, masks, shampoos, deodorants and body powders.

Hypo-allergenic products contain none of the substances the FDA identifies as allergy producing. However, a person may still be allergic to something in the product and also might not be allergic to a product not designated as hypoallergenic. Each individual reacts to products in a unique way.

SAFE BODY CARE PRODUCT ALTERNATIVES

Henna is the only hair coloring recognized as safe by the FDA. The different shades can be achieved by blending powders from three different botanicals all recognized as henna. Growing conditions and the area it is grown in can also affect the color. Neutral henna can be used if no color is desired. One henna treatment will last 3-4 weeks. Henna is also an excellent hair conditioner.

Highlighting can be achieved through shampoos, rinses and mousse based upon herbs which can enhance light and dark tones. Although the effect is temporary and subtle, it is non-toxic.

Toothpaste can also contain questionable ingredients. Commercial toothpaste may contain saccharin, salt, synthetic phosphates, petroleum glycerine, various preservatives, and artificial colors and flavors. Look for toothpaste free of all artificial flavors, colors, and sweeteners. Herbal oils such as cinnamon, mint, anise, or fennel can be used as natural flavoring agents. Chalk, dolomite, or baking soda can be used as abrasive agents. Fluoride is an option for those desiring its topical application for protecting teeth from decay. Each person should be aware of the level of fluoride present in their community water supply. Individuals living in communities with high amounts of natural fluoride (2-8 ppm) need no further source of fluoride. Too much can cause mottling of the teeth. Fluoride added to municipal systems is generally at a level of 1 ppm.

Antiperspirants & deodorants are often assumed to be the same product, but their effects are quite different. **Antiperspirants** inhibit underarm sweating while deodorants either inhibit the bacteria that cause odor or simply mask the odor. Since antiperspirants affect the body's function, the FDA classifies it as a drug. Aluminum chlorohydrate or aluminum-zirconium chlorohydrate are used to diffuse into the sweat glands and retard the flow of perspiration ranging from 15-50%, depending on the person and the product. Keep in mind that perspiration is one method to rid the body of toxins and to cool the skin and that antiperspirants will alter these normal functions considerably.

Many people are allergic or sensitive to aluminum compounds and/or perfumes added to the formula. Aerosol sprays, so popular because of their convenience, may cause lung damage after years of use. Each time an aerosol spray is used, it creates a fine mist in the air near the mouth and nose and is inhaled. Of the two types of aluminum compounds used in antiperspirants, the FDA only allows aluminum chlorohydrate to be used in aerosol antiperspirants since the zirconium compound was shown to cause lung tumors in laboratory animals. Some studies show possible links between excessive accumulation of aluminum in the body with brain disorders including Alzheimer's disease.

Deodorants are often combined with antiperspirants but also can be found as a single product. The FDA considers deodorants cosmetics since they control body odor without affecting sweating. Like antiperspirants, some people may be allergic or sensitive to some of the chemicals or perfumes used.

Regular bathing will control and prevent most body odor. For additional protection, choose aluminum-free formulas based on clay, vegetable oils, herbal scents, and natural fragrances. Not only are they effective deodorants and antiperspirants, but they have less potential to be toxic to the body or irritating to the skin.

Sun protection - our ancestors practiced it intuitively all along. The custom of wearing hats and bonnets, parasols, long skirts, long sleeved clothing, and pants protected them from the potentially harmful rays of the sun. Whether they realized the significance of what they were doing or whether it was merely conforming to the cultural norms, values, or current fashion, scientists today are affirming their practices with solid data.

Sunlight is a necessary element in life. It regulates the pineal gland, is responsible for the body's manufacture of vitamin D, stimulates the immune system, and even effects our emotional well-being. However, overexposure to these same ultraviolet rays can destroy skin cells, thereby causing cancer and premature aging of the skin. Even if a person never "lays out" in the sun, there is still the potential for overexposure with outside activities such as exercising, gardening, and mowing the lawn. However, the good news is that we can handle twice as much sun when active.

A great deal of summertime sun is a fact of life. There are a number of ways to adapt to the increase in ultraviolet rays that naturally occurs due to the particular angle of the sun to the earth and to the increased time that is usually spent outside in the summer months. Avoid the midday sun between 11 A.M. - 3 P.M. (daylight savings time) when the ultraviolet rays are at their peak. Wear a hat and protective clothing. Dry, tightly woven clothing can block 70-80% of the rays. And, use a good sunscreen, even on cloudy days or if you spend most of your time in the shade. Clouds and shade decrease the UV rays only by about 50%.

Sunscreens scatter a varying amount of UV rays. They do not protect indefinitely against sunburn or skin damage or promote tanning; they simply extend your safe exposure time in the sun.

Melanin is our natural protective mechanism in the skin. The darker the skin, the more protection a person has from UV rays. Melanin reacts to the prolonged exposure of UV rays by darkening or, in other words, tanning. The amount of melanin pigment in skin cells is genetically determined. Fair skinned, blue eyed individuals, especially red heads, have much less melanin than brown eyed, dark haired individuals who have the ability to produce even more melanin, and thus tan more easily. However, even people who have more melanin need to monitor the amount of time they spend in the sun and use a good sunscreen.

Make sure any sun protection product you buy has its **SPF rating** listed. SPF is the abbreviation for **'Sun Protection Factor'** which was developed by the FDA as a way to compare the effectiveness of various sun products. The SPF rating on a product indicates how much longer a person could stay in the sun without burning than if no protective means were used. The number listed after the abbreviation is the multiple of the time it would take for you to develop a burn. For example, if you burn in 10 minutes without a sunscreen, theoretically, a product with SPF 12 would allow you 120 minutes in the sun without burning. Notice the word, "theoretically". A sunscreen's effectiveness depends on how it is used. Start out gradually with short exposures to the sun and apply ample amounts frequently. Sunscreens penetrate the skin more thoroughly if applied at least 1/2 hour before exposure to the sun. Reapply at least every 40 minutes and after swimming and heavy perspiring. For maximum protection, don't forget the tops of the ears, nose bridge, forehead, wrists, and soles of the feet.

Don't worry, there is no need to purposely let yourself burn in order to calculate how long it takes you to burn so you can decide which SPF factor you need. In general, everyone should start exposures to the sun with the higher rating levels. SPF ratings can range from the little protection available in SPF 2 to a complete sunblock in products with SPF 15-21. A product needs SPF of 5 or more to qualify as a real sunscreen. SPF 15-21 was designed for those who always burn & never develop a tan, especially freckled redheads. Those who can burn easily but can get somewhat tan should start out with a sunblock and gradually switch to SPF 12, if desired. SPF 8 can be used by those who tan gradually and burn moderately and also by individuals with olive complexions who tan moderately and burn minimally. SPF 4 should be the minimum protection even for those who rarely burn or with very dark or black skin pigmentation.

PABA (an essential vitamin for certain animals but not for humans) is an effective sunscreen and quite often the primary protective factor in a sunproduct. Because it is water soluble, it needs to be applied often and carefully since it can stain clothing. Octyldimethyl PABA is not water soluble and, therefore, can last longer. PABA may cause allergic reactions in sensitive people, however, sunscreens without PABA are available. Supplementing with PABA internally has not been proven to prevent burning.

Other features found in some sunscreens include various moisturizers, aloe vera, jojoba oil, comfrey, and collagen, all designed to soothe and maintain soft skin. Studies have shown that the addition of vitamin E to sunscreens reduces even more of the damage caused by UV rays due to vitamin E's role as an antioxidant that neutralizes the the highly reactive oxygen molecules that damage cells.

Cocoa butter and **baby oil** are often used by sunbathers, however, these function only as lubricants and not as sunscreens. Baby oil based on mineral oil also depletes the body of vitamins A, D, and E. In contrast, zinc oxide, the source of the "white nose syndrome" seen on many life guards, is a very effective sunscreen.

Don't forget the lips! As with body sunscreens, apply a **lip balm** that contains PABA 1/2 hour before exposure to the sun and use frequently. Colored lipstick offers partial protection. Try using a lip balm underneath lipstick for complete protection.

Some people suffer from phototoxicity, an allergic reaction from the combination of the sun and a substance that causes skin irritation or a generalized exaggerated sunburn. Birth control pills, antibiotics, tranquilizers, diuretics, anti-hypertension drugs, and perfumes are the most common culprits. The syndrome usually ends after elimination of the cause. Check with your doctor if experiencing any problems with phototoxicity before terminating a prescribed medication on your own!

If you are looking for that tanned look without exposure to the sun, avoid **chemically based bronzers**. These are based on beta-carotene and canthaxanthin which give an orangish cast to the skin. There are several reported cases of severe nausea, diarrhea, stomach cramps, and painful skin eruptions with these products. In addition to its potential to leave fatty deposits in the blood, skin, and liver, excess canthaxanthin leaves deposits on the retina that can interfere with night vision. A natural alternative bronzer is based on the extract of walnut shells which darkens the top layer of the skin. These are not permanent, washing off easily with water, but definitely much safer.

So what if after all this advice you get a burn, anyway? Take a soothing bath with the addition of apple cider vinegar, baking soda, or oatmeal. Aloe vera and comfrey salves are also cooling and help the healing process.

Moderation in exposure time and proper protection will enable you to fully enjoy the time you actually spend in the sun and for the rest of your life.

Soaps are a mixture of alkaline salts of fatty acids most commonly derived from animal fats, coconut oil, or olive oil. This mixture is then milled which is a manufacturing process involving compression.

Hard milled means the bar was processed twice. **French milled** soap has been milled three times. A milled soap is longer lasting and has a thicker lather due to the reduced water content.

Superfatted soaps have extra fats or oils added for use with dry skin. They have a creamy feeling and have a thicker, longer lasting lather.

Transparent soaps or **glycerine** soaps are made from alcohol and at least 10% glycerine. Glycerine soaps are not milled so they melt faster and make less lather. On the other hand, they tend to rinse off easier than other soaps.

Synthetic soaps are based on petroleum derivatives and, technically, are not soaps at all. They are less alkaline than regular soaps, clean very well, and leave no filmy scum. Sensitive skins generally react well to this type of cleanser. Soaps listed as a beauty bar or cleansing bar are synthetic soaps.

Castile soaps are named for the region in Spain where they were originally made. It is a basic soap in liquid or bar form made from olive oil, coconut oil, and an alkali salt. Castile soap is good for normal to oily skin but may be too drying for those with dry skin. The liquid castile is very versatile. It can be used to hand wash clothes, to wash surface sprays off fruits and vegetables, and as a shampoo and toothpaste.

Other soap ingredients— Herbs, oatmeal, almond meal, clay, jojba oil, vitamins A and E and various scents are just a few additions which further expand the choices beyond these basic types of soap.

Hairsprays have been suspect for years. Just as the use of aerosols in deodorants can cause lung problems, so it goes with inhalation of aerosol hairsprays. Recently, methylene chloride was banned by the FDA for use in hairsprays. This chemical was used in many hairsprays as a propellant, solvent, flame retardant, and agent to help dry and set the resin in the spray that holds the hair in place. Studies on rats have shown that inhalation could be potentially carcinogenic in humans. Based upon the estimate of a person using hairspray once per day for 5 seconds and remaining in the same area for 5-10 minutes after each use, calculated risks range from 1 out of every 1000-10,000 people developing cancer. For hair stylists, the risks increase to 1 for every 100-1000.

Methylene chloride is not a necessary ingredient in hairsprays, so hair sprays will continue to be made. However, no matter what chemical is contained within the product, inhalation is still an issue. Fortunately, non-aerosol holding sprays using natural herbal gums, can provide a good non-stiff alternative.

No body care product can effectively substitute for a poor diet, lack of exercise, or erratic lifestyle. Good quality products teamed with concern for one's body will make an obvious difference in the way one looks and feels.

HOUSEWARES

Besides the usual measuring spoons and cups, can openers, and other basic kitchen gadgets, houseware departments offer some unique and handy kitchen tools.

A porcelain grater is shaped either in the form of a minature grater or in the likeness of a long, white daikon radish! It has sharp, effective teeth that are excellent for grating fresh ginger root, the daikon radish, and other root vegetables.

A **suribachi** is a ceramic mortar with a ridged bowl that "catches" and grinds foods as you press with the wooden pestle in a circular motion. Use it to mash, blend, puree, grind nuts, seeds, or herbs, or to add seasonings to a small amount of soups or sauces before returning it to the pot.

A **sushi mat** is a mat made from slender reeds of bamboo bound with durable undyed string. Use it to roll sushi (nori wrapped rolls of rice or noodles with vegetables and sometimes fish) or to cover cooked foods, allowing them to breathe and yet keep warm.

A good quality **knife** should be the first purchase when outfitting a kitchen. The best knives have blades made from **high carbon steel.** High carbon steel blades have an extremely sharp edge which is kept sharpened with a sharpening rod or stone. These blades must be wiped dry after each use to prevent rusting and discoloration from acidic foods.

High carbon stainless steel knives will neither rust nor stain, but even though a fairly sharp edge can be maintained, it does not match the sharpness of a high carbon steel knife.

Superstainless steel knives are those that are advertised merely as stainless steel. Once the original sharpness is gone, you'll need to buy a new knife since they cannot be sharpened.

A **juicer** is a machine that can be appreciated for years. Since it is a somewhat major investment and features vary according to the juicer, it is important to know the basic differences among juicers and also your specific requirements for a juicer.

There are two basic types of juicers available, centrifugal and masticating, each supplying unique features. Use the following guide to help decide which juicer will fit your needs.

Centrifugal juicers such as Acme and Phoenix extract juice by grating and spinning the fruit or vegetable to separate pulp from the juice. A centrifugal juicer makes a clear, light, smooth juice with less pulp at a high extraction rate. While easy to clean, pulp extracted by Acme juicers needs to be removed from its removable internal basket after producing two quarts of juice. Phoenix juicers eject the pulp instead of collecting it and, therefore, can be cleaned when all juicing is completed.

Centrifugal juicers also vary in whether stainless steel or plastic, non-porous materials are used in the juicer's construction. Both models of Acme juicers have stainless steel internal parts, while the more expensive model also has a stainless steel top and bowl.

Phoenix is made primarily from non-porous materials.

Warranties range from 5-10 years, depending upon the model and brand.

Centrifugal juicers are generally the best choice if a person is mainly interested in making juices.

Masticating Juicers, such as Champion Juicers, chew, rub, and break up the cells and fibers of fruit or vegetables. The juice is then extracted through pressure. Masticating juicers have a lower extraction rate since a fair amount of juice remains in the pulp that is ejected during the process. The juice tends to contain more pulp than a centrifugal juicer and, because of that, it has a stronger flavor.

Advantages to a masticating juicer are that it is better at juicing greens than a centrifugal juicer and is multi-purpose. In addition to making juice, it grates, purées, and produces nut butters.

Juicer parts are made from a non-porous nylon material while the blades and screen are stainless steel.

Champion juicers carry a 5-year warranty. Other masticating juicers may have similar terms.

A masticating juicer is the best choice if a person is interested in its multi-purpose aspects.

NOTE: Some juicers that are marketed are nothing more than glorified blenders. The "juice" that is made is merely a purée.

Good tools make cooking enjoyable!

AFTERWORD

Quality of life, harmony within ourselves, pleasant relationships with others, and happiness...While changing to a better diet or becoming more aware of environmental issues isn't the entire answer, it's a positive start, affirming that you and everyone else really do deserve the best.

The options are available to you.

Rediscover, experience, and enjoy the possibilities.

BIBLIOGRAPHY

Armstrong, David. *The Insider's Guide to Natural Foods.* Bantam Books: New York, NY, 1983.

Ballantine, Rudolph, M.D. *Diet & Nutrition: A Holistic Approach.* Himalayan International Institute: Honesdale, PA, 1978.

Belleme, Jan and John. *Cooking With Japanese Foods.* East-West Health Books: Brookline, MA, 1986.

Bruder, Ray. *Discovering Natural Foods.* Woodbridge Press: Santa Barbara, CA, 1982.

Center for Science in the Public Interest. *Chemical Additives in Booze.* CSPI: Washington, D.C., 1982.

Colbin, Annemarie. *Food and Healing.* Ballantine Books: New York, NY, 1986.

Cooperative Whole Grain Educational Association. *Uprisings: The Whole Grain Baker's Book.* The Mother Earth News, Inc.: Hendersonville, NC, 1984.

Dadd, Debra Lynn. *Nontoxic and Natural.* Tarcher, Inc.: Los Angeles, CA, 1984.

Editors of East-West Journal. *Shopper's Guide to Natural Foods.* Avery Publishing Group, Inc.: Garden City Park, NY, 1987.

Estella, Mary. *Natural Foods Cookbook.* Japan Publications: New York, NY, 1985.

Firkaly, Susan Tate. *Into the Mouths of Babes.* Betterway Publications: White Hall, VA, 1984.

Frazier, Anitra w/ Eckroate, Norma. *The Natural Cat.* Kampmann Publishing Co.: New York, NY, 1983.

Freeland-Graves, Jeanne & Peckham, Gladys. *Foundations of Food Preparation 5th Ed.* MacMillan Publishing Co.: New York, NY, 1987.

Gerras, Charles. *Rodale's Basic Natural Foods Cookbook.* Rodale Press: Emmaus, PA, 1984.

Goldbeck, Nikki and David. *American Wholefoods Cuisine.* New American Library: New York, NY, 1983.

Hillman, Howard. *Kitchen Science.* Houghton-Mifflin: Boston, MA, 1981.

Jackson, Michael. *World Guide to Beer.* Running Press: Philadelphia, PA, 1977.

Jacobsen, Michael F. *The Complete Eater's Digest and Nutrition Scoreboard.* Anchor Press/ Doubleday: Garden City, NY, 1985.

Kushi, Aveline. *Complete Guide to Macrobiotic Cooking*. Warner Books: New York, NY, 1985.

Lappe', Frances Moore. *Diet for a Small Planet*. Ballantine Books: New York, NY, 1982.

Lichine, Alexis. *New Encyclopedia of Wines and Spirits*. Kropf Publishing: New York, NY, 1982.

MacNeil, Karen. *The Book of Whole Foods*. Vintage Books: New York, NY, 1981.

Peckham, Gladys & Freeland-Graves, Jeanne. *Foundations of Food Preparation 4th Ed.* MacMillan Publishing Co.: New York, NY, 1979.

Pennington, Jean & Church, Helen Nichols. *Food Values of Portions Commonly Used*. 14th Ed. Harper & Row: New York, NY, 1985.

Pitcairn, Richard H. and Susan Hubble. *Dr. Pitcairn's Complete Guide to Natural Health for Dogs and Cats*. Rodale Press: Emmaus, PA, 1982.

Reed, Patsy Bostick. *Nutrition: An Applied Science*. West Publishing Co.: St. Paul, MN, 1980.

Robertson, Flinders, & Godfrey. *Laurel's Kitchen*. Bantam Books: New York, NY, 1976.

Robertson, Flinders, & Ruppenthal. *The New Laurel's Kitchen*. Ten Speed Press: Berkeley, CA, 1986.

Rohe', Fred. *The Complete Book of Natural Foods*. Shambhala: Boulder, CO, 1983.

Rombauer, Irma S. and Becker, Marion Rombauer. *Joy of Cooking*. Bobbs-Merrill Co.: Indianapolis, IN, 1964.

Rosenthal, Sylvia. *Fresh Food*. Tree Communications: New York, NY, 1978.

Rosso, Julee & Lukins, Sheila. *The Silver Palate Cookbook*. Workman Publishing: New York, NY, 1982.

Rosso, Julee & Lukins, Sheila. *The Silver Palate Good Times Cookbook*. Workman Publishing: New York, NY, 1985.

Seamens, Dan and Wollner, David. *Shopper's Guide to Natural Foods*. East West Journal, Inc.: Brookline, MA, 1983.

Shurtleff, William and Aoyagi, Akiko. *The Book of Miso*. Autumn Press: Brookline, MA, 1976.

Shurtleff, William and Aoyagi, Akiko. *The Book of Tofu*. Ballantine Books: New York, NY, 1975.

Tapley, Weiss, et al. *Columbia University College of Physicians & Surgeons Complete Home Medical Guide*. Crown Publishers, Inc.: New York, NY, 1985.

Tierra, Michael. *The Way of Herbs*. Unity Press: Santa Cruz, CA, 1980.

Whitney and Hamilton. *Understanding Nutrition.* West Publishing Co.: St. Paul, MN, 1987.

Wood, Rebecca Theurer. *Whole Foods—A Guide for Employees of Natural Food Stores.* Wood & Associates: Boulder, CO, 1983.

PERIODICALS:

American Health
Bon Appetit
Business Week
Complementary Medicine Magazine
Consumer's Report
Consumer's Research Magazine
Cook's: The Magazine of Cooking in America
Diabetes and Nutrition News
East-West Journal
FDA Consumer—U.S. Government Printing Office
Food and Wine
Fruit and Vegetable Facts and Pointers — (United Fresh Fruit & Vegetable Association Newsletter)
Gourmet
Macromuse
Medical Self Care
NASFT Showcase (from the National Association for the Specialty Food Trade)
Natural Foods Merchandiser
New Farm Magazine
Nutrition Action
Nutrition Today
Spring (no longer in circulation)
The Smithsonian
Soya Newsletter: Marketing & Technological News of Soyfoods Industry
Tufts University Diet & Nutrition Letter
Twinlab Nutrition Update
University of California, Berkeley Wellness Letter
Vegetarian Times
Women's Sports and Fitness

Special thanks go to the following people for sharing their extensive knowledge:
Dr. Margaret Briley— University of Texas: Austin, Department of Nutrition
Joe Burrow— FDA Milk Safety Branch, Division of Cooperative Programs
Susan Finn— Pet Food Institute: Washington, D.C.
Peter Golbitz— editor: Soya Newsletter
David Goodwin— Whole Foods Market
Kirby Graham— Whole Foods Market
Thomas Harding— Organic Crop Improvement Association
Ric Jensen— Texas A & M University Communications Specialist
Dr. Joann Lupton— Texas A & M University, Department of Human Nutrition
Paul Reynes— Chairman of National Pet Food Committee
Catherine Richardson— Protein Technologies International
Lenwood Scholtz— Texas Department of Health: FDA Division
I.J. Shinkir— Office of Texas State Chemists
Billy Sims— Quality Control Engineer-Texas Farm Products, Nacogdoches, TX
Susan Templin— USDA Consumer Information Service
Bud Wright— Texas Farm Products, Nacogdoches, TX

INDEX

CHART INDEX

RECIPE INDEX

RECIPES BY CATEGORY